WHEN
HOPE AND HISTORY
RHYME

WHEN
HOPE AND HISTORY
RHYME

Natural Law and Human Rights
from Ancient Greece to
Modern America

Douglas R. Burgess Jr.

At the time of publication, all URLs printed in this book were accurate and active. Charlesbridge and the author are not responsible for the content or accessibility of any website.

An Imagine Book
Published by Charlesbridge
9 Galen Street
Watertown, MA 02472
(617) 926-0329
www.imaginebooks.net

Library of Congress Cataloging-in-Publication Data
Names: Burgess, Douglas R., Jr., author.
Title: When hope and history rhyme: natural law and human rights from
    ancient Greece to modern America / Douglas R. Burgess Jr.
Description: [Watertown, MA]: Charlesbridge Publishing, 2022. | Includes
    bibliographical references. | Summary: "A study of how the struggle over
    natural law and human rights has transformed the relationship between
    state and citizen from antiquity to the present."—Provided by publisher.
Identifiers: LCCN 2021004959 (print) | LCCN 2021004960 (ebook) |
    ISBN 9781623545062 (hardcover) | ISBN 9781632892355 (ebook)
Subjects: LCSH: International law and human rights—History. | Natural
    law—History. | United States—Politics and government.
Classification: LCC KZ1266.B87 2022 (print) | LCC KZ1266 (ebook) | DDC
    340/.11209—dc23
LC record available at https://lccn.loc.gov/2021004959
LC ebook record available at https://lccn.loc.gov/2021004960

Display font set in Compacta Std and Copperplate
Text type set in Adobe Caslon Pro
Printed by Berryville Graphics in Berryville, Virginia, USA
Production supervision by Jennifer Most Delaney
Jacket design by Ronaldo Alves
Interior design by Connie Brown

Printed in the United States of America
(hc) 10 9 8 7 6 5 4 3 2 1

For my father, Douglas R. Burgess Sr.,
who taught me to honor the truth

History says, *Don't hope*
On this side of the grave,
But then, once in a lifetime
The longed-for tidal wave
Of justice can rise up
And hope and history rhyme.

—*Seamus Heaney*

Where the mind is without fear and the head is held high;

Where knowledge is free;

Where the world has not been broken up into fragments by
narrow domestic walls;

Where words come out from the depth of truth;

Where tireless striving stretches its arms towards perfection;

Where the clear stream of reason has not lost its way into the
dreary desert sand of dead habit;

Where the mind is led forward by thee into ever-widening
thought and action

Into that heaven of freedom, my Father, let my country awake.

—*Rabindranath Tagore*

CONTENTS

WHEN
HOPE AND HISTORY
RHYME

— Introduction —

In the Oval Office of the Obama White House was a carpet of the president's own design. Inspirational quotations circled its perimeter, including one from Dr. Martin Luther King Jr.: "The arc of the moral universe is long, but it bends towards justice." In January 2017, Donald Trump promptly had the carpet removed.[1]

It was well he did. One can only imagine the golden letters enduring four years of neglect and debasement, pressed down by the heels of countless sycophants, quislings, criminals, and a few outright traitors. Yet the most indelible marks would have been left by the president himself. Historians will need decades to sort through the pile of Donald Trump's enormities, a heap so vast and varied that its commission in a mere four years beggars belief. What stands out most are the gravity-bending contradictions: deep cynicism coupled with infantile incompetence, amorality and extremism, xenophobia and a fondness for dictators, belligerence and an unquenchable thirst for praise. President Trump was a man who flirted with authoritarianism yet lacked the courage of even a Stalin or Pinochet to pull the trigger himself.

There is a pattern here. The Trump administration was marked by a wholesale retreat from all responsibility: personal and presidential, foreign and domestic. The federal government withdrew protections from its most vulnerable citizens and actively moved to disenfranchise many more. Its foreign policy amounted to a refutation of all international obligations. Having led the world in the promulgation of human rights for seventy-five years, the United States walked off the stage. The vacuum was quickly noticed. The governments of Russia, China, Turkey, and others acted swiftly to consolidate their power, moving against minority groups and political opponents that had long sought refuge from the United States. As a result, four years of "strongman" Trump weakened the United States and emboldened its enemies in exact proportion.

Not since the Second World War had the cause of human rights reached such a nadir. It therefore became the imperative and urgent task of the next administration to craft a new understanding of right and justice for the next century, with a commitment to the United States' reengagement with the world. If nothing else, the four Trump years cogently demonstrated the folly of isolationism; however, there is also a danger of overcorrection. Neoconservatives hark back to the Cold War presidencies of Dwight Eisenhower and Ronald Reagan for inspiration, when America was a "city on a hill" shining its democratic beacon around the world. But after Trump, any attempt to blithely reassume the mantle of moral supremacy would be met with ridicule. The United States must earn its allies' trust. This can only be done through good faith and commitment to a clearly articulated vision of the world we seek to create.

To some extent, the rebuilding has already begun. Joe Biden came to the presidency with as comprehensive an understanding of world affairs as any president in history, combined with a genuine commitment to human rights. This commitment, we may assume, springs in part from his Catholic upbringing—which taught him the value of every living soul—and from the innate decency of the man himself. Through word and action, President Biden demonstrated his core belief that every person is deserving of equal rights under the law; he also believes that the United States must hold other nations to account for their abuses. In a *New York Times* interview prior to the election, he declared unwaveringly, "When I am president, human rights will be at the core of US foreign policy."

While that task may be great, President Biden has advantages—some more apparent than others. Trump's appalling record on human rights had one unintended benefit. For the first time in decades, human rights are no longer viewed through the narrow prism of Western democratic values. The conversation has changed. Moreover, the language of rights is no longer exclusively the province of states or nongovernmental organizations (NGOs). The global pandemic of 2019–21 accelerated a process already well underway, as new alliances formed and transnational communities coalesced around shared values. Forced confinement produced a moment of pause and reckoning that led many to question assumptions they had long taken for granted. The result was an upsurge of social activism. In the United States, for example, the murder of George Floyd detonated a powder keg of suppressed rage against racial injustice, fueled by the president's reactionary response. Hundreds of thousands took to the streets. Yet in the midst of a social and economic crisis greater than any in living memory, something new and extraordinary emerged. "I can't believe I'm gonna say this," activist and author Ta-Nehisi Coates declared in June 2020, "but I see hope. I see progress."[2]

The expression of that hope, the very idea of progress, is rooted in a profound faith in natural rights. At rallies, vigils, and marches throughout the United States, protestors articulated an ancient truth transcending class and race: no one should fear the state that protects them. But why should that be so? On what basis do we claim a "right" or demand that the state honor it? The answer, not coincidentally, also provides the path for American reengagement on human rights.

◆ ◆ ◆

Imagine the law as a great game board with each individual moving along a preset course. These courses constantly overlap, and when they do the game provides exact rules for what happens next. But who sets these rules? Do they need to be fair? And what's the point of the game anyway?

Consider: if the state sets the rules, it also decides what "fair" means. Consequently, the point of the game is whatever the state decides it to be. Law, as Michel Foucault observed, is neither moral nor immoral but simply the articulated will of the state. But what if the rules were set not by any state or group but instead by an external authority: Nature, or God? Then "fairness" becomes an objective standard, not subject to human malleability. Likewise the point of the game, of following the law, is not merely obedience to the state but adherence to a higher set of values universally recognized to be an objective good.

That is natural law. Today natural law serves as the foundation of most legal systems, international law, and human rights. Yet there has been little attempt to examine its interrelationship with statecraft; for most scholars it remains a charming philosophical concept quaintly removed from the hurly-burly of actual governance. This is a dangerous misapprehension. Natural law is vital in both senses of the word: necessary, and very much alive. It is no less relevant today than in Marcus Tullius Cicero's time; in fact, we need it more than ever. But like a great edifice forgotten in the midst of an even larger city, other structures have grown up around it and obscured its presence. Part of this book's purpose is thus archaeological: brushing aside the weeds and revealing the beauty of the structure within.

The larger project, however, is to determine when and how we stumbled from the path toward universal right under natural law and, more importantly, how to return. Return we must, for natural law is preconditioned on a progressive view of human development. An objective, absolute law is the yardstick by which humanity measures its own progress. In an earlier era this was termed "civilization," a concept freighted with imperial connotations and disastrous results. But at its core natural law is neither Western nor imperial: it speaks to the best within us through its claim that all humans, regardless of birth or culture, are imbued with an impulse toward justice. As we seek justice for ourselves, we perceive the necessity to grant it to others, which is understood as right. Progress, by this definition, is measured by the extension of right and justice in all places and among all peoples. For this reason, natural law is sometimes derided as utopian: endless striving toward an impossible and ephemeral goal. But that misses the point. Even if humanity never reaches the Platonic state of universal right—even if it was never intended to—the upward climb is a goal unto itself. Thus Mr. Coates can see progress even in the midst of turmoil and be quite correct.

It is all very well to speak in general terms of "natural law," but what is this law or laws? How do we know it when we see it? When Thomas Jefferson declared that the rights to life, liberty, and the pursuit of happiness were "self-evident," he was indulging in a charming bit of Enlightenment obfuscation. In truth there is scarcely anything less self-evident than natural right, as evidenced by the many centuries of debate over its existence and character—a debate that is not ended by any means.

Approaching this subject from a twenty-first-century perspective, as I did when I first encountered it, is rather like walking into a theological disputation among acolytes of a complex and arcane religion. It is all too easy for a novitiate to become lost in the lacunae of positivism versus originalism, universalism versus relativism, and so on. Indeed, the sheer weight of scholarship on natural law makes Jefferson's assertion of self-evidence almost laughable. Nineteenth-century English philosopher Jeremy Bentham, for one, did laugh: he described the whole idea as "simple nonsense, rhetorical nonsense, nonsense upon stilts."[3] To the utilitarian mind, the concept of a perfect, divine law awaiting human discovery like some lost temple in the wilderness smacked of religious superstition, or worse. Moreover, even if we accept the existence of natural rights, we are still left with two paramount questions that have plagued scholars for centuries: where do these rights come from and what exactly are they?

As to the first, natural law was predicated from antiquity to the Renaissance on the concurrent existence of a benevolent deity. Even the eighteenth-century *philosophes* grudgingly allowed for divine instigation as one theory among several. Human beings, Jefferson wrote, do not simply enjoy their rights, they are so "endowed by their Creator."[4] Similarly, when the Revolutionary Assembly met in Paris in 1789 to draft the *Rights of Man and of the Citizen,* it acknowledged that it met "in the presence and under the auspices of the Supreme Being."[5] Yet as early as the seventeenth century, scholars following Hugo Grotius began carving an alternative path for natural rights: emerging not from the mind of God but the collective or individual mind of humanity itself. We were endowed, yet we also endowed ourselves. More on that later.

As to the exact nature of these rights, Jefferson's list reflects a general consensus. Sir Edward Coke, Thomas Aquinas, John Locke, Samuel von Pufendorf, William Blackstone, and the Marquis de Lafayette all endorsed the quartet of life, liberty, security, and property. You may well ask, why these rights in particular? Why not speech, or religion, or voting, or privacy? Before embarking on the story of natural law, it is vital to remain grounded in its essential tenets. Let us clear away, for the present, all scholastic debate and consider instead the moment when we take ownership of our rights, which is at birth. As we lie naked before the world, what do we possess? This is another way of asking what we have been "endowed" with, what is innate to us. These possessions did not come via any human agency, and therefore we exert a claim over them independent from the community. This is the basis for the idea of a "right"—something that is ours and no one else's and therefore meriting protection. So what are these possessions, or rights?

First, we have our life. It is uniquely our own; it can be sacrificed but not transferred, taken but not appropriated. This sounds like a grand statement of the obvious, until one considers how few of our possessions contain that immutable quality. The "gift of life" came not from the community but from nature, however one wishes to define the concept. As we are endowed with it, and it is wholly and intractably ours, we must have the right to defend it.

Second, we have our will. This may not matter much to a three-minute-old infant, yet tucked away inside its brain are millions of neurons busily firing and making choices—choices that become increasingly complex as we mature. As with our lives, our wills cannot be transferred to another. We can be compelled to act contrary to our inclination, but we cannot be compelled to think the opposite of what we know to be true. As the saying goes, "A man convinced against his will is of the same opinion still." Nor, obviously, can we lend our will or transfer it. The ability to make choices is understood as the essence of liberty.

Third, we have a body. At the risk of redundancy, it must be stated that this too is ours and no one else's. We can give someone a lock of hair, or even a kidney, but these are merely pieces of the whole, which is not itself transferable. It is uniquely ours in precisely the same way as our lives and wills. If it is ours, then we must have the right to protect it from harm. This forms the basis of the third pillar, security.

But what of property? No child has ever come into this world clad in a three-piece suit clutching a stock portfolio.[6] How can we claim ownership of things external to ourselves and therefore mutable and transferable? The simplest answer is that the tools with which we are born are not sufficient to keep us alive. We require food and shelter, clothes and medicines. If they are elemental to our survival they must therefore fall under the "right to life" provision outlined earlier. But what about an iPhone, or a winter home in Palm Beach? What "right" do we have to things that aid our comfort but not survival? This question clearly bothered Jefferson, who shied away from defining property as an essential right and opted for the pleasanter if vague "pursuit of happiness" instead.

An interesting if somewhat circumlocutory answer comes to us by way of William Blackstone's *Commentaries on the Laws of England*, published in 1765. "The right of personal security," he writes, "consists in a person's legal and uninterrupted enjoyment of his life, his limbs, his body, his health, and his reputation."[7] Life and limb, certainly, but reputation? Yet Blackstone's logic is sound. As with the rest, a person's reputation is a possession that can be owned but never transferred. Just as someone can injure your body or take your life, they can do irreparable damage to your honor. Iago tells Othello:

> Good name in man and woman, dear my lord, Is the immediate jewel of their souls: Who steals my purse steals trash; 'tis something, nothing; 'Twas mine, 'tis his, and has been slave to thousands: But he that filches from me my good name robs me of that which not enriches him and makes me poor indeed. (*Othello*, Act III, Scene III)

Reputation is not contained within the body yet nevertheless is tethered to it. Any harm to it radiates to ourselves, like signals along a wire. From this connection it is possible to imagine a similar relationship with other possessions; they are all, in a sense, extensions of ourselves. Therefore the law understands theft, arson, damage, and vandalism as "injuries" done to those things that radiate out from each of us. In this materialistic age we move about like tiny planets ringed with the innumerable satellites of our acquisitions, which collide and trespass over one another and keep generations of corporate attorneys very busy indeed.

Life, liberty, security, and property are grand and vague concepts. Each can be narrowly or broadly defined, as one wishes. "Liberty," for example, has become a catchall phrase for everything from political participation to—in its most extreme form—resistance to any kind of legal restraint.

Liberties are often confused with privileges, which are themselves more closely related to property. Property too is quicksilver. How total is our dominion over our possessions? Can we kill someone for attempting to steal them or for trespassing upon them?

◆ ◆ ◆

These complexities are only the beginning of the debate. As the centuries progressed, new understandings of rights competed with, convoluted, and in some cases consumed natural law. Nineteenth-century revolution and reform led to a new category of "positive" rights, which now form the backbone of a non-Western critique of "negative" natural ones. Nor can the impact of politics be ignored. Even as delegates met in San Francisco in 1948 to draft the Universal Declaration of Human Rights, a formidable challenge arose in the twin cataclysms of Cold War and decolonization. Manichaean global politics dictated that human rights be conflated with Western liberalism and democracy, contrasted with the alleged "barbarity" of the Soviet Union, and sold wholesale by the United States and its allies. Conversely the Soviets, by rejecting Western democratic values, went a long way toward rejecting all human rights as well. Decolonization—or rather the legacy of several centuries' colonization—wove like a caduceus within this conflict. Long-nourished resentment against imperial oppressors flared into open rejection of "Western imperialist" notions of justice and right. The Soviet Union is gone and the colonies long since freed, yet these resentments and political divisions remain intact.

Even if legitimate questions may be raised about the United States' Western-centric concept of human rights, its development has been a core principle of American foreign policy since the Roosevelt administration. Divergences broke along party lines: broadly speaking, Republican presidents favored a limited concept of right analogous to political freedom, while Democratic ones favored a more holistic model embracing social as well political rights. Universally acknowledged, however, was the pivotal role and responsibility of the United States in fostering rights around the world. That acknowledgment came to a halt in 2017. President Trump and his advisers sneered at "theological" attachment to principles. A profile of former National Security Adviser John Bolton in the *Atlantic* illustrates this philosophy:

> Bolton's return to power has allowed him to pursue his great passions in life, which are outmaneuvering his adversaries, foreign and domestic, and getting America out of treaties. ("So many bad deals to kill," Bolton once wrote, "so little time.")… He said that America has slowly constrained its range of action, through foolhardy entanglements with international institutions such as the United Nations.[8]

President Trump initially focused on undoing his predecessor's legacy, withdrawing the United States from the Trans-Pacific Partnership, the Paris Agreement, and the Iran nuclear pact. Emboldened, and with a nativist's deep suspicion of foreign "entanglements," he began to sever as many international cords as he could reach. Here, as with much else, the president's motives ranged from vindictive to reactionary to genuinely cruel. Others were merely incomprehensible. Piqued by other nations' refusal to laud his diplomatic genius, Donald Trump struck at the very pillars of the global order, blustering about withdrawing from the World Trade Organization and NATO or threatening to revoke the lease on the United Nations building.

Less widely reported, but no less disquieting, were the actual withdrawals from UNESCO and the UN Human Rights Council—the latter announced the day after the UN high commissioner denounced the forced removal of migrant children from their parents at the US border. Concurrently, the State Department received new protocols making asylum more difficult than at any time since before the Second World War, when Breckinridge Long crafted "a paper trail from here to Berlin" to block Jewish refugees. Even those unmoved by such policies could not fail to be shaken by the president's personal diplomacy. Beyond disparaging allies and cosseting enemies, Trump displayed a frightening indifference to and even affinity for human rights abuses. At various points in his presidency he staunchly defended atrocities and acts of political violence by the governments of Russia, North Korea, China, Brazil, Saudi Arabia, Hungary, and the Philippines. Often there seemed in the president a genuine wistfulness that he could not deal in like fashion with his enemies.

American presidents have been faulted for not doing enough for human rights, but Donald Trump stands alone in wishing their negation. A perfect corollary to his efforts abroad was the creation of a working group at home, euphemistically titled the "Commission on Unalienable

Rights," whose stated goal was to distinguish "genuine" rights from "ad hoc rights created by politicians and bureaucrats." Most commentators believed the goal was to so weaken the definition as to make it unenforceable, freeing the United States from any obligation to intervene or even object to human rights abuses. Fortunately, as with many of the president's half-baked notions, it came to nothing.

Taken in sum, the policy of the Trump administration on human rights combined a quixotic attempt to barricade the United States from the world (in some aspects literally) with a cynical dereliction of American responsibility. The first year of the Biden presidency was mostly triage: assessing the nature of the wounds, the depth of their severity, and applying emergency treatment. Now we have reached a watershed moment where this administration, and this nation, can begin to articulate a new and lasting vision of human rights. The auspices are favorable: the president is enthusiastic and committed, the global community is mainly receptive, and there is no overarching conflict monopolizing our foreign policy. But there are dangers as well. Our allies still regard us warily, wondering whether the isolationist policies of the Trump years will return again—possibly in the unlovely form of Donald Trump himself. It has been some years since the United States made a declarative act defending human rights abroad, beyond the usual boilerplate. Even under President Obama, offending nations learned to expect little more than a strongly worded note—the infamous "red line" on Syrian atrocity being an obvious case in point. It is easy enough to call for a return to universalism or fantasize about a utopia where all rights are enjoyed by all. But the path toward that goal requires mindfulness of past missteps and a commitment to a permanent set of values that transcends any one political party or administration. Specifically, this book will advance three propositions:

1. In order to progress beyond stale debate, the United States must decouple itself from a Western democratic understanding of human rights.

In some ways the modern conception of human rights is frozen in amber, trapped in the ideological and political conflicts of the last century. The struggle with Nazism established clear fault lines: "fascism" and "democracy" were not simply contrasting political ideologies but umbrella terms covering every kind of law and value. Human rights, rejected wholesale by the Nazis, came to be associated with democratic states and ultimately democracy itself. This trend was reinforced during the Cold War, when communism replaced fascism as ideological foil and "freedom" became synonymous with right. Political freedoms in particular were given pride of place in a global discourse led by the United States, codified in such documents as the Universal Declaration of Human Rights. Thus the term "freedom" was transformed: defined for centuries as personal liberty, it now came to include and necessitate full participation in democratic government.

This idea, now decades old, is cancerous. Conflating basic rights with liberal democracy perpetuates the falsehood that only certain forms of government are conducive to rule of law, or that democracy is a necessary precursor to the establishment of human rights. Worse yet, it reinforces the counterargument that human rights are a tool of neoimperialism among Western powers, negating the power of the rights themselves. And so the old arguments get rehashed again and again, in the United Nations, in G-8 summits, even apparently in the Methodist Church.

Disentangling basic human rights from Western democratic values is no easy task. When Franklin Roosevelt ordered his State Department to draft the first international bill of rights in 1940, the results were as predictable as they were disappointing. Despite being international in scope, no non-Western sources were consulted or employed, and the final product was nearly indistinguishable from the Bill of Rights in the US Constitution. The delegation that drafted the 1948 Universal Declaration of Human Rights was certainly more multiethnic, yet it met in San Francisco under the aegis of American encouragement and very much in the shadow of the late President Roosevelt (Eleanor Roosevelt served for a time as chair). The declaration similarly adopted language drawn verbatim from both Western and specifically American sources: FDR's Four Freedoms speech, the Declaration of Independence, and the Constitution.

Just as problematic as definition are issues of enforcement. America's role as global policeman, a legacy of the Cold War, has placed it in the invidious position of choosing which rights to preference. Again not surprisingly, political rights take precedence. Moreover, uneven enforcement (often predicated on whims and political inclinations of each president) means that there are few absolutes: neither allies nor hostile nations know which infractions cross the nebulous "red line"—largely because we don't know ourselves. Definition and enforcement are interwoven with realpolitik calculations, meaning that ultimately the United States chooses to enforce those rights abroad that are most convenient or politically advantageous at home. One does not need to be a cynic to doubt Ronald Reagan's vision of the "shining city on a hill" under these circumstances. Indeed, as Samantha Power argues, decades of ad hoc enforcement and bad faith have so eroded America's voice on issues of human rights that we have devolved back to pre-1945 conditions, where state malefactors act with impunity and no fear of legal repercussions.[9]

Ironically, the Trump administration's abandonment of human rights gave other voices an opportunity to emerge. After the United States exited the stage, other nations—South Africa, Canada, Botswana, Germany, Taiwan, Jordan, Bhutan, France, Argentina, the UK, and many more—came forward. This is not to suggest that the rest of the world suddenly discovered natural law when Trump abandoned it. International law is a conversation dominated for decades by a small coterie of speakers, most especially the United States. With that voice effectively silent, others could at last be heard. As the conversation continues it transforms, which we must recognize as we reenter it. A suddenly reengaged United States trumpeting about democratic values and "West vs. the rest" will sound, in effect, like a crusty Cold Warrior in a very different century.

For our voice to be heard, we cannot speak as the presumptive moral arbiter of the world—a title we might perhaps have enjoyed in 1945 but not for very long and certainly not today. The waning light of Wilson's "moral diplomacy" was extinguished entirely by Donald Trump; any human rights policy that predicates itself on American exceptionalism—however idealistic or well intentioned—will be treated with scorn by our allies and indifference by others. However, if we address the global community not as hegemon or even primus inter pares but rather one among equals, we can ultimately exert greater influence than ever before. A modest, ecumenical approach encourages trust and allows us to avoid the accusation of neoimperialism. This means abandoning the much-cherished idea that "human rights are American rights" and arguing instead for international coalition and covenant. Thus do our perceived weaknesses become strengths.

On the other hand, modesty must not be mistaken for timidity. Willingness to seek coalition may be misinterpreted as a sign of diminished authority, encouraging endless debate and perpetuating the very tropes of cultural relativism that we seek to abolish. For this reason, the United States must be clear and absolute in its own definition of fundamental rights and its willingness to enforce them. This brings us to the second proposition:

2. The United States and other nations must distinguish between fundamental rights based on natural law and other rights.

In a 2002 study, Upendra Baxi examined the problem of "too many rights": an oxymoron on the face of it, like too much of a good thing, but not so. Consider the Universal Declaration of Human Rights discussed earlier. The declaration has thirty articles and no key describing their order of importance. Is right to life of equal importance to right to leisure? Are safe working conditions and political participation to be given the same weight? What happens when two or more "fundamental" rights conflict? The declaration has been described as an aspirational document designed more to encourage than direct; it is not, strictly speaking, law. Not a single nation was in compliance with all its provisions in 1948 and none is today. Yet even as a guideline it has serious flaws. Moreover, for all the decades of subsequent legislation and covenant, there are still no recognized categories of rights in international law, no prioritization—in effect, only a list.

The problem with too many rights is that, given the impossibility of honoring them all, states select which to prioritize. China, for example, argues that ensuring the right to adequate standards of living for its citizens necessitates sacrificing some personal liberties. This argument may have merit, but it is a slippery slope: if individual states and governments choose which rights to follow, ultimately there are no "fundamental" rights at all, and the very concept becomes analogous with subjective state policy. For cultural relativists this is both inevitable and correct. Why should we presume the international community knows more about the rights and needs of a people than that people's own leaders? The answer, of course, is that if this argument is taken to its logical conclusion, law becomes the will of the state and the very concept of right disappears.

Too many rights also leads to confusion, frustration, and cynicism for those states and organizations trying to uphold them. Consider this: at one time in mid-nineteenth-century America, temperance, postal reform, and a dozen other causes competed alongside abolitionism, feminism, and social welfare for the attention of would-be reformers. Those passionate about blue laws or banning mail delivery on Sundays believed their cause was no less righteous or necessary than abolishing slavery. Many reformers, indeed, espoused multiple campaigns at the same time. Yet this diffuseness of focus worked against their intent, slowing progress and spreading the movement too thin.

Very much the same problem exists today in human rights. While individual NGOs may direct their attention on specific rights abuses, governments often have broader, vaguer understandings of when to object or intervene. No one would seriously suggest military intervention to ensure that a state provided paid vacations for its citizens, yet there is little guidance on the difference between this right (Article 24 of the Human Rights Declaration) and the right to life (Article 3). Far from establishing priorities, human rights proponents seem determined to move in the opposite direction. The 1993 World Conference on Human Rights declared that "all human rights are universal, indivisible, and interdependent and interrelated," a statement that sounds grand but, with reflection, becomes nonsense. Which rights, whose rights, and what happens when they conflict? How exactly is Article 27 (the right to copyright one's own work) inextricably linked to Article 16 (the right to marry)? Compounding this inanity, the conference blithely concluded: "The international community must treat human rights globally in a fair and equal manner, on the same footing, and with the same emphasis."[10] Right.

There are, of course, certain things a government may do that constitute crimes: the International Criminal Court holds jurisdiction over genocide, crimes against humanity, war crimes, and crimes against peace. But prosecuting a crime is not the same as upholding a right. Does a state have to commit mass murder in order to provoke other states to protect the rights of its citizens? Conversely, adherence to basic human rights becomes increasingly untenable when they are lumped indiscriminately alongside the whole. As Peter Stearns writes, "Groups wary of basic rights definitions may balk further when they realize the list may prove inexhaustible.... Societies favorable to a basic rights list, at least after some period of habituation, will inevitably splinter anew when new rights are claimed."[11]

There is a pressing need for clarity on the difference between fundamental and secondary rights. Yet the answer is already self-evident. Fundamental rights are those which no state may deny its citizens; secondary rights are those which are important yet aspirational—goals rather than foundations. But how can we distinguish between the two? Moreover, even if the United States were to do so, why should any other state accept its distinctions?

The answer lies in promulgating a list of fundamental rights that are not purely American, or even Western. This is natural law. Since antiquity, scholars have identified four principal rights under the law of nature: life, liberty, security, and property. This short, powerful list transcends ethnicity, border, status, and time. Indeed it is difficult to find any society whose laws do not reflect an acknowledgment. Yet it is all too easy to bring to mind examples past and present when a state has denied each or all to its citizens. A narrowed focus on these fundamental rights will allow the United States to argue for baseline compliance and rally the community of nations to prevent, halt, or adjudicate abuses.

This is not to suggest that we should abandon all other rights that fall outside the narrow boundaries of the "big four." We must and should continue to press for the enlargement of rights around the world through all the channels available to us: economic, political, and even personal. What this does mean, however, is prioritizing some rights above others. Build the foundation, in other words, before the ceiling. The core of US policy on human rights must be a commitment to upholding natural law rights within its borders and using every means available to compel other nations to do the same. Hence the third and final proposition:

3. The United States and other nations must pledge to absolutely enforce natural law rights.

"Speak softly and carry a big stick." The advice of Teddy Roosevelt's apocryphal tribesman has never been more relevant than today, as for decades the United States has done precisely the opposite. Diplomatic protest in the wake of an atrocity has become synonymous with "thoughts and prayers" after a mass shooting, and just as cynical. Yet imagine for a moment if the reverse were true. Imagine the United States reentering the conversation in a post-Trump world modestly, abandoning its eagle-screeching rhetoric for a gentler approach. The great advantage to natural law is that even if one disagrees with its philosophical foundations, it is well-nigh impossible to deny the necessity of the four basic rights it espouses. Encouraging international comity on these rights places the United States as one among equals. Yet it also recognizes America's unique potential to bring the full weight of its political, economic, and military pressure to bear on recalcitrant states.

There are several ways to encourage or ultimately compel a state to obey international law. At the easier end of the spectrum are rhetorical tools like shaming, bringing notice, or international condemnation. Then come economic sanctions, either partial or total. Finally, in the case of the most grievous abuses, military intervention. The United States must commit to employing any and all of these measures. In practice, this means a recognition that the law supersedes all other international or commercial agreements. We cannot continue to trade with a nation that tortures its citizens, even if that trade is beneficial to our own economy. We must not shirk from calling out a state for abusive practices, even if it is an ally. Finally, crucially, we must be willing to use military force to stop the most flagrant abuses of natural law. This does not mean assuming (or reassuming) the mantle of world policeman. As one partner among many, the US would naturally encourage international response to human rights abuses. But a willingness to act unilaterally, even against our own self-interest, sends a clear and powerful message to the rest of the world.

There is nothing radical in this. All state law is composed of three elements: edict, enforcement, and consequence. The edict must be supported by sufficient force to ensure compliance as well as the certainty of punishment for failure to do so. Thus the law acts primarily as a deterrent. But international law falls short of this tripartite structure, having only the code. There is scant motive for compliance and no effective deterrent from abuse. By pledging to uphold a set of narrowly defined fundamental rights around the world, the United States will add the final two elements. This was precisely what Franklin Roosevelt intended in his plan for the United Nations, and indeed what early secretaries general saw as its ultimate aim. Recommitting the United States to upholding natural law merely resets the clock to 1945, revivifying not only the central mission of the United Nations but the United States' role within that organization as well.

If this vision still seems utopian, it should. The momentous task of resuming the upward path of natural law begins with a recommitment to the idea of an upward path itself. The locus is not within governments but within the individual mind. Hence the purpose of this book is to introduce the reader to a different way of thinking about the law and their relationship with it, one that is both profoundly arduous yet hopeful as well.

With that in mind, let us begin.

— 1 —

THE MIND OF JUPITER

On January 6, 2021, Richard Barnett, age sixty, of Gravette, Arkansas, entered the office of the Speaker of the House in the nation's Capitol building. "I wrote her a nasty note, put my feet up on her desk," he claimed proudly, identifying himself by name to journalists. He was joined by several hundred others, brandishing flags and homemade weapons, rampaging through the Capitol—screaming, looting, vandalizing, and urinating on the floor. The mob surged past Capitol police, past the silent disapproving statues of Henry Clay and Daniel Webster, and into the very sanctum of American democracy: the House and Senate chambers. Some wore shirts emblazoned "Camp Auschwitz," while others bore the legend "6MWE"—"Six Million [Jews] Wasn't Enough." They lost themselves in opulent corridors and hammered against barred doors, mimicking scenes from every palace coup in history. On the floor of the House, Democratic representative Ruben Gallego stood atop a chair and directed his colleagues toward the exits, calmly instructing them how to don gas masks. As deranged faces appeared through broken windows, Republican representative Markwayne Mullin—a former mixed martial artist—placed himself foursquare before them and demanded they stand down. A few minutes later the doors gave way and jubilant QAnon rioters took selfies in the evacuated chambers. In a recorded message, Donald Trump told them: "We love you. You are very special." In a follow-up tweet, he added: "Remember this day forever!"

Of that there is no doubt. The storming of the Capitol will be remembered as a nadir of democracy, when Americans gave in to their baser selves and proved they were no more immune to the blandishments of populism than Germans, Italians, Latin Americans, or even ancient Romans had been. This lesson was not lost on the United States' allies or her enemies. "All my life America has stood for some very important things—an idea of freedom and an idea of democracy," UK Prime Minister Boris Johnson declared, and "so far as he encouraged people to storm the Capitol and insofar as the president has consistently cast doubt on the outcome of a free and fair election, I believe that that was completely wrong." For others, however, there was a more insidious message. The United States, which under Donald Trump had already abandoned any pretense of defending human rights around the globe, now punctuated that surrender in spectacular fashion. "The US has lost its moral authority to preach democracy and human rights to other countries," said Charles Santiago, an opposition lawyer in Malaysia. "It has become part of the problem."[1] Even more disturbing was this statement from the president of Zimbabwe: "Last year, President Trump extended painful economic sanctions placed on Zimbabwe, citing concerns about Zimbabwe's democracy. Yesterday's events showed that the US has no moral right to punish another nation under the guise of upholding democracy. These sanctions must end."[2]

Since Woodrow Wilson first spoke of a "moral diplomacy," the United States held itself as an exemplar of right, justice, and good government for the world to emulate. It used its military and economic supremacy to propagate that vision, and—as with Zimbabwe—punished nations that failed to live up to it. At the definitional core of American foreign and domestic policy was a single word: freedom. Yet in the United States that most fundamental right had seemingly lost all meaning. In the aftermath of the Capitol incident a counternarrative emerged: the rioters were not an antidemocratic mob championing a would-be dictator, not at all. "These are people that understand first principles," Fox News host Pete Hegseth maintained. "They love freedom and they love free markets and they see exactly what the anti-American left has done to democracy."[3]

It is tempting to dismiss these words with contempt, as part of the same Orwellian gaslighting that has gone on for years among a certain segment of the American political right. But that would be undervaluing them. If Mr. Hegseth may tell his viewers that suppression is freedom, and they believe him, we must consider whether "freedom"—or indeed, any other fundamental right—is properly understood at all. This was made explicit by Republican representative Chip Roy of Texas, a former chief of staff to Senator Ted Cruz, who broke with his caucus over its refusal to certify Joe Biden's electoral victory. On the night of January 6, with the detritus of a failed putsch still around him, Mr. Roy reduced the problem to elementals: "We are divided about even 'life, liberty and the pursuit of happiness.'" These natural law rights were once the bond that held the nation together, he went on, but now they "tear us apart because we disagree about what they even mean."[4]

A right without definition is, by definition, no right at all. If Mr. Roy is correct, then the first and most critical task is not promulgating a new vision of human rights around the world but rediscovering for ourselves what those rights truly are. We must begin by tracing each one from its inception, considering whence it came and how it was shaped over time. Only by relearning the law can we rediscover the true definition of a natural right. Only by understanding those rights can we hope to avoid the dark vision of anarchy offered by the events of January 6.

❖ ❖ ❖

Each natural right forms the basis of an entire discipline of legal study. But when were they first articulated, and how? Natural law skeptics like Jeremy Bentham argued that if such rights were indeed imbued in us since time immemorial, one might expect to find them equally observed in all cultures at all times. Otherwise what does "universal" denote? It may be reductive to say so, but knowledge of justice does not equate with universal pursuit. On the contrary, the earliest forms of law reflect more elemental necessities: restraining and punishing conduct harmful to the community, on the one hand; reinforcing the will of the sovereign on the other.[5] The fourth-century BCE Greek philosopher Xenophon declared that "whatsoever the ruling part of the State, after deliberating as to what ought to be done, shall enact, is Law."[6] Law was the will of the state, neither moral nor immoral, just nor unjust. Many centuries later, Michel Foucault would take a similar view, arguing that law is simply the manifestation of a power relationship between the community and the individual.[7] This definition brings to mind at once the image of Thomas Hobbes's leviathan: a body politic composed of millions of individual cells, each a citizen-subject. Acting in concert, the collective imposes its will on the individual through law.

Yet even in antiquity this was not the only view. Consider Xenophon's contemporary, Demosthenes: "Every law is a discovery and gift of the gods, and at the same time a decision of wise men, and a righting of transgressions, both voluntary and involuntary, with the covenant of a State, in accordance with which it deems all persons in the state to live their lives."[8] There is a great deal to unpack in this concept. The idea of law as "a discovery and gift of the gods" is the essence of natural law, yet Demosthenes is careful not to deny human agency. Wise men, having "discovered" the law, are tasked with interpreting and employing it justly. Law, far from the amoral will of the sovereign, becomes something profoundly organic—a base material discovered in nature (placed by a benevolent deity) which, if understood and utilized, produces great good. Several centuries before Cicero—and a great many more before Thomas Aquinas or William Blackstone—Demosthenes had already provided as workable a definition of natural law as any before or since.

Classical scholars grappled with another aspect of natural law: the idea that humankind is imbued with the impulse for justice. Plato introduced the idea of a perfect form of law within each person, translating into the essential goodness of humanity. Aristotle accepted the concept in part: humans were indeed imbued with knowledge of a natural law, he maintained, yet the state of placid acceptance assumed by Plato did not mesh with the realities of the world. Even if that knowledge was innate, it must be cultivated. Thus the role of natural law in society was not stationary but active—specifically, a forward momentum. As each individual must learn that which exists within himself, so too must society. As society comes to understand and accept the natural law, it moves ever closer to the Platonic ideal. From Aristotle, therefore, comes the progressive model inherent in our understanding of natural law today.[9]

As for natural laws themselves, they have proved remarkably universal both in definition and application. Contrary to the relativist position that natural law is a Western construct, one finds elements of it in nearly every ancient civilization and its laws. The Chinese philosopher Mencius, living in the same era as Xenophon and Demosthenes, propounded the belief that human society is ordered by heaven according to logical principles. The purpose of sovereigns, therefore, is to uphold divine law and administer it for the benefit of their people. If they do not do so, says Mencius, the people have the right to rebel: "The people are of supreme importance, the altars to the gods of earth and grain come next; last comes the ruler. When a feudal lord endangers the altars to the gods of earth and grain he should be replaced."[10] Thus Mencius has been described as a kind of Confucian John Locke, advancing social contract theory centuries ahead of its time. But this is only partly true. Mencius shares Locke's views on the necessity for good (or "benevolent") government and the conviction that rulers who deny it are violating a sacred trust. "Is there any difference between killing a man with a knife or killing him with misrule?" King Hui of Liang asks Mencius. "There is no difference," Mencius answers.[11]

But Mencius differs from Locke in the emphasis placed on the innate character of humankind, from which springs the law itself. Divine law, or "mandate," is instilled in every person; hence to know the law is merely to follow one's own nature. This Platonic view contrasted sharply with the prevailing Confucian belief that society established standards of good and evil conduct and shaped each individual accordingly. "Human nature is like the *ch'i* willow," rival philosopher Kao Tzu declares. "Dutifulness is like cups and bowls. To make morality out of human nature is like making cups and bowls out of the willow." Mencius disagrees. "Can you make cups and bowls by following the nature of the willow?" he replies. "Or must you mutilate the willow before you can make it into cups and bowls? If you have to mutilate the willow to make it into cups and bowls, must you then also mutilate a man to make him moral?"[12]

In ancient India, the *Dharmashastras*, or Hindu codes, laid down precise (although inconsistent) rights and duties for each person, including the rights to life, liberty, security, and property. These were so closely aligned with Western views of law that they became the basis of a standard Indian legal code drafted by British colonizers during the Raj. According to the *Mahabharata*, a Sanskrit epic often compared to the Christian Bible in its cultural impact, "the purpose of Law is the stability of society, the maintenance of the social order, and the general welfare of the subject."[13] Comparisons like these cannot be taken too far. The Dharma also mandated a rigid caste system and vast inequalities between the sexes. Nevertheless, as Indian scholar Chakradhar Jha writes, "the foundation of the society of ancient India rested on enlightened states with popular sovereignty, organized administrative and judicial systems, assurance of fundamental rights and liberty of the people [and] rights in property."[14] These early antecedents still resonate today and give the lie to claims of the "Westernization" of natural law. During the debate over the drafting of the Universal Declaration of Human Rights, political scientist S. V. Puntambekar soundly rejected the idea that natural rights were unique to Greco-Roman scholarship. "Both Manu and Buddha," he wrote, "propounded a code as it were of ten essential human freedoms and controls or virtues of good life." The list was strikingly familiar, not only to natural law scholars, but to those who remembered FDR's famous speech: among them were *Ahimsa* (freedom from violence), *Asteya* (freedom from want), *Aparigraha* (freedom from preventable sickness), *Akrodha* (freedom from intolerance), *Jnana* (freedom of conscience), and *Vidya* (freedom from fear).[15]

No religion or society, however, reflects the principles and adoption of natural law more fully than Islamic civilization. The Quran states that humankind possesses *fitri*, an innate knowledge that Allah exists, and an impulse toward justice. This knowledge is gained through a process of deductive reasoning; the harmony between reason and divine revelation, the *tawhid*, is absolute. Islamicist scholar A. Ezzati writes, "While Western rationalism developed outside Christianity and mainly against Christianity, Islamic rationality grew out of Islam itself."[16] As human nature is instilled by Allah, it must be in harmony with natural law; thus Islam recognizes both natural order, *takwin*, and divine law, *tashri*, as complementary and correlated within both the individual mind and society as a whole. Islamic scholar Muhammed al-Sharastani, writing in the twelfth century, described the relationship in almost Aristotelian terms:

> The world order moves towards good, because it proceeds from the origin of good, and good is what everything desires.... When the first being knew the perfect good *in potentia*...it emanated from Allah, and that is the eternal providence and will. Thus good came within the divine decree essentially, while evil came accidentally.... Ultimately, evil *per se* is privation, the loss of a thing's true and perfect nature.[17]

Islam recognizes four essential elements, or laws, of human nature. The first, as discussed above, is knowledge of Allah. The second is freedom, which is divinely ordained. As a creation of Allah, the individual is subservient only to Him and cannot be enslaved or pressed upon in any way without offending the deity. Thus both law and government, under Islam, follow Rousseau's precept that each individual should enjoy as much freedom as within a state of nature, subject only to the necessity of living within a community. The third element is equality. In common with Christianity, Islam views all humans as works of divine creation and therefore fundamentally equal: "Whosoever gives life to a soul, shall be as if he had given life to mankind altogether." Indeed, contained within the verses of the Quran is an impassioned declaration for universalism that seems tragically removed from the present state of affairs: "Oh mankind! We created you from a single pair of male and female, and made you into nations and tribes, so that you may know each other, not that you may despise and discriminate against each other."[18]

If the third element, equality, resembles its Christian counterpart, the fourth and final is starkly different. This is humankind's freedom from original sin. Man is a rational animal, placed on earth to perfect his existence and that of the community. He is imbued by Allah with reason, justice, and goodness. He has, in short, all the tools to fashion paradise not only on the ground before him but within his own mind. Thus Professor Ezzati concludes: "A just society is the society which is just to itself and to the entire creation at the same time. In Islam the laws governing nature are not separable from those governing man and human society. The divine order/harmony/balance is applied to man as well as to the entire creation."[19]

❖ ❖ ❖

Contemporaneous with the development of rationality in the Quran was a similar philosophical movement in Greece. Stoicism embraced the idea of a rational universe operating under fixed laws; as with the teachings of Islam, man's harmony with nature depended on understanding and following these laws as closely as possible. In contrast, however, the Stoics were only superficially interested in the divine aspect of natural law; they posited that such law came from "the gods" yet this concept remained amorphous. Obeying the law honored the gods, certainly, but that was not the primary reason for so doing. Instead, aligning oneself with natural law placed the individual in harmony with nature itself. This was, ultimately, a secular philosophy delineating a certain mode of living. Stoics were known for their deference to the will of fate; "stoicism" has entered the lexicon as a synonym for resignation and endurance of great trials.

Stoicism transformed legal understandings in the West. If natural law was indeed universal, and personal harmony could be achieved only by following it, then it followed logically that all state laws must share in that universality and harmony. As Zeno of Citium described it: "A well-admired republic is founded on the principle that human beings should not be separated within cities and nations under laws particular to themselves, because all humans are compatriots...and because there is only one life and one order of things."[20] The implications were profound. If individual harmony depended on following natural law, so too should community harmony. Therefore law could not be the will of the state or sovereign but rather adherence to a universal standard that united all humankind. From an individual philosophy, Stoicism evolved into an egalitarian foundation for law and statecraft. The causal chain was logical: "For this universe is obedient to God, and land and sea are submissive to the universe, and human life depends on the just administration of the laws of the universe, and human life depends on the just administration of the laws of order."

These words were written by the greatest and most prolific of the Stoics, Roman statesman Marcus Tullius Cicero. "This, then, as it appears to me, has been the decision of the wisest philosophers," Marcus tells his brother Quintus and friend Atticus in Book II of *De Legibus,* "that law was neither a thing to be contrived at by the genius of man, nor established by any decree of the people, but a certain universal principle which governs the entire universe, wisely commanding what is right and prohibiting what is wrong. Therefore they call that aboriginal and supreme law the Mind of Jupiter, enjoining or forbidding each thing in accordance with reason."[21] The setting for this exchange is idyllic: Marcus, Quintus, and Atticus stroll through the gardens at Arpinum on a sunny afternoon in May. Their conversation reflects this refined atmosphere—a placid philosophical discourse in which Cicero inevitably assumes the role of sage while the others act as adoring acolytes ("With what conciseness, brother, have you brought before our eyes the duties and offices of the magistrates!"). At times Cicero seems almost like a sovereign laying down the law to his subjects. "Let the orders of the senate be free from reproach and scandal," he pontificates, "and let them be an example of virtue to all."[22]

But the setting is as false as the script. If Cicero enjoyed the peace of Arpinum, it was only to temporarily escape the turmoil of Rome—and perhaps preserve his own life. He wrote these words at a time when the republic was tearing itself apart. Rivalry between the two most powerful men in the Senate, Julius Caesar and Gnaeus Pompeius, or Pompey, had escalated toward civil war. The Senate split into factions: the *optimates*, or Old Guard, supported Pompey, while the *populares*, or New Men, supported Caesar. Cicero, who had served a term as consul and was widely reckoned the foremost orator of the age, found himself caught in the middle. It was a position he would retain for the remainder of his life, through Caesar's victory over Pompey, his brief tenure as dictator, and his ultimate assassination. At each twist and turn, Cicero's support would be sought from both sides, and with each decision he made new enemies. Having ultimately thrown his lot with the losing side twice—Pompey over Caesar and Caesars's assassins over his avengers—Cicero's name fell on a proscription list written by Mark Antony and Gaius Octavian. His carriage was intercepted not far from the gardens at Arpinum and he leaned his head out to the executioner, saying, "There is nothing proper in what you are doing, soldier, but do try to kill me properly."[23]

Cicero's personal history matters because it informs the nature of his writings. His two greatest works, *De Republica* and *De Legibus*, were both composed during times of personal crisis. In the former he was an unhappy exile in Cilicia, having fallen from power after his consulship due to the machinations of Publius Clodius. During the latter he was anxiously awaiting the outcome of a civil war he had long predicted and dreaded. The detached, almost dreamlike quality of the books deliberately distances them from the realities of Rome. Cicero is not Machiavelli, writing a practical handbook of governance. He is attempting, in the model of the Stoics, to find some rational core to the chaos around him. Thus he argues:

> True law is right reason in agreement with Nature; it is of universal application, unchanging and everlasting.... We cannot be freed from its obligations by Senate or People, and we need not look outside ourselves for an expounder or interpreter of it. And there will not be different laws at Rome and at Athens, or different laws now and in the future, but one eternal and unchangeable law will be valid for all nations and for all times.[24]

This was law beyond the corruptive influence of human touch, yet as immediate and intimate as the contents of one's own mind. It transcended not only Rome's present troubles but Rome itself, uniting all humanity and all ages in one glorious holistic sphere. Remote it might be, but not unreachable. The gardens of Arpinum were a dream, and a very specific one—a dream of the future. Cicero knew the utopia he described was not the world in which he lived. He was, to paraphrase the Broadway musical *Hamilton*, planting seeds in a garden he would never see. The juxtaposition of his views on law and governance and the reality of his surroundings suggests another evolution in the understanding of natural law: that it is fundamentally progressive and aspirational. The republic might be disintegrating, yet somewhere in the ether the law remained inviolable. Too wary and shrewd to reference the present, Cicero made his case by invoking the distant past: "Again, though in the reign of Tarquin there was no written law concerning adultery, it does not follow that Sextus Tarquinus did not offend eternal law when he committed rape on Lucretia.... [The] existence of moral obligation is co-eternal with that of the divine mind."[25] An eternal law is also an eternal promise—that in some distant time, long after the present troubles are ended, a perfect society may yet emerge. Contrasted with the senseless brutality of civil war was the perfect logic of the gods:

> It is impossible that the divine mind can exist devoid of reason, and divine reason must necessarily be possessed of a power to determine what is virtuous and what is vicious.... Therefore the true and supreme law, whose commands and prohibitions are equally authoritative, is nothing other than the right reason of the Sovereign Jupiter.[26]

That was all very well, but how was mankind to access the mind of Jupiter? Through their wits, says Cicero: "For those creatures who have received the gift of reason from Nature have also received right reason, and therefore they have also received the gift of Law, which is right reason applied to command and prohibition.... As the divine mind, or reason, is the supreme law, so it exists in the mind of the sage, so far as it can be perfected in man."[27] By this understanding, natural law is a twofold creation: the law itself and the tool—"divine reason"—needed to reach that law. The first is both eternal and immutable. The second is neither. The sage who employs reason and logic to understand divine law is nevertheless hampered by his own humanity and his times. "So far as it can be perfected in man" is a telling phrase, implying that mankind's understanding is not perfect, may never be so, yet is perpetually evolving toward that state. This was a necessary qualifier for a man who looked with despair on the irrationality and chaos of his own era yet retained unshakeable faith in the essential rightness and orderliness of the universe. Even if the republic fell, as it ultimately would, the law fashioned by the "right reason of Jupiter" would await the next generation to rediscover it. In this belief, Cicero was a true Stoic.

The dichotomy between natural law theory and Roman reality was multilayered. If law was indeed universal, and all human beings had been given a codex within their own minds to unlock its secrets, there must be an essential equality among all persons. Zeno and Cicero both subscribed to this view. Yet neither questioned the existence of slavery in Greco-Roman society. If all humans were instilled with the divine spark, how could one enslave another? Enslavement was the antithesis of natural law: slaves had no right to property, liberty, or even their own bodies. "Nature's laws do forbid us to increase our means, wealth and resources by despoiling others," Cicero declared.[28] Yet Cicero owned slaves, as did practically every member of his class. Nor was the conundrum confined to slaves alone: foreigners, women, and children all had fewer "rights" under Roman law. Thus it is hard not to conclude that "right" was more akin to "privilege," and far from establishing Stoic egalitarianism, Roman law actually reinforced caste, gender, and social distinctions.[29]

The trajectory of natural law itself is similarly murky. The idea of a transcendent law superseding even the will of the state might be considered far-fetched during the late Republic; in the Empire it was sedition. It is not surprising, therefore, to find imperial jurists backpedaling from the now-extreme views of Cicero. Gaius, writing during the placid Antonine era, nevertheless felt it prudent to declare that "what natural reason dictates to all men and is most equally observed among them is called the law of nations, as that law which is practiced by all mankind."[30] This lowest-common-denominator approach could offend no one. A few decades later, Severan scholar Paulus rendered natural law almost meaningless, as that which "is always equitable and good."[31] The most complete legal tract emerging from this era comes from Ulpian, head of the imperial chancellery under Septimius Severus and Caracalla, two emperors not known for their tolerance of dissent. Almost as if apologizing for Cicero's heresy, Ulpian proffered a new definition of natural law that not only distinguished it from the law of the state but removed it from the realm of humanity altogether:

> Natural law is that which nature has taught all animals; this law indeed is not particular to the human race, but belongs to all animals.... The law of nations is that law which mankind observes. It is easy to understand that this law should differ from the natural, inasmuch as the latter belongs to all animals, while the former is particular to men.[32]

Nevertheless, even if jurists in the Imperial era were reluctant to define natural law, they may have been groping toward its application. Legal historians argue that the empowerment of magistracies to protect public morals, intervene in private affairs, and maintain good order collectively represent a very modern concept: the protection of rights. The term *humanum*, or humanity, which Cicero used extensively in his discussion of universal law, suddenly began to appear in imperial legislation in the second century AD. "The goods these laws aim to protect are by their content similar to the rights we can read in modern human rights declarations," scholars Jacob Giltaij and Kaius Tuori recently argued. "[I]f we proceed from a more open-ended concept of human rights…there is utility in the role and structure of those rights that can justifiably be called human rights, even when researching this concept in the ancient context."[33]

These discrepancies and disparities are not to be wondered at. It requires vast effort to stand amidst the ruins of the Roman Forum today and reassemble them in the mind into anything coherent. A broken bit of carving or truncated column is often all we have from what was once a great temple. Reconstructing Roman law is no less daunting; of its vast catalog of jurisprudence only a tiny fraction survives. Cicero and Ulpian cite sources long since lost, and the survival of their own words owes as much to random chance as to the brilliance of their reasoning. We cannot look to Rome for a completely realized human rights law. Yet the few broken fragments that remain hint at the greater whole, and beneath the rubble of centuries it is just possible to distinguish a formidable foundation.

❖ ❖ ❖

If Stoicism represents the first great evolutionary leap in the history of natural law, the rise of Christian scholasticism is certainly the second. It is tempting to argue that the Catholic Church did nothing more than restore the author back into the manuscript, replacing "Nature" with "God" in a manner indistinguishable from Islam. Thus "natural laws" become God's laws, and the medium of communication is not pure reason but the revealed word of the Bible. Gratian's *Decretum,* or canonical law, from the year 1140 states unequivocally: "Mankind is ruled by two laws: Natural Law and Custom. Natural Law is that which is contained in the Scriptures and the Gospel." But in truth the relationship between natural law and Christianity was much more complex. Medieval scholastics did not abandon logic in favor of blind faith; rather, they attempted to find a middle path to reconcile reason and piety. As historian A. P. d'Entreves describes it:

An immense task lay ahead of the medieval man. The present had to be secured, the past reconquered. The lesson of Roman law was that the greatest of all legal systems had been based purely on reason and utility; the lesson of Aristotle, that the State is the highest achievement of man and the necessary instrument of human perfection. How could Roman law be accepted as the universal law of Christendom?... There must be a system of natural ethics. Its cornerstone must be natural law.[34]

That need was supplied by the thirteenth-century theologian St. Thomas Aquinas. A Sicilian nobleman who entered the Franciscan order and studied at the University of Paris under the legendary Albertus Magnus, Aquinas had greater access to written knowledge than almost any man living. This is significant, as we are speaking of an era when pre-Christian writings were regarded as heretical and access to them was strictly controlled by the Catholic Church. Just as the church appropriated the marble of the Forum to build its cathedrals and kept much of the "blasphemous" statuary in catacombs hidden from view, classical texts were stored under lock and key within private monastery collections. If not quite the daunting fortresses depicted in Umberto Eco, they were certainly a far cry from contemporary libraries. Their educational purpose was not philosophical but instructional, teaching young novitiates proper Latin and penmanship; Cicero, Aristotle, Suetonius, Livy, and Ovid were basically copybooks.

Thomas Aquinas would certainly have read these, and many more, but unlike most of his peers he actually *read* them. As he did, the stark outlines of a metaphysical conundrum appeared. If all "true" knowledge was contained within the Bible, what to make of the writings of a man like Cicero who had lived before Christ? Were all pre- and non-Christians damned for their ignorance, their writings contaminated as well? This did not accord with Aquinas's view of a just God. Nor was he alone in this opinion. A quiet revolution was building within the church among scholars seeking to reconcile biblical and secular truth, which would ultimately be known as scholasticism. At the heart of this debate was natural law.[35]

Aquinas understood the debate over natural and divine law as part of an even greater question: what is humankind's relationship with God? Echoing Muslim scholars of an earlier era, Aquinas argued it was at its core a logical one. "Supposing the world to be governed by divine Providence...it is clear that the whole community of the universe in governed by divine reason. This rational guidance of created things on the part of God... we can call the Eternal Law."[36] Eternal law was not biblical law. It was not merely commandments but a mechanical system of infinite complexity that controlled the universe and everything within it, including humanity. But humanity was set apart from every other created thing by one distinction: its ability to understand, in some small part, the mind of God. That understanding was the basis of the unique bond between them—a bond not merely of faith but of reason. "Of all others," Aquinas writes, "rational creatures are subject to divine Providence in a very special way; being themselves made participators in Providence itself, in that they control their own actions. So they have a certain share of divine reason itself."[37] Thus individual will and the ability to make choices was not only a gift from God but a tiny fraction of God's own power that set humanity apart from all creation.

Aquinas's depiction of natural law was both a reiteration of Cicero's and an evolution beyond it. For both, the mind of God is rational and can be accessed only by logic and reason. But Aquinas goes further: the discovery and implementation of natural law does not merely align the community with celestial harmony but is the basis of all personal morality. Each ethical choice is either an acceptance or rejection of God's law; to deny that law is to deny reason itself. Roman gods were remote and capricious, only peripherally interested in the doings of humankind; Aquinas's God, in contrast, has given humanity the unique ability to strive toward His own perfection (and, we may assume, remains actively interested in the process). In a neat inversion of Ulpian, Thomian natural law is not the law of animals but the law that distinguishes man from beast and places him closer to the divine.

It is not hard to see how Aquinas's construction of natural law posed serious challenges to orthodoxy. First and foremost, it moved the locus of truth from the received word of the gospel to the individual mind; Christians were not merely to accept but to *decide*. Moreover, Aquinas reintroduced the Ciceronian idea of transcendent law superseding all others, even the sovereign. "Man is bound to obey secular rulers to the extent that justice requires," he declares in his *Summa Theologica*. "For this reason if such rulers have no just title to power, but have usurped it, or if they command things to be done which are unjust, their subjects are not obliged to obey them."[38] This was not merely heresy but treason. "And if human law is at variance with any particular with the Natural law," he concludes, again echoing Cicero, "it is no longer legal but rather a corruption of law." This statement resonates down the centuries. From this fundamental idea of justice would eventually come John Locke's theory of the social contract. Ultimately, natural law would become the litmus test to determine the fidelity of states and justify revolution. Even as early as the end of the thirteenth century, English jurist Henry de Bracton declared the sovereign to be under the law: "Justice is the constant and unfailing will to give each his own right."[39]

Thomas Aquinas exposed the fault lines within medieval legal, social, and spiritual philosophy. Yet ultimately the Catholic Church was grateful: by constructing a faith based on reason, he allowed the church to evolve and still retain its centrality in its parishioners' hearts and minds. Moreover, scholastic influence revolutionized legal education. Prior to the establishment of formal schools of law, instruction on the continent centered around two principal texts: Gratian's *Decretum*, discussed above, and the *Decisions and Digest of the Emperor Justinian*. *Libra extra,* papal decretals and bulls, were sometimes added to keep practitioners up to date. This sparse canon reflected the neat division in the Catholic mind between *res spiritualia* and *res temporae,* spiritual matters and secular. Any additional questions could be referred to the relevant biblical passage.

Over time, however, the list grew. Students demanded access to both local laws (understandably, as that would form the bulk of their practice) and, crucially, to classical texts that might inform their understanding of Justinian's text. Cicero began to circulate once again. Those who studied law at university might also find themselves reading the works of Aristotle and Aquinas. Consequently, as R. H. Helmholz writes, "students thus began with texts that stated the assumption that God had implanted certain principles of conduct and justice in the hearts of men.... [They] would have heard that a fuller understanding of the law would come if they drew conclusions from morality fashioned from the law of nature.... One function of legal education was to teach students how to do this."[40] The results were profound. Once legal training required a knowledge and understanding of natural law, the concept departed the theoretical realm and became intermeshed with statecraft. The same statesmen who fashioned their nation's laws began their professional career with a foundation in that law's moral, societal, and spiritual purpose.

As the law's philosophical universe expanded, conflicts hinted at during the Roman Republic flared to life once again. If Roman jurists had been content to overlook the inconsistencies of a natural law society that possessed slaves, their medieval and Renaissance descendants could not. Indeed, Cicero's universalism became a rallying cry for the small band of academics, jurists, philosophers, and clerics who wrote against slavery and colonization. As early as the seventh century, Saint Isidore of Seville insisted on inserting the phrase "common liberty of all" into Gratian's *Decretum*, which it appears he borrowed from Cicero. The parallels were striking: if slavery was inconsistent with pagan natural law, surely it must also be with the Christian/Thomian view that saw each human being as a reflection of God.[41] Marsilius of Padua, writing in the fourteenth century, marveled at Cicero's prescience and regarded *De Officiis* as "an explicit lesson about the responsibility that follows from a recognition of the common bond of humanity."[42] The "lesson" would continue to fascinate and inspire scholars for centuries. In 1588, Jesuit theologian Luis de Molina wrote of a "concord of free will with the gifts of divine grace," arguing controversially that God's will works with rather than within humankind. The capacity for individual choice is thus divinely offered and therefore a basic right.[43]

Equally vexing to scholars was the problem of conquest. If all humans were fundamentally equal in the sight of God, as both Cicero and the Catholic Church declared them to be, what justification could exist for colonization? The most obvious was that the colonized—for example, the Mesoamericans under Spanish rule—were *not* human, in the understood meaning of the term. They had (in Spanish eyes) no civilization, no morality, and most importantly no knowledge of Christ. Nonsense, wrote jurist Francisco de Vitoria in the fifteenth century. Drawing equally from Cicero and Aquinas, Vitoria argued in *De Indes* that there existed a universal law of nations which "is, or is derived from, natural law." The whole world—not just the Judeo-Christian part of it—was united in a commonwealth of morality. What of an individual raised in a "barbarian" land with no knowledge of God or Christ? Vitoria's answer was classically Ciceronian: even that person not knowing the true God was nevertheless created by God and instilled with the same divine reason as everyone else. He or she could make rational choices that were also, by definition, moral.[44]

Vitoria's argument is double-pronged. First, as children of God, indigenous peoples and all persons are possessed of the same capacity for morality. Second, as moral beings participating in a universal society, they cannot be dehumanized through conquest. Vitoria was not writing in a vacuum. He and other European scholars were responding to the reality of Spanish colonization in the New World and reports of horrors and atrocities committed there. Among the most outraged and influential commentators was Franciscan cleric Bartolome de las Casas, whose *In Defense of the Indians* was an outright indictment of Spanish rule. In contrast to paternalistic claims that the natives were incapable of governing themselves, Casas shot back:

> Now if we shall have shown that among our Indians of the western and southern shores (granting that we call them barbarians and that they are barbarians) there are important kingdoms, large numbers of people with settled lives in a society, great cities, kings, contracts of the law of nations, will it not stand proved that the Reverend Doctor Sepulveda has spoken wrongly and viciously against peoples like these, either out of malice or ignorance of Aristotle's teaching.... From the fact that the Indians are barbarians it does not necessarily follow that they are incapable of government and have to be ruled by others, except to be taught about the Catholic faith.[45]

In these words we can read the political evolution of natural law from theory to practice, and finally to legal defense. Casas's argument shares its logical core with prosecutor Robert Jackson's at the 1945 Nuremberg Tribunals: if there is a natural law that binds all humanity, any attempt to deny an individual's humanity is a breach of natural law. The premise seems simple enough, but there are caveats: "Except to be taught about the Catholic faith." Casas was writing in an era when the Catholic Church reeled under the assault of Protestantism, a challenge we will explore in the next chapter. Catholics, including Casas and his opponent

Dr. Sepulveda, viewed the world as a battlefield between the forces of good and evil, perhaps even a prelude to the Last Judgment. There were no bystanders in this fight. The Mesoamericans, for all their cities and kings, could not be left "barbaric." Like outposts of empire, they had to be converted and rallied to the cause of the True Faith. This was not only for the sake of the church but for their own salvation. Church doctrine mandated that anyone not receiving the sacraments should suffer everlasting damnation: the frescoes of Michelangelo and Hieronymus Bosch brought these horrid images vividly to life. A compassionate Catholic must save as many souls as he could before they passed into the afterlife.

Similarly, even those outraged by the practice of Spanish colonization did not necessarily discount the premise altogether. Belonging to a universal commonwealth brought privileges and obligations to both sides, Vitoria argued. Just as the Mesoamericans had the right to their freedom, so too did others have the right to pass unmolested through their territory and seize whatever might be of use to them, provided the hosts did not need or want it. *Ius communicandi,* the right of intercommunication, sounds innocuous enough. Yet it is not surprising that colonizers capitalized on this concept, using it to justify wholesale theft on the grounds that the native peoples did not understand the value of the precious metals beneath their soil and therefore had no right to them. Arguments like these would enjoy a long pedigree. Nineteenth-century imperialists frequently maintained that they were doing nothing more than maximizing the value of "abandoned" goods; moreover, in contrast to claims of universalism, they insisted upon a moral imperative (similar to Casas's "except") to bring the "barbaric" world into the light of civilization so that it might better participate in the community of nations.

By the end of the Renaissance, the interplay between statecraft and natural law had provided a foundation for the emergence of a modern conception of rights. The Magna Carta of 1215 speaks of justice, not right; the two concepts are fundamentally different. Justice is a reflection of the community, the "better ordering of our kingdom," as the Magna Carta describes it. Right is inherently personal and individual. There were no "rights" in ancient Rome: one's treatment in law and society was determined by their social position. Yet Cicero's declaration of a universal brotherhood under natural law opened a path for precisely that understanding, a fact later chroniclers from Thomas Aquinas to Hugo Grotius made explicit. Domingo de Soto, writing in the sixteenth century, provides a telling example. At the basis of any just system of law, he argued, was the right to preserve one's life from arbitrary, capricious, or cruel termination; all other rights flow from that necessity. The possession of one's life includes all its attributes, most especially body and will. Therefore, de Soto reasoned, individuals must have rights of security and liberty as well.

This contrasted sharply with prevailing notions of justice, even in his own age. Cicero had declared that "the security of the people is the magistrate's highest law" and for centuries all understandings of justice mirrored that communitarian perspective. "Every day," Juan de Robles wrote, "free men lose thousands of liberties without fault, but not without cause." Such sacrifices were necessary to the maintenance of the good of the whole. Robles compared the body politic to an actual body in which each individual is merely part of the whole. "If it is necessary for the good of the community that we lose our liberties and lives, it is just that they should be lost."[46] Soto disagreed. In the absence of natural law, human communities might well be described as body politics, but under that law the individual remained apart and sacrosanct. "A limb does not have a being distinct from that of the whole; nor of itself can it sustain right or injury. But a man, albeit he is part of a commonwealth, is nevertheless a subject existing for the sake of himself."[47] States could not claim that the good of the many outweighed the good of the one (although they did); proper justice, by this understanding, flowed from universal deference to individual rights, not the other way around. If sovereigns violated this trust, they offended not only the individual but, under natural law, the entire human community and God himself. It is not difficult to imagine where this argument could lead. By the eighteenth century natural law had evolved far from its original theoretical auspices into a radicalized, weaponized form.

It became the language of revolution.

— 2 —

THE TREE OF LIBERTY

In the nave of the Church of St. Nicholas in the Lesser Town of Prague, there is a statue. It purports to be St. Cyril of Alexandria, an unlovely fifth-century character who earned his sainthood through quarreling with the church's enemies and expelling Jews from the city. Cyril stands tall, whiskered and mitered in this early-eighteenth-century depiction, holding a golden staff to the throat of the unfortunate heretic Nestorius. Nestorius lies pinned and prostrate, face turned upside down toward the viewer, terrified. A smug little smile plays on the saint's lips as a cherub clutches his robe and urges him on.

The symbolism of the statue is heavier than its marble. The Catholic Church vanquishes its foes with merry, righteous ruthlessness. But this was an image forged in anxiety, when over a century of conflict with Protestant heresy had left the church weaker than ever before. By the turn of the eighteenth century, England, the Netherlands, Switzerland, many of the German principalities, and all of Scandinavia had adopted Martin Luther's reforms. Across the Atlantic, English Protestant colonies held the balance of power over their French and Spanish neighbors. Even in Bohemia, as it was then known, the long shadow of the Hussite movement remained. In all likelihood the statue was placed there to remind parishioners of the penalty of recidivism—as if they could forget.

The spread of the Protestant faith had a greater impact on the trajectory of natural law than any movement before or since.[1] It helped create an entire language of right based on the fundamental power of choice, reinforced egalitarian principles inherent in the law yet largely dormant since Cicero's time, and provided the rational and spiritual foundation for rebellion. Initially, however, none of these outcomes seemed likely. Martin Luther was not a champion of enlightened skepticism; quite the contrary. One of Luther's principal critiques of the Catholic Church was its presumption to know God's mind by the sale of indulgences and the forgiveness of sins through clerical intervention. Luther's God was unknowable, and thus Luther drew clear distinctions between the Gospel, *Evangelium,* and Law, *Gesetz.* Law was a creation of man intended to better order his community, nothing more. Natural law philosophy, which posited that God's mind might be reached through reason, struck Luther as heretical; in that one regard he and the Catholic Church were united.[2]

But it did not take long for Protestantism to outgrow these narrow bounds. Philip Melanchthon, a disciple of Luther, broke with his mentor on the issue of natural law and reason. Philosophy alone might not provide the answers to essential truths, he admitted. "But moral philosophy is part of divine law. For it is the law of nature itself…. And it is certain that the law of nature is truly the law of God concerning those virtues that reason understands."[3] Such rational virtues do not stand apart or in opposition to those of the Ten Commandments, he insisted. Rather, all revealed wisdom in the Bible merely reinforced what humans already knew within their hearts; natural law and biblical law were one and the same. Alberico Gentili, an Italian Protestant living in sixteenth-century England, poetically described natural law as "a particle of divine law" left behind after Adam and Eve's expulsion from the Garden of Eden.[4]

This seemingly mild critique was in fact a clarion call for succeeding generations. Protestantism's philosophical and spiritual core lay in its name: to protest is to challenge the status quo. It is a profoundly individual decision. Protestantism emerged as an idiosyncratic revolutionary movement more than a countervailing orthodoxy, which accounts for its otherwise astonishing growth. It was never a monolithic faith; schisms and challenges were woven into the fabric. From the sixteenth to the early eighteenth centuries, these schisms widened into gulfs and finally distinct sects—Methodism, Congregationalism, Anglicanism, Quakerism, and so on—all unique, yet all "Protestant." This heterodoxy meant that each individual, in challenging the Catholic Church, was in effect placing his or her own beliefs against the whole. A stubborn streak of contrariness and individuality was practically a prerequisite.

Consider the Puritans. They abandoned England in the 1620s because they believed the Church of England had become infected by popery, and they founded their colony in Massachusetts as a "city on a hill," where all like-minded nonconformists could find refuge. Yet almost from the beginning there were problems. The colony was overseen by a governor and council of elders whose primary task was to ensure all inhabitants followed biblical law; sin, in these messianic times, meant the colony might be one step closer to divine wrath. But how to impose religious conformity on a community of nonconformists? Sectarian heresy was rife, with numerous communities hiving off from Massachusetts to form their own "havens" beyond the walls. Ultimately the crisis became so acute that Governor John Winthrop allowed dissident leader Roger Williams to establish a second colony, Rhode Island, as a kind of inverted Massachusetts. Rhode Island had universal tolerance and a rigid separation of church and state. Not only nonconformists but Jews, Muslims, Catholics, Quakers, and nonbelievers were welcomed.[5]

The case of Massachusetts illustrates the latent power of Protestantism: it encouraged, even mandated original thought. Individuals had to reckon for themselves their relationship with God, and in so doing redefined their relationship with the rest of God's creation. This instilled a lack of deference not only to church but also, inevitably, to state. Until the seventeenth century, the idea of state justice was barely questioned. Sovereigns were honor-bound to be fair and evenhanded in their administration of law, but the rationale lay in the ancient idea of keeping the kingdom in harmony with nature (as per Cicero), not deference to individual rights. The difference is one of agency: here the sovereign has a duty to act, but the citizen/subject does not have the right to demand. Cicero was explicit on this point. "We would not, however, limit ourselves to requiring from the citizens submission and obedience towards their magistrates;

we would also enjoin them by all means to honor and love their rulers…. If anyone shall disturb the public harmony, let them be punished as a criminal."[6]

Protestantism slowly but surely worked a transformation within the collective mind. Cicero declared that "the security of the people is the highest law." That phrase, restated and reworked through millennia, has come to embody the collectivist view of law as preservation of the community over individual rights. But when individuals begin to question their role within the cosmos, the universal center shifts from the collective to the one: what is *my* relationship with God and society? What do *I* believe to be true? If deference to a higher authority is no longer possible, the only avenue left is individual reason. Thus Western society not only implicitly accepted the Stoic premise of natural law but also began to seriously consider what that law entailed. Teleologically, these questions took the form of what God expects of us and what we expect from Him. If God conferred certain blessings (and obligations) on each of us, no secular or clerical authority could supersede them. Thus "God's blessings" gradually evolved into *rights*.[7]

The term "right" was not invented in the seventeenth century, but the modern definition certainly was. The Magna Carta speaks of "ancient rights and liberties," but these were more properly understood as customs that had the force of law. "Liberty" in the medieval era simply meant the ability to do that which one was not otherwise constrained from doing. Yet liberty, defined as freedom of choice, was at the heart of the Protestant Reformation. Under its auspices, God instilled in each individual an implicit knowledge of Himself. One must have the power to choose—and therefore the *right* to choose—in order to reach that understanding. Rejection of certain practices was a choice, as was the adoption of others.[8] The Protestant faith, indeed, consisted of an endless vista of choices—for this reason, ministers even today commonly describe the faith as a constant struggle.

❖ ❖ ❖

If the Protestant Reformation led to the first essential characteristic of modern natural law, the primacy of the individual, the scientific revolutions of the seventeenth and eighteenth centuries provided the second: rationalism. Logic had been at the core of natural law philosophy since the Stoics, but the perceived dichotomy between reason and faith meant that the law's defenders were constantly having to prove they were not heretics—or, worse, atheists. Scientific rationalism, founded on the principle of demonstrable proof, swept aside these stale debates. It is generally believed that the rise of scientific methods challenged religious orthodoxy, pitting secular values against spiritual. This is reductive at best. Scientists and scholars of the seventeenth century did not set out to topple the Judeo-Christian God from His throne; on the contrary, most were assiduous in maintaining that the universe they uncovered reinforced rather than refuted His presence.[9] This was a rational sphere, where both heaven and earth moved in perfect, orderly, precise motion. Such clockwork precision suggested a divine intelligence; rather than the mysterious, unknowable figure of the Middle Ages, God became a great tutor sharing his infinite wisdom. This view meshed perfectly with Cicero's "mind of Jupiter." The laws of humanity were no less rational than those of the cosmos. Natural law thus became enfolded within a holistic philosophy embracing physics, biology, astronomy, mathematics, and behavioral science.

Dutch philosopher Hugo Grotius was the first to apply this new scientific method to natural law, with far-reaching results. Rather remarkably, he did so on commission: in 1605 the Dutch East India Company had been accused of some illegal business off the coast of Malaysia and offered him a handsome fee if he could prove that their actions, while an affront to Portuguese law (that is, the law of their victims), were quite consistent with *ius gentium,* the Law of Nations.[10] First, however, he had to demonstrate that there *was* a law of nations. In *De Iure Praedae* (On the Right of Conquest) and his better-known *De Iure Belli et Pacis* (On the Laws of War and Peace), Grotius developed a starkly modern interpretation of natural law that extended from the individual soul all the way to congress between nations.

As with any experiment, he began by introducing doubt. Does natural law even exist and, if so, what evidence is there to support that claim? Aristotle defined justice as a virtue that considered only the other's good. As human nature was fundamentally moral, a community composed of moral persons would reach justice by consensus among themselves. Grotius disagreed: whether humans were moral or not, surely one sought his own good first. And, if so, how could there still be justice? Clearly the individual reasoned that in order to enjoy justice himself he must be willing to give it to others. This concept, which humanists defined as "sociability," reversed the understood trajectory of the law. Rather than flowing from the community into each individual (as both Roman and medieval scholars posited), Grotius claimed it flowed from the individual into the community. Justice began in the mind. It was not a moral choice but a rational one.[11]

The truly radical aspect of this idea was that it didn't require God. No divine being was needed to instill a moral code within each human mind to guide its choices: the mind, in a rational universe, would reach the same conclusion anyway. "Measureless as is the power of God," Grotius wrote, "nevertheless it can be said that there are certain things over which that power does not extend.... Just as even God cannot cause that two times two should not make four, so He cannot cause that which is intrinsically evil not to be evil."[12] This was the voice of scientific reason. If only one logical result is possible, that logic is immune from all the devils and angels in the firmament. It is worth remembering that these words were written in 1625, one year before and a few hundred miles away from the infamous trials of Wurzburg and Bamberg, which saw the mass execution of over a thousand accused witches. Heresy was a real and acknowledged crime. Perhaps recognizing this, Grotius softened the hammer-blow of his conclusion as best he could: "What we have been saying would have a degree of validity even if we should concede that which cannot be conceded without the utmost wickedness, that there is no God, or that the affairs of men are of no concern to Him."[13] *Etiamsi daremus non esse Deum,* "Such things as these would still be true even without God."

Removing God from natural law allowed the concept to stand or fall on its own merits. The tenets of that law emerged from the rational choices each person made in order to exist within a community. Thus, in an early foreshadowing of Jefferson's "self-evidence," Grotius argued the law spoke for itself. Sounding much like Rene Descartes describing a proof, he wrote of his method:

> I have made it my concern to refer to the proofs of things touching the law of nature to certain fundamental conceptions which are beyond question; so that no-one can deny them without violence to himself. For the principles of that law, if you only pay strict attention to them, are manifest and clear, almost as evident as are those things which we perceive by our own senses.... With all truthfulness I aver that, just as mathematicians treat their figures as abstracted from bodies, so in treating law I have withdrawn my mind from every particular fact.[14]

At the center of Grotius's argument was the fundamental nature of liberty. Scholars had never reached a working consensus on whether liberty was a law, a right, or a condition. Thomas Aquinas looked askance at the whole idea, allowing only that there was nothing in the natural law to expressly deny it. Luis de Molina, writing at the end of the Renaissance, offered an interesting twist: just as man owned his life and body, so too was he "the owner of his own liberty, and therefore, even standing solely under natural law, he can alienate it and drive himself into slavery."[15] The implication is that people can only sell their liberty (Molina is likely referring to indentured servitude, not slavery) if they own it in the first place. This was something, but not very much. His contemporary Hugues Doneau, writing just a decade before Grotius, traced the concept of liberty back to Ulpian. Just as natural law was common to all creatures, so too were all creatures, man and beast, born free. "Servitude is contrary to nature, as long as we understand nature as the first condition in which men were created, common even to brute animals."[16] As a philosophical construct this was problematic: did not humans "enslave" animals all the time—horses, oxen, cattle—to say nothing of even worse treatment? Would not Doneau object if someone told him his horse was "free"?

Liberty as a condition hardly qualified as a natural law. Accordingly, Grotius dismissed the idea. A beast in the wild might be free, in the sense that no constraints were placed on it, but it did not enjoy "liberty." Liberty was an *awareness* of one's own freedom. Only a human with a rational mind could understand and appreciate this gift. From that awareness came the ability to determine action—or, as the Protestants would have it, make choices:

> God made man *autexousios,* that is, free and *sui iuris*
> [independent], in such a way that each man's actions and the
> use of his goods should be subject to his own will and not to
> another's. And that is approved by the consensus of all the
> nations. For what else is that natural liberty than the faculty of
> doing what it pleases anyone?[17]

From Grotius's reference to the "use of his goods" came another
advance in natural law, property. Reflecting the new individualism of
the seventeenth century, Grotius defined "right" as a power relationship
between the self and all things, internal and external. Thus one exerted
power *(dominium)* over one's body, mind, and possessions equally. This
right was inviolable unless it conflicted with another's—in other words,
if your *dominium* over a piece of property was challenged by another
claim. This was radical indeed. The disparities of wealth and poverty
in seventeenth-century Europe were great, and ordinary subjects had
few property rights. It is not surprising, then, that over a century before
the American revolutionaries built their revolution upon Grotius's concept of liberty, the English Levellers of the mid-seventeenth century
advocated the radical philosophy that every human had an absolute
right to that which they themselves created. As Max Weber argues,
this was entirely consistent with the Protestant work ethic emerging
at that time. Protestants, Weber writes, believed that as God gave His
blessings through the land, only by fully utilizing that land could they
honor God.[18] Richard Overton, an English pamphleteer and prominent Leveller, related this sacred trust to the very right to life itself
and emerged with a holistic political philosophy grounded squarely in
natural law:

> To every individual in nature is given an individual property
> by nature not to be invaded or usurped by any. For everyone,
> as he is himself, so he has a self-propriety, else he could not
> be himself; and of this no second may presume to deprive of
> without manifest violation and affront to the very principles of
> nature and of the rules of equity and justice between man and
> man.... No man has power over my rights and liberties, and I
> over no man's.[19]

The essential inviolability of the individual, which lay at the heart of both Protestant and Grotian philosophy, was the nexus by which natural law translated into reform, and ultimately revolution. Until the seventeenth century, bound up as it was in abstract notions of "justice," natural law remained almost as remote and unknowable as the mind of God itself. Moreover, the task of divining it was, as Cicero had argued, exclusively the province of state magistrates. But if Law began not in the mind of God but in the rational mind of mankind, as Grotius claimed, individuals—magistrate, serf, or slave—were like a sovereign state unto themselves. For the first time, their "rights" were understood not in relation to a state, but inherent to themselves. One did not enjoy these rights as a man or a citizen or a property owner, but simply as a human being. This introduced a radical new concept into law: equality. If each person on earth is born with the rights to life, liberty, security, and property, such rights transcend nationality, gender, religion, and caste. Justice became redefined as the protection of these rights.

This was a profoundly dangerous idea, for many reasons. To start with, it placed clear limits on what a state could do to its citizens in the name of "law." If law existed for the purpose of upholding rights, any law which failed or did the opposite was not, by definition, a law at all. An obvious example was torture. State-sanctioned torture to obtain confessions or evidence in law was ubiquitous throughout the Western world well into the eighteenth century. Not only that; condemned criminals were often subjected to prolonged agony prior to their execution. Sometimes these horrors were enacted in public before a jeering crowd. These cruelties reflected a prevailing view of criminality in which criminals placed themselves against the state or community, almost as a private war. Each crime was an offense against the body politic, and thus torture and execution were a form of collective catharsis; "justice" became a pageant in which the suffering and death of the criminal mirrored the enjoyment and satisfaction of the populace.[20]

But if every person enjoyed natural rights under the law, those rights must extend to criminals as well. Among them, as Grotius identified, was freedom from bodily harm. This natural law foundation coincided with a great societal shift in Western Europe in the eighteenth century, "a sense of the separation and self-possession of individual bodies, along with the possibility of empathy for others," as historian Lynn Hunt describes it.[21] Accordingly, the Baron de Montesquieu condemned the practice of judicial torture in his *Spirit of Laws*, published in 1748. The gruesome breaking and death of a sixty-four-year-old French Protestant in 1762 led Voltaire to pen a *Treatise on Tolerance on the Occasion of the Death of Jean Calas*, which for the first time invoked the phrase "human right" in connection with state practice.

Neither, however, went as far in their reasoning as Italian scholar Cesare Beccaria. Montesquieu and Voltaire viewed torture largely from the perspective of the state; states, they claimed, as custodians of civilization, must not engage in uncivilized conduct. Beccaria distinguished himself by viewing the practice from the vantage of the condemned criminal whose rights were being abridged. Torture was not only barbaric but "useless cruelty."[22] It served no purpose other than bloodlust and violated the condemned person's sacred rights for the amusement of the crowd. Moreover, if the state could not violate a person's body without also violating his or her natural rights, he reasoned, how could it take a life? The state did not give the subject his life any more than his body or his freedom; what right then did it have to take it? Only if the subject could be assumed to have entered into a social compact with the state could such a thing be allowed, but "who has ever willingly given up to others the authority to kill him?"

Capital punishment, Beccaria argued, like torture, was not only savage but "useless": the same end could be achieved through incarceration. A rational state, like a rational individual, must choose the wisest course and not be guided by vengeance or bloodlust. Therefore all punishments meted out by the state must be proportional to the crimes committed: anything in excess "is not punishment, but abuse." To those who argued that the death penalty was indeed useful as a deterrent, Beccaria had two responses: first, that a lifetime in prison was infinitely worse than a moment of pain; second, that any useful gains would be more than outweighed by "the example of savagery it gives to man." While not going quite so far as his Italian contemporary, English jurist William Blackstone agreed in principle. Criminal law, he wrote, must "be conformable to the dictates of truth and justice, the feelings of humanity, and the indelible rights of mankind."[23]

❖ ❖ ❖

Yet it was liberty, not life or security, that came to dominate natural law discourse in the seventeenth and eighteenth centuries. Liberty was the most dangerous right of all: broadest to define, easiest to breach. A state could hardly take someone's life or property, or cause them bodily harm, without it being instantly recognized for what it was. But what exactly constitutes a breach of liberty? This was particularly problematic as law abjures conduct seen as harmful to the community and may also require other conduct that is beneficial. These are limitations on choice or, if you prefer, freedom. The state's "right" to restrain conduct rests on the perceived harm or benefit to the whole, but if that were the only basis it would be scarcely any different from Cicero's conception of law as "the security of the people." Instead, as scholars of the Enlightenment argued, the citizen-subject should enjoy as much freedom as possible except when their enjoyment impinges on the rights of another. But that balance is almost as impossible to find now as then.

Surely, however, any definition of the right to liberty would include freedom from slavery. Yet it was during the seventeenth and eighteenth centuries that the transport of slaves from Africa to the New World peaked, transforming the American continents and reshaping European economies. By the time Grotius wrote *De Jure Belli et Pacis* in 1625, the Spanish in the Americas had been enslaving the indigenous population for over a century and had recently begun importing African slaves to augment the labor force. Soon their example would be followed by the English colonies of St. Kitts and Barbados, which spread in turn to the Carolinas, until by the end of the century nearly every Atlantic colony had a captive population. In 1644, Grotius's erstwhile employers, the Dutch West India Company, opened their first slave-trading post at Offra, in present-day Benin.

Grotius did not condemn slavery himself, taking refuge instead in Aristotle's patronizing line that "certain persons by their nature are slaves."[24] The implication was that even though they were nominally free, like all humanity, their culture and/or biology predestined they would "choose" slavery. This obvious fallacy was not lost on later scholars. The antislavery movement that emerged during the eighteenth century drew its inspiration partly from natural law and partly from Christian thought—indeed it might be considered the linear descendant of such long-dead voices as Francisco de Vitoria and Bartolome de las Casas. The precept that God instilled in each person a gift of divine reason never jibed well with slavery and conquest. By the end of the seventeenth century, Christian theology, like natural law philosophy, had largely come to reject slavery outright. Protestants and Catholics accepted equally that God created humanity in His image and instilled it with morality. One Protestant sect, the Quakers, developed this idea yet further, believing each person to be possessed of an Inner Light, "that of God within man." This was not just a moral code but a fragment of the Divine Singularity that bound all humankind together in a single community. It should not be surprising, then, that Quakers were among the first to organize anti-slavery societies in England and the American colonies.[25]

There was also a rational, secular argument against the practice. Criminal reform was predicated on the idea of the relationship between the sovereign and the citizen. But what were the state's obligations to noncitizens? They had entered into no social compact with the state. Was the state obliged to respect their natural rights as well? Of course it was, for two reasons. First, natural rights were universal, transcending government and nationality. Just as one individual could not violate another without offending the natural law, neither could the citizens of one state violate another. Second, states were proscribed from "barbarous" conduct: the state, as a reflection of the community, must at all times uphold that community's law. Cruelty was not constrained by geographic boundaries. By denying their captives' liberty, the European states debased themselves just as surely as if they had enslaved their own citizens. Francis Scott Key, appearing before the Supreme Court in a slave-trading case in 1825, argued forcefully that whether the practice was universally criminalized or not, it was universally criminal. "By the law of nature," he declared, "all men are free." Key lost the case. "The African slave trade is contrary to the law of nature," Justice John Marshall wrote, "but it is not prohibited by the positive law of nations."[26] The wide gulf between theory and practice ensured that it would be many decades before Western society came to accept the unlawfulness of slavery; as late as the 1860s Southern slave owners still thumbed through their Bibles to find justification in scripture. Nevertheless, the melding of Christian belief and natural rights provided the necessary foundation, without which it is difficult to imagine how the practice could have ceased.

The politicization of natural rights, especially liberty, had even more radical consequences. It began with an unanswered question nearly two thousand years old. In *De Legibus*, Cicero maintained that "if a state has no law, it is not for that reason to be reckoned a state at all,"[27] and underscored this idea with a copious list of "virtues" for a proper magistrate. As he would with all things, Cicero sought balance: the people required and deserved justice, while the magistrate required and deserved obedience. "We would not, however, limit ourselves to requiring from the citizens submission and obedience towards their magistrates; we would also enjoin them to by all means honor and love their rulers." Minus the Orwellian overtones, Cicero's model for an ideal state looks contractual: each side has responsibilities and expectations. If citizens broke faith by committing a crime, the state had the right to compel or punish them. Even social dissent was cancerous: "If anyone shall disturb the public harmony, and foment party quarrels, let him be punished as a criminal."[28]

Yet Cicero's contract seems curiously one-sided. While the penalties for citizens are clear, what would happen if the state ceased to uphold the law? Would its citizens have the right to declare it was no longer a state and refashion a new government in its place? It is tempting to say yes, but there is nothing in *De Legibus* to support this view. The closest Cicero ever comes to acknowledging the possibility is in an oblique reference to the lawless state of Rome under King Tarquin, when he argues that natural law nevertheless continued to exist even when it was not being followed. The implication, however slight, is that a tyrant is an aberration that must be borne until the natural and normal state of harmony inevitably returns. This Stoic forbearance would have been small consolation for Tarquin's subjects, or indeed for Cicero himself under the dictatorships of Sulla and Caesar.

The emergence of natural-rights philosophy in the seventeenth century reanimated the old conundrum. Cicero's contract was between two collective entities: the citizenry (*civiae*) and the magistracy (*gubernacula*). In an age of rights, however, the contract was between each individual and the sovereign. Could that contract ever be annulled? Who could do so, and how? The question took on an air of urgency in 1641, when relations between King Charles I and his recalcitrant parliament broke irrevocably. The English Civil War, fought between 1641 and 1649, saw king and parliament raise rival armies to settle on the battlefield the question of which had the ultimate authority to rule.

Charles I maintained his claim derived from divine right, customary law, and practical necessity. The sovereign was the embodiment of law, the safeguard of liberty. Without him the people had no law and no rights. At his execution in 1649, his last words conveyed a warning to his countrymen:

> And truly I desire their Liberty and Freedom as much as any Body whomsoever. But I must tell you, that their Liberty and Freedom consists in having of Government: those Laws, by which their Life and their Gods may be most their own. It is not for having share in government that is nothing pertaining to them. A subject and a sovereign are clean different things, and therefore until they do that, I mean, that you do put the people in that liberty as I say, certainly they will never enjoy themselves.[29]

Thomas Hobbes agreed. Writing in support of the king, he saw the root of the problem in Grotius's definition of liberty. Grotius had identified liberty as a right alongside life, security, and property; all were natural laws that must and should be reflected in the positive laws of the state. But, said Hobbes, liberty was not like the others. Liberty was not law but its antithesis, a kind of void that he defined as absence of restraint. "Natural liberty is a Right not constituted but allowed by the Laws; for the Laws being removed, our liberty is absolute." States could not create laws to safeguard liberty, for every law constrained it still further: "Law is a Fetter, Right a freedom, and they differ like contraries."[30]

Hobbes's argument was subtler and more complex than it sounds. The right to liberty was indeed distinct from other rights; one could enjoy one's life and limb to their heart's content without disturbing anyone, but unfettered liberty was indistinguishable from anarchy. Something could not be a natural right, he reasoned, if its enjoyment threatened or nullified all other so-called natural rights. In natural law, liberty was not unrestrained freedom but "the liberty each man hath to use his own power, as he will himself, for the preservation of his nature, that is to say, of his own life."[31] Self-preservation was for Hobbes the essential fount of natural law. It must be so, for "it is neither absurd, nor reprehensible, neither against the dictates of true reason for a man to use all his endeavors to preserve and defend his Body and the members thereof from death and sorrows…. Therefore the first foundation of natural right is this, that every man as much as in him lies endeavor to protect his life and members."[32]

Human beings had a natural right to self-preservation, but human nature precluded its practice without some form of restraint. Man loved his liberty, but he loved exerting his authority as well. This logic led inexorably to Hobbes's famous (and cynical) conclusion that the only way to preserve natural law rights was to surrender all authority to an artificial body, the state:

> The final cause, end, or design in men (who naturally love liberty and dominion over others) in the introduction of that restraint upon themselves in which we see them live in commonwealths is the foresight of their own preservation…. For the laws of nature of themselves, without the terror of some power to cause them to be observed, are contrary to our natural passions, that carry us to partiality, pride, revenge, and the like. And covenants without swords are but words, and of no strength to secure a man at all.[33]

In some ways Hobbes's argument is similar to Cicero's; both recognized the necessity of a state to articulate the natural law and compel obedience. By translating justice to right, Hobbes was merely updating the old Stoic concept for a new and different age. He would have agreed with Cicero's famous dictum that "the security of the people is the highest law." And like Cicero, Hobbes left no escape clause from the social compact he envisioned. The state, once brought into being, could not be undone. If individuals were allowed to challenge its laws on the grounds that their "liberty" was breached, no state could exist at all, for every law was a restraint upon liberty. Only if the state wholly ceased protecting the security of life and person could it be construed to have ceased its function, and Hobbes could imagine no circumstance where a state would wish to annihilate its own people. In 1644 this was a practical impossibility anyway; it would take another three centuries for technology to make it feasible.

John Locke, writing several decades later in the aftermath of the "glorious revolution," sought to reconcile abstract theory with political reality. His times were no less galvanic than Hobbes's. Prompted by the birth of a Catholic heir presumptive in 1688, a cabal of lords and parliamentarians deposed King James II and invited William of Orange, *stadtholder* of the Netherlands, to take the throne. Despite its widespread popularity among the English people, the revolution could scarcely be described as a legal enterprise. An English Bill of Rights, passed by Parliament under the watchful gaze of King William III and Queen Mary in 1689, attempted to make it so ex post facto. The bill began by citing a long list of charges against James, "all [of] which are utterly and directly contrary to the known laws and statutes and freedoms of this realm," before advancing the astonishing claim that James II had "vacated" the throne of his own will, forcing Parliament to appoint a successor.

The legal argument was twofold: the king had broken the law, and he had abandoned the kingdom. The state being effectively broken, the Bill of Rights reestablished it under a new contractual basis. William III and his successors would be pledged to uphold a list of "rights," constitutional limitations on their power. In some aspects this was a reworking of the Magna Carta, pressed on King John by his rebellious barons in 1215. Both spoke of the king's obligation to uphold "ancient rights and liberties." But the Bill of Rights went much further, placing the king in a subordinate position to Parliament and effectively redefining the English "state" forevermore: "Now in pursuance of the premises the said Lords Spiritual and Temporal and Commons in Parliament...do pray that it may be declared and enacted that all and singular the rights and liberties asserted and claimed in the said declaration are the true, ancient and indubitable rights and liberties of the people of this kingdom, and so shall be esteemed, allowed, adjudged, deemed and taken to be...in all time to come."[34]

No one could dispute that Parliament had the power to do as it did, but was it legal? Thomas Hobbes (and James II and presumably his late father, Charles I) would say no. Both the Magna Carta and Bill of Rights were essentially ransom notes forced upon the monarchy after a civil war. They were not "contracts" in the proper sense, as only one party had been obliged to sign them. John Locke, who had returned from exile to take up a position in William's government, nevertheless claimed them valid. He began his analysis by restating the accepted truth, that superseding the laws of king and Parliament was another, higher law: "The State of Nature has a Law of Nature to govern it, which obliges every one: And Reason, which is that Law, teaches all Mankind, who will but consult it, that being equal and independent, no one ought to harm another in his Life, Health, Liberty, or Possessions." He even agreed with Hobbes, up to a point:

> And that all Men may be restrained from invading others Rights, and from doing hurt to one another, and the Law of Nature be observed, which willeth the Peace and Preservation of all Mankind, the Execution of the Law of Nature is in that State, put into every Man's hands, whereby everyone has a right to punish transgressors of that Law to such a Degree as may hinder its Violation. For the Law of Nature would, as all other Laws that concern Men in this World, be in vain, if there were no body that in the State of Nature had Power to Execute that Law.[35]

The temporal, corporeal state was necessary to constrain humankind's passions and enforce the natural law. Locke rejected, however, Hobbes's conception of freedom and law as opposites. Granted that freedom was not "a liberty for every man to do what he wants," it nevertheless had a meaning beyond just preservation of the self, as Hobbes claimed. The individual under natural law must not be "subject to the arbitrary Will of another, but freely follow his own."[36] The key word was "arbitrary." Curtailment of action must be justified, and the only justification possible was in defense of natural laws, including the freedom of others. "The end of Law is not to abolish or restrain, but to preserve and enlarge Freedom," Locke concluded, for "where there is no Law, there is no Freedom."[37]

Locke also challenged the monolithic image of the sovereign portrayed in Hobbes's *Leviathan.* For Hobbes, state and sovereign were one and indivisible; for Locke, they were two separate entities. The king was, ultimately, a man, and thus as prey to illogical passions as any other man. As head of state, his capacity for great good and great harm was magnified by his office. Therefore when an outraged citizenry rose up and deposed a tyrant, they set themselves against the man, not the state. "In transgressing the Law of Nature," wrote Locke, "the Offender declares himself to live by another rule than of reason and common Equity...so he becomes dangerous to Mankind.... And in this case, and upon this ground, every Man hath a Right to punish the Offender, and be the Executioner of the Law of Nature."[38]

This was political dynamite. Locke was finally and explicitly answering the question left by Cicero. The social contract between state and citizen was inviolable and insoluble, but it was maintained by fallible humanity. The people need not suffer a despot out of some blind deference to order, for a despotic king was merely another individual in a state of nature who had amassed more sharp sticks and stones than anyone else. "I shall desire those who make this Objection," Locke declared,

> to remember that Absolute Monarchs are but Men, and if Government is to be the Remedy of those Evils, which necessarily follow from Men's being Judges of their own Cases, and the State of Nature is therefore not to be endured, I desire to know what kind of Government that is, and how much better it is than the State of Nature, where one Man commanding a multitude has the Liberty to be Judge in his own Case, and may do to all his Subjects whatever he pleases, without the least liberty to anyone to question those who Execute his Pleasure?[39]

Despite or perhaps because of their radicalism, Locke's *Two Treatises of Government* went largely unremarked during his lifetime. It was only in the middle decades of the eighteenth century that they resurfaced, thanks to a new generation of natural law scholars led by Swiss philosopher Jean-Jacques Burlamaqui. Their work, along with the political tracts of Montesquieu, Diderot, Rousseau, and others, transformed the discourse on rights from retrospective to aspirational: coupled with Enlightenment ideas on the perfectibility of man, natural rights provide a blueprint for the ideal state.[40] This concept was both new and ancient. A progressive view of humanity had always been integral to natural law; as it comes to know the "mind of God" over millennia, human society moves closer to the celestial. But never before had this concept been employed to justify revolution.

❖ ❖ ❖

The American colonies proved fertile ground for arguments of this kind. Protestant individualism was nowhere stronger than in Puritan Massachusetts, a colony which through its charter had attained a measure of independence from the English crown since its foundation. This was coupled with an equally strong streak of utopianism: Puritans had determined in the 1630s to create a "city on a hill" to serve as both refuge and beacon for their benighted brethren across the Atlantic. Whether the experiment was a success was a matter of debate, but the ideals remained. As historians Leonard Levy and Alfred Young have argued, "Puritan political theory, like Puritanism itself, left a lasting influence on American development.... The social compact theory and representative government...natural law and rights...and the exceptional importance of the individual—all may be found in Puritan political ideas."[41]

This argument must not be taken too far. Puritanism was neither the largest nor the most dominant faith in the English Atlantic, and Massachusetts was something of an anomaly in its charter government. What was universal to every colony, however, was a melding of English and distinctively local law. Acts of Parliament, acts of King-in-Council, and directives from the Board of Trade arrived weekly in every colony, to be placed in the hands of the colonial governor for immediate implementation. What happened next was less certain. Governors often chose to ignore, dismiss, or deliberately misconstrue these instructions while assiduously claiming in reports to London to be following them to the letter. There is no question they saw their colonies as socially, economically, and legally distinct from the mother country. This distinction can best be seen during great political crises like the English Civil War and the Glorious Revolution. Following the latter, New England colonists eagerly arrested their crown-appointed governor, Edmund Andros, and demanded a return of their charter rights. The situation in New York descended into even greater anarchy as mutual claimants jockeyed for power. Even in times of relative placidity, the colonies guarded their legal autonomy. An act to create admiralty courts in the colonies in 1698, for example, provoked Rhode Island governor Walter Clarke to warn the colonial assembly that to recognize the admiralty commission was to surrender their charter rights and privileges, and that "we had better like men spend the one half of our Estates to maintain our privileges" sooner than be "brought into bondage and slavery."[42] One year later his successor, Governor Samuel Cranston, was still refusing to acknowledge the commissions: "Let us not fall into the bonds of slavery. A word to the wise is sufficient."[43]

At the heart of colonial law was a paradox. When colonists insisted on their rights "as Englishmen," they referred to the so-called unwritten constitution: a body of codified and customary law stretching back centuries which included, though was not limited to, the Magna Carta and English Bill of Rights. Englishmen rightly viewed their legal system as the truest expression of natural law presently in existence. William Blackstone, writing at the mid-eighteenth century, wrote that all law derived from the law of nature, which translated into the rights to life, liberty, security, and property. But, he lamented, only England seemed to be aware of that fact: "These [rights] were formerly, either by inheritance or purchase, the rights of all mankind; but in most other countries of the world being now more or less debased and destroyed, they at present may be said to remain...the rights of the people of England."[44] This was a harsh judgment on other nations' law, but it had a kernel of truth. Englishmen and -women considered themselves the "freest" of all citizens of the world in the eighteenth century, the legacy of two convulsive revolutions and a constitutional monarchy.

American colonists shared this view. "Every British subject born on the continent of America, or in any other of the British dominions, is by the law of God and nature, by the common law, and by act of parliament...entitled to all the natural, essential, inherent and inseparable rights of our fellow subjects in Great Britain," James Otis declared in 1764.[45] But to that body of customary law they also added their charters and whatever local law had been erected within the colony. Therein lay the paradox. Colonial law was not British law but an amalgam. On what foundation did local law rest, especially (as was often the case) when it conflicted with the mother country's? If the colonies ignored the law being transmitted from London (as they often did), could they still lay claim to legal status as Englishmen?

Natural law filled the void. If local law had no basis under English jurisprudence, and indeed might contradict it, it could still be held valid if it reaffirmed natural rights, which were universal. "Thanks be to God," Reverend Samuel Langdon told his Massachusetts brethren in 1775, "that he has given us, as men, natural rights independent of all human laws whatever, and that these rights are recognized by the grand Charter of British Liberties."[46] Some of them, at any rate. Less than a year later, an anonymous pamphleteer suggested that this cherry-picking of English law was not only justified, but essential. Colonists "carry with them only so much of English laws as is applicable to their own situation," he argued, and if "their native rights as freemen" were violated, they could and must assert their "natural rights."[47]

More august voices lent their support. If the colonies had the right to create such local laws as did not offend the natural law, surely they also had the right to reject any British law that did. Philadelphia jurist James Wilson tackled the subject of parliamentary authority in 1774 in a brief but tightly argued essay. Of Parliament, he asked rhetorically: "Have they a natural right to make laws by which we may be deprived of our properties, of our liberties, of our lives?" Clearly not, as these were natural rights themselves. Wilson, a Scotsman by birth and well versed in both Grotius and Locke, grounded his argument in the familiar claim that all persons—colonist or Englishman or Chinese, for that matter—are born "equal and free: no one has a right to any authority over another without his consent."[48]

From Boston, staunch patriot John Adams concurred. A lawyer himself, Adams had spent much of his adult life learning and arguing over Massachusetts law—an impenetrable morass of custom and local practice; acts of assembly; gubernatorial proclamations; cases; charter rights; residual Puritan *iuris ecclesiastici;* and, of course, British law. This was every bit as confusing as it sounds. Nor was it singular. In December 1697, the Board of Trade issued a formal request for a copy of all laws currently in effect in Rhode Island.[49] What came back was, according to a board member, "a blind copy of their laws,"[50] which was "full of incoherence and nonsense jumbled together and confused. The Government themselves cannot tell when they have the whole: how then can the people be supposed to know what is Law amongst them?"[51] For Adams, however, this was the source of the law's strength. He granted that colonial law was a distinct and diverse genus whose only common ancestor was natural law. "How then," he demanded, "do we New England men derive our laws? I say not from parliament, not from common law, but from the law of nature, and the compact made with the King in our charters."[52]

The American pre-Revolutionary legal landscape was thus a hodgepodge of Protestant individualism, Puritan utopianism, Grotian philosophy, Lockian social contract theory, British *ius gentium*, and local practice, all bound up in a rather woolly but deeply felt adherence to natural law and rights. Nowhere was this curious admixture better expressed than in the Declaration of Independence. Thomas Jefferson freely admitted that he drew from numerous sources when drafting the declaration, not least his own *Summary View of the Rights of British America*.[53] In its first sentence the declaration pays deference to both Protestant and Enlightenment concepts when it speaks of the necessity "to assume among the powers of the earth, the separate and equal station which the Laws of Nature and of Nature's God entitle them." This was not a secular invocation; the rights to life, liberty, and the pursuit of happiness did not merely exist in nature but were "endowed by our Creator," an idea that (as we have seen) traces itself back through Melanchthon to Aquinas and Cicero. Nevertheless, the subsequent passage was strikingly modern and illustrates just how far natural law concepts had evolved:

> That whenever any Government becomes destructive to those ends, it is the Right of the People to alter or abolish it, and to institute new Government, laying its foundation on such principles and organizing its powers in such form, as to them shall seem most likely to effect their safety and happiness.[54]

The Declaration of Independence was galvanic, more so after it became clear the American Revolution was going to succeed. "I have lived to see the rights of men better understood than ever," one patriotic clergyman exulted, "and nations panting for liberty, which seemed to have lost the idea of it."[55] The Marquis de Condorcet echoed this theme of lost utopia, writing in 1789 that the Declaration of Independence was "a simple and sublime exposition of these rights that are at once so sacred and so long forgotten."[56] Forgotten by whom? Never before had natural rights been the explicit basis for revolution. But the desire to link modern revolutions with "ancient rights and liberties" was understandable. The French revolutionary assembly underscored this predisposition by promulgating a Declaration of the Rights of Man and of the Citizen, which effectively forbade citizen and state alike from "forgetting" natural rights:

> The representatives of the French people, organized as a National Assembly, believing that the ignorance, neglect, or contempt of the rights of man are the sole cause of public calamities and of the corruption of governments, have determined to set forth in a solemn declaration the natural, unalienable, and sacred rights of man, in order that this declaration, being constantly before all the members of the Social body, shall remind them continually of their rights and duties.[57]

By the end of the eighteenth century, natural law had irrevocably transformed into natural rights. The concept, which had once been an abstraction, now became the basis upon which all Western governments were founded and the test whereby all state law was judged. This seemed to bode well for a new body of laws grounded in the basic rights of life, liberty, security, and property. But there were crosscurrents. How could one speak of universal freedom when a significant part of the world's population was enslaved? How could French revolutionaries continue to maintain the pretense of a natural law republic throughout the Reign of Terror? As a new century began, these questions remained unanswered. But the author of the Declaration of Independence, for one, was unperturbed. "The tree of liberty must be watered from time to time with the blood of patriots and tyrants," he once remarked. "It is its natural manure."

If so, the next century promised a deluge.

— 3 —

THE CIVILIZATION GAME

In February 1901, a month after the start of a new century, Samuel Clemens took a moment to reflect on the last. He was perhaps the most qualified man to do so. Clemens, aka Mark Twain, had seen more of the Victorian world than anyone, traveling across the United States in the days before the transcontinental railroad and around the world (twice) in his old age. He had met emperors and Borneo tribesmen. He had journeyed on every kind of vehicle from rickshaw to ocean liner—even an automobile. He quickly adopted the contemporary obsession with machinery and invested in several disastrous flops. He was possibly the greatest after-dinner speaker in history.

But most of all, through his endless perambulations and interactions with a good part of the globe, Twain had seen more of that elusive animal called civilization than any of his peers. By 1901 he had seen too much. With his usual caustic wit, he told his fellow Americans: "Extending the Blessings of Civilization to our Brother who Sits in Darkness has been a good trade and has paid well, on the whole; and there is money in it yet, if carefully worked—but not enough, in my judgement, to make any considerable risk advisable." The imagery was biblical—Matthew 4:16. "The people who sat in darkness have seen a great light." It was a favorite quotation among missionaries and empire builders. Rudyard Kipling invoked it in his famous exhortation of the "White Man's Burden":

> Take up the White Man's Burden,
> And reap his old reward:
> The blame of those ye better
> The hate of those ye guard—
> The cry of those ye humor
> (Ah slowly) to the light:
> "Why brought ye us from bondage.
> "Our loved Egyptian night?"

Twain was unimpressed. He had seen how the English ruled their empire with a combination of condescension and brutality. He quoted a recent dispatch from a private in the Boer War: "We tore up the hill and into the intrenchments, and the Boers saw we had them; so they dropped their guns and went down on their knees and put up their hands clasped, and begged for mercy. And we gave it them—*with the long spoon.*" The long spoon was a bayonet. Twain was similarly unsparing in his judgment of the German, Spanish, and Russian empires, but his greatest vitriol was reserved for his countrymen. A year earlier he had admitted: "I [once] wanted the American eagle to go screaming into the Pacific…. But I have thought some more, since then…. We have gone there to conquer, not to redeem. And so I am an anti-imperialist. I am opposed to having the eagle put its talons on any other land."[1] The base hypocrisy of the so-called "blessings of civilization" was now more apparent than ever. "Having now laid all the historical facts before the Person Sitting in Darkness," Twain wrote acidly, "we should bring him to again, and explain them to him. We should say to him:

> They look doubtful, but in reality they are not. There have been lies; yes, but they were told in a good cause. We have been treacherous; but that was only in order that real good might come out of apparent evil. True, we have crushed a deceived and confiding people; we have turned against the weak and the friendless who trusted us…but each detail was for the best…. This world-girdling accumulation of trained morals, high principles, and justice, cannot do an unright thing, an unfair thing, an ungenerous thing, an unclean thing. It knows what it is about. Give yourself no uneasiness; it is all right.[2]

How had things gone so disastrously wrong? How had the concept of natural rights, which seemed in 1800 to herald a new Age of Enlightenment, become so warped by 1900 as to be an instrument of oppression? Twain, though an eyewitness to the result, had not been present at the start. The Victorian era was the watershed moment when social reform and imperialism buried natural law beneath an avalanche of dubious new "rights" and supplanted it on the global stage with the amorphous concept of civilization. The consequences remain with us to this day.

❖ ❖ ❖

By 1794, translations of the Declaration of Independence, the American Bill of Rights, and the French Declaration of the Rights of Man had circulated throughout Latin America, inflaming *insurrectos* like Simon Bolivar and Jose de San Martin. Bolivar, "El Liberator," dictated the 1812 constitution of Colombia, which guaranteed "the rights of man and citizen…in full enjoyment of their liberty and independence."[3] Thomas Jefferson, now in his dotage at Monticello, declared himself delighted.

A similar transformation had taken place in England and on the Continent. The Prussian *Allgemeines Landrecht* (General Law of the Land) stated in its preface that "the general rights of the individual rest upon his natural freedom to pursue and promote his own welfare, without injury to the rights of others."[4] The Napoleonic Code, established in 1804, declared that "the exercise of civil rights is independent of the quality of citizen, which is only acquired and preserved conformably to the constitutional law."[5] As with Blackstone, it divided the laws into categories conforming to natural rights of life, liberty, and property and proceeded to spell out the civil law in each with exhaustive detail. Unlike revolutionary declarations, however, there was no invocation to that "universal and unchanging law, the source of all positive laws, none other than natural reason." The code was a much more workmanlike document. "The laws," it began bluntly, "are executory throughout the whole French territory, by virtue of the promulgation made thereof by the first consul."

In these early years of the nineteenth century, even revolutionary language continued to be couched in familiar terms of natural right. The

Chartist movement, which flamed briefly in England in the late 1830s, sought a new constitution for the British people modeled in part on the American example. "The universal political right of every human being," it maintained, "is superior and stands apart from all customs, forms, or ancient usage; a fundamental right not in the power of man to confer, nor justly to deprive him of."[6] In an 1837 petition, Chartists called for, among other things, universal suffrage and equal representation in parliament. The movement collapsed almost as quickly as it arose, but it is significant that the first workers' revolt in Victorian England was grounded firmly in Enlightenment concepts of political right.

That would soon change. Observing the revolutions that peppered the Continent between 1820 and 1848, German economist Karl Marx drew some conclusions. Even revolutionaries, he declared, were immersed in "a cult of law, a cult of the State."[7] They argued for radical change using the same ossified lexicon as their oppressors. Natural rights, Marx concluded, were nothing but a bourgeois construct designed to maintain its control over humanity through the promulgation of false goals for the masses. "Freedom" was defined in political rather than social terms, but real freedom, according to Marx, began with self-sufficiency. What good did it do a man to have the right to vote if he was denied the ability to feed his family, or himself?

Marx's contemporary, Friedrich Engels, agreed. Universality was a myth—and a convenient one, as it kept the working class falsely content with their lot. Rights, he maintained, "varied so much from nation to nation and from age to age that they have been in direct contradiction to each other."[8] Morality was a construct as well, emerging from a particular class at a particular moment in history. Contrary to religious teachings or Enlightenment philosophy, Engels declared, "all moral theories are the product, in the last analysis, of the economic stage which society has reached at that particular epoch. And as society has hitherto moved into class antagonisms, morality was always a class morality."[9]

Events favored this new relativism. The disparities between rich and poor in the West had always been great, but not so great that a universal language of rights was incompatible. There had been a merchant class and a planter class, and lesser cognates of each. As such, a townsman and a farmer might have different lives, but they understood one another.

This basic comity was all but destroyed in the nineteenth century. The rise of factories and mechanized labor during the Industrial Revolution transformed villages into cities and cities into slums. Under the factory system workers became "wage slaves," often earning just enough to pay the rent for a home owned by the factory and goods purchased from factory stores. The insatiable appetite for coal to run machinery, railways, and steamships consigned an entire generation into the mines, where conditions were even more hellish than in factories. On transatlantic liners the classes were divided into rigid socioeconomic strata that brought Marx's theories into relief: at the very top, first class dwelled in sybaritic luxury; second class, the bourgeoisie, lived just beneath; and under them the cattle stalls of steerage. But below them all, in the stygian depths, an army of stokers and trimmers worked in infernal heat, smoke, and dust keeping the boilers alight. This floating city, Marx's microcosm, quite literally ran on the back-breaking labor of the men at the bottom.[10]

From these stark inequalities came a new understanding of rights. "Property is theft!" Pierre-Joseph Proudhon declared in 1840.[11] Rights bound humanity together, he wrote, but property by its very nature created divisions. In a state constructed on Enlightenment principles of law, as Jean-Jacques Rousseau once argued, the individual should exist in as much liberty as in a state of nature. Each person within the state enjoyed the same liberty and security as any other, but the right to *own* property was not the same as the right to property itself. No one had any natural rights to property, only the same theoretical right to acquire it. Yet, as Proudhon argued, right and ability were not synonymous: the working classes often had no ability to purchase land, even if they had the "right" to do so. Conversely, Marx and Engels charged, the natural right of property had become an economic weapon wielded by the ruling classes against the proletariat. There was some truth in this. As historian Douglas Hay argues, property rights in eighteenth- and nineteenth-century England allowed for the establishment of a punitive legal structure designed to maintain class divisions. [12]

Numerous legal texts from Grotius to Blackstone spoke of citizens' "enjoyment" of their natural rights. But according to Marx and Engels, the rights to life, liberty, and security required a foundation of economic and social security in order to be enjoyed. From this basic premise came an ultimate division between that which the state may not deny the individual (natural, or "negative," rights) and that which the state has the obligation to provide (social, or "positive" rights). Now Pandora's box was opened. If the state had certain positive obligations toward its citizens, what were they? Not all answers emerged from the Marxist handbook. In an age of reform, starch-shirted Victorian crusaders argued passionately for the "right" of the working class to an education, to public libraries and universities, to parks and museums and other temples of the spirit. The horrendous conditions of the slums sparked calls for the right to clean water, natural light, and fireproof buildings. And, of course, working conditions in the factories brought forth an entirely new language of rights: wage minimums, workday hours, child labor, safe conditions, and so on.

Not all (nor even most) of these cries for reform came from socialists. Victorians saw the charitable state as an extension of the charitable home: just as each person sought the good for themselves and their family, Christian duty required that they seek it for the community as well. Public buildings became temples dedicated to this new reformist zeal, from libraries modeled on the Parthenon to firehouses with garish neo-Gothic battlements. This was the architecture of ennoblement: each building symbolized the higher purpose behind its function. Railway stations were quite literally cathedrals to progress. Even prisons, hospitals, and insane asylums were transformed into palaces of rehabilitation. Thus the definition of "rights" gained almost limitless elasticity: a right was anything that, if enjoyed by all, served the public good.

New rights encouraged new claimants. Unmoored from natural law, this new generation argued that each individual within a society could advance certain rights subjective to their station. Hence the factory worker enjoyed certain rights *as* a worker, which would be neither needed nor sought by an aristocrat. In that year of revolutions, 1848, another revolt was taking shape that would ultimately eclipse them all. At the Seneca Falls Convention, Susan B. Anthony and Elizabeth Cady Stanton offered a devastating summary of how their rights as women had been trampled by men for millennia. It was all the more fascinating for its joint advocacy of traditional rights under natural law and new positive ones:

The history of mankind is a history of repeated injuries and usurpations on the part of man toward woman, having in direct object the establishment of an absolute tyranny over her.... He has compelled her to submit to law, in the formation of which she had no voice. He has withheld for her rights which are given to the most ignorant and degraded men—both natives and foreigners.... He closes against her all the avenues of wealth and distinction which he considers most honorable to himself.... He has denied her the facilities for obtaining a thorough education, all colleges being closed against her.[13]

The nineteenth-century extension of rights was not merely in response to Marx or Engels; social advocates like Thomas John Barnardo and Florence Nightingale did not speak through a mouthpiece of Marxism. Advocacy was broader and more diverse than any political or economic theory could encompass. But it is certainly true that socialism and communism emerged from the same overarching societal impulse that dominated the age: reform. Reform could mean all things to all people. For Chartists in England and their contemporaries in the Dorr War in Rhode Island, it meant extending suffrage; for Stanton and Cady, it meant egalitarianism between the sexes; for the myriad Christian and secular organizations throughout America, Britain, and the Continent, it meant anything from temperance to postal laws to clean hospital beds.

❖ ❖ ❖

Yet for much of the century, on the international scene, reform meant slavery. As discussed in the previous chapter, slavery had long been a sore point for legal theorists, as it appeared to violate not just one but every natural right. Grotius abandoned his customary cool logic to make the utterly spurious claim that Africans chose to be slaves. A highly selective understanding seemed to reinforce this view: the Spanish and Portuguese, arriving in West Africa in the early 1600s, discovered a common practice among tribes of enslaving those captured in battle. This had been common in the West also, when Rome paraded her captives through the streets of the Forum, but such unpleasant realities were best forgotten. One of the crowning ironies of the seventeenth and eighteenth centuries was that both slavery and the theory of natural rights flourished in perfect juxtaposition.[14]

Aside from Quakers and other splinter sects, the first significant voice of dissent came from none other than William Blackstone. In the first edition of his *Commentaries,* published in 1765, Blackstone declared that "a slave or a negro, the moment he lands in England, falls under the protection of the laws and with regard to all natural rights becomes *eo instanti* a freeman."[15] This was charming but untrue. No such understanding existed in England, where slaves—especially in major cities like London—were commonplace. Moreover, Blackstone draws an odd distinction between English soil and English law: even if such persons were freed once they reached England, what about all those territories under English jurisdiction? These included Barbados, Jamaica, Virginia, and the Carolinas, all of whose economies depended upon slave labor.

Blackstone's edict was finally given form in a 1772 case, *Somerset v. Stewart.* On the question of whether a slave was presumed free upon arriving in Britain, Lord Mansfield declared he must be: no law establishing the legality of slavery had ever existed in the country, and in the absence of law one must look to those rights and freedoms that did exist. These spelled out quite clearly the natural rights of all persons—black or white—within England. Mansfield was careful to draw a distinction between the isles and the colonies, where such positive law legitimizing slavery had been enacted by colonial assemblies. Nevertheless, the *Somerset* case had the effect of a warning knell. Slavery was "so odious" and contrary to natural law, wrote Mansfield, that it could only persist until right-thinking legislators disposed of it.[16]

At the beginning of the nineteenth century, this legal reform became a crusade. A faction of Parliament, led by the charismatic William Wilberforce, campaigned to extend Mansfield's ban to the whole of the British slave trade. Their efforts bore fruit with the passage of the Slave Act of 1807, which declared the trade an offense to natural law and the law of nations. But that was only the beginning. It soon became clear that banning British merchants merely encouraged other nations to carry slaves—a fear that had been articulated forcefully by opponents of the bill in Parliament. Hence after 1807 Britain turned her efforts to enforcing a general ban throughout the world.[17] This sweeping policy must be understood in context. From the French Revolution of 1789 to the defeat of Napoleon Bonaparte at Waterloo in 1815, the whole of Europe and much of the globe was convulsed by war. Britain's slave-trade ban was only as effective as its ability to compel other nations to follow suit, which was limited. Denmark freed its slaves in 1794, but few others joined it. France, which had abolished slavery under the revolutionary government that same year, reestablished it under Napoleon in 1803. Also in 1794, the United States Congress set a deadline for the ban of the slave trade by American vessels (though not slavery itself) by 1808. In 1806 President Jefferson, a slave owner himself, urged the Congress to hurry things along: "I congratulate you, fellow-citizens, on the approach of the period at which you may interpose your authority constitutionally, to withdraw the citizens of the United States from all further participation in those violations of human rights which have been so long continued on the unoffending inhabitants of Africa."[18] Jefferson's invocation of "human rights" is fascinating but vague: is it the natural rights of the Africans that are being violated, or is it the deleterious effect on the souls of the slave trader that has him concerned?

Britain's ban on the trade continued to reverberate. An 1823 case before the Supreme Court, *In re Antelope*, argued the claim that the slave trade was an offense to the law of nations, no different than piracy, and thus illegal even in states which had not officially abolished it. Claimants raised the example of pirates who as *hostis humani generi* (enemies of the human race) were subject to universal jurisdiction—in effect, international criminals. So too, they maintained, were slavers. The Marshall court reluctantly disagreed. While it concurred that the trade was abhorrent to natural law, that understanding had not become so universal as to elevate it to the law of nations. It left open the possibility for such an understanding in the future, however.[19]

By the 1820s the abolitionist campaign altered focus. How could Britain abolish slavery within its borders and its fleet, yet allow it in colonies under British law? This was a delicate matter, as reformers soon discovered. Attempts to enforce the trade ban encountered fierce local resistance in the Caribbean, where planters in Trinidad and Barbados openly bartered with smugglers as colonial governors looked the other way. Parliament passed strengthening legislation in 1811 and 1815 imposing criminal fines for purchasing contraband slaves, but this had little effect. In the 1820s the Colonial Office adopted a different tack, encouraging gradual emancipation by drafting a model law and circulating it through the colonies. Except for tiny Nevis, every British colony ignored the bill or openly rejected it.[20]

Such intransigence hardened the government's resolve. When the Whigs returned to power under Charles Grey in 1830, they did so under a banner of reform. The Reform Act of 1832, hailed as the most sweeping reordering of government since the Glorious Revolution, extended the franchise and abolished the so-called "rotten boroughs" that had allowed privileged families to elect themselves unopposed to Parliament. In 1834, Grey channeled this same spirit of reform toward the colonies. Frustrated by colonial foot-dragging, Parliament finally declared the abolition of slavery throughout the empire on August 1, 1834. As historian G. M. Trevelyan grandly phrased it, "All slaves under the British flag were to become free. On the last night of slavery, the negroes in our West Indian islands went up to the hill-tops to watch the sun rise, bringing them freedom as its first rays struck the waters."[21]

Emancipation in the empire and Britain's efforts to curtail the slave trade around the globe were a milestone in the history of natural law. For the first time, a nation had advanced the proposition that natural rights were enforceable the world over and undertook to do exactly that. Moreover, the sweeping abolition of slavery in the colonies represented a stern moral lesson: some behavior, no matter how deeply ingrained in local society or beneficial to local economies (or even, indeed, to the British economy) was simply beyond the pale of the law. This should have been an unalloyed triumph, an extension of the same principles that animated the legal and political revolutions of the last century. Yet the precedent held another meaning. Once reform had been introduced to the empire through the abolition of slavery, it cleared a broad path; "reform" was a suitably elastic term for almost any social, political, economic, religious, or cultural interference.

❖ ❖ ❖

The implications were not lost on William Wilberforce. The same man who ended the British slave trade turned his attention to India in 1813. Decrying the "moral pollution" of Hindu and Moslem society, he declared in a breathless rush: "Must we not...endeavor to raise these wretched beings out of their present miserable condition, and above all, to communicate to them those blessed truths which would not only improve their understandings and elevate their minds, but would, in ten thousand ways, promote their temporal wellbeing and point out to them a sure path to everlasting happiness?" [22] That was a tall order even for an empire. Fortunately for Wilberforce, his brother-in-law, James Stephen, had recently been appointed undersecretary and chief counselor to the Colonial Office. Described by one historian as "an unbending busybody" in whom "pedantry and priggishness were more than balanced by a sense of moral obligation toward alien races under the British flag," Stephen soon gained the nickname Mr. Mother Country. [23] Championing Edmund Burke's principle that Britain should adopt a policy of benevolent trusteeship toward her colonies, Stephen and his colleagues in the Colonial Office went further. They resolved to raise the banner of reform in every British territory, until the whole of the empire was legally, culturally, and morally indistinguishable from Britain herself.

This secular crusade mirrored an ecclesiastic one of even longer heritage. "Behold!" cried Reverend Samuel Marsden, wading ashore in New Zealand in 1814 and encountering a group of bemused Maoris, "I bring you glad tidings of great joy which shall be to all people!" Long before the British government (or any government, for that matter) became concerned with the manners and souls of their imperial subjects, Protestant missionaries had already staked their claim. This reformist zeal traced itself as far back as the Puritan colony of Massachusetts: its colonial seal featured a Native American with a ribbon of speech pouring from his mouth and encircling him like ectoplasm: "Come Over And Help Us." [24] Nor was the English case singular. A papal edict of 1492 gave unlimited title of any conquered lands to Spain and Portugal, provided they convert the indigenous populations to Catholicism. The Protestants were simply following the same path.

While such efforts had been underway for centuries, Christian proselytizing in the late eighteenth and nineteenth centuries emerged from the same rich soil of reform as abolitionism. In less than a decade during the 1790s, London alone produced the Baptist Missionary Society, London Missionary Society, Church Missionary Society, and British and Foreign Bible Society. These societies were often far in advance of the British government in what they saw as the protection of native peoples. In 1837, for example, the Colonial Office proposed the New Zealand Association, which provided for the establishment of an inspector of natives and pledged that 10 percent of all lands would be set aside as native reserves. Not good enough, the Church Missionary Society answered. If the government could only "let the Mission have its free and unrestricted course for half a century or more…the great political and moral problem will be solved—of a people passing from a barbarous to a civilized state."[25]

It is worth considering for a moment what that transmutation actually entailed. Theoretically, any aboriginal that embraced Christianity was "civilized," but they could not do so unless they could read the Bible for themselves. Nor could they participate in the greater community until they learned its language, manners, and dress. The Age of Reform in the colonies thus welded preexisting Christian norms of morality and cultural practice with a more generalized and secular "civilization" that included recognition and adoption of natural rights. The result—with railway lines and other modern mechanical marvels thrown in—was a holistic vision of reform extending to every aspect of aboriginal life.

The wondrous thing about civilization was that, having absorbed Christian values, it no longer depended on Christianity. Even a confirmed skeptic like John Stuart Mill found a utilitarian argument in favor of imperialism. "This mode of government," he wrote in 1861, "is as legitimate as any other, if it is the one which in the existing state of civilization of the subject people, most facilitates their transition to a higher stage of improvement."[26] In another article published the same year, he developed this secular civilizing philosophy yet further:

> It is a step, as far as it goes, towards universal peace and generally friendly cooperation among nations…and in the case of the British possessions it has the advantage, specially valuable at the present time, of adding to the moral influence and weight in the councils of the world, of the Power which, of all in existence, best understands liberty.[27]

The logical gymnastics required for such a statement—that the nation that best understands liberty is best equipped for world domination—must be understood in the context of its time. In an age of railroads and steamships, telegraphs and stock exchanges, the developed world had little patience for the undeveloped. "The right of savages to the soil they occupy," German socialist Eduard Bernstein wrote, was conditional on its use. If they did nothing with it, they derived no use from it, and therefore were not owners but squatters.[28] Bernstein may thus be credited for having provided, ex post facto, a justification for Andrew Jackson's Indian Removal Act of 1830. Another prominent socialist, Irish playwright George Bernard Shaw, lampooned the smug certainty of the colonizers with his customary caustic wit. The Englishman, he wrote,

> is never at a loss for an effective moral attitude. As the great champion of freedom and national independence, he conquers and annexes half the world and calls it Colonization. When he wants a new market for his adulterated Manchester goods, he sends a missionary to teach the natives the Gospel of Peace. The natives kill the missionary: he flies to arms in defense of Christianity … and takes the market as a reward from heaven.

Yet Shaw, too, endorsed colonization, so long as it was a force of "civilization."[29]

Civilization, like its brother reform, had no ontological reality; it could mean all things to all people. Socialists saw well-organized states administering vast territories for the good of all; capitalists saw untapped markets; missionaries saw a holistic community of the saved, and so on. Inasmuch as the old, narrow timbers of natural law could still be found within this monumental edifice, they were best identified in the late-nineteenth-century concept of "liberal imperialism." Liberalism, which in England represented the voice of social justice and equal protection under the law, had global potential. Recall Blackstone's snarky comment that, although natural law existed everywhere in the world, England was the only nation that recognized the fact. The logical argument went thus: As Cicero once posited that only rational minds could discern natural law, thus it followed that only rational cultures could do so. A society hidebound by collective ignorance or superstition was as willfully blind to the law as a child. Just as the state bore the responsibility of educating every child, so too must the empire educate its unlettered multitudes. The first and best way was by example. "By bringing European gentlemen into direct and immediate contact with those of our new subjects who are yet unacquainted with our character," an early colonial wrote from Delhi, "their minds would be conciliated and a groundwork laid for the introduction of our financial and judicial system."[30]

It is easy to read smugness into such declarations and dismiss them accordingly. Yet however they might sound today, one cannot deny the fervency with which such views were held by the lawgivers or the determination they brought to the task. British officials tasked with bringing law to the hinterlands often found themselves confronting beliefs and practices more appalling than any early Christian missionary could have imagined. And, like St. Boniface among the Frisians, they soon learned that condemnation alone would not get them very far. When company representative John Campbell reached southern Orissa, he found the Kond peoples routinely kidnapping children from other villages, drugging them, and cutting them to pieces in religious rituals. Campbell's response was a miracle of restraint. "The superstition of ages cannot be eradicated in a day," he lectured his superiors. Rather than condemn, he sat amongst the Konds and shared with them that ancient Britons had once sacrificed humans also. "We were fools then and ignorant." Then, adopting the tone and tenor of the Konds themselves, he made each of them take a handful of rice and earth and solemnly declare, "May the earth refuse its produce, rice choke me, water drown me, and tiger devour me and my children if ever I break the oath…to abstain from sacrifice of human beings." It worked.[31] His example was soon followed by dozens of other administrators, and many egregious cultural practices, including ritualized murder and mutilation, began to decline. Even today it is hard to argue against the efforts of men like Campbell; such examples echo more recent debates over female genital mutilation, for example, and how far states may go in condemning or curbing it. That ethical problem did not exist for empire builders in the nineteenth century. "High-principled aristocrats from Britain's political elite," historian Lawrence James describes them. "They saw themselves not as India's conquerors but as its emancipators."[32]

Intertwined with yet distinct from Christian proselytizing, Liberal imperialism borrowed from enlightened rationalism and Victorian reform to present a vision of the world disenthralled from ancient superstition and barbarity, joined together by glittering bands of commerce and law. At the apogee of the empire this became a rallying cry: export Bibles and shirtwaists and railway lines and *rights*. A global empire meant not only that Britain had the ability to universalize natural rights but the obligation to do so. The Liberal politician Archibald Primrose, fifth Earl of Rosebery, expressed it thus: "We have to consider what countries must be developed by ourselves or by some other nation, and we have to remember that it is part of our heritage to take care that the world as far as it can be moulded by us, shall receive an English-speaking complexion, and not that of other nations."[33] In 1900, as a new century loomed, Lord Rosebery looked with paternal pride upon the imperial achievements of the last. Chief among these, he argued, was the spread of English law:

> How marvelous it all is. Built not by saints and angels, but the work of men's hands cemented with men's honest blood... not without taint and reproach incidental to all human work, but constructed on the whole with pure and splendid purpose. Human and yet not wholly human, for the most heedless and the most cynical must see the finger of the Divine.[34]

Even as Britain's political leaders placed themselves among the cherubim and seraphim, the architecture of empire served to reinforce these lofty aspirations. T. Robert Smith addressed the London Society of Arts in 1873 on the subject of public buildings in New Delhi. These, he insisted, must "be European both as a rallying point for ourselves, and as raising a distinctive symbol of our presence to be beheld with respect and even with admiration by the natives.... [Such buildings must] embody the idea of law and order which has been produced out of chaos by the British administration."[35] Victoria Railway Station in Bombay, completed in the jubilee year 1887, was a product of this philosophy. Railways, like the law, combined pragmatic, symbolic, and societal purposes. Ostensibly they facilitated the movement of goods, people, and, if necessary, soldiers. Yet overlying this basic function was a high gloss of progressive morality: train tracks cleaved like gleaming scythes through ignorance, poverty, and paganism, enveloping every community they reached in the greater civilization. "Railways," reformer Charles Trevelyan declared in 1854, "will be the great destroyer of caste, and the greatest missionary of all."[36]

Accordingly, British architects in Bombay demolished an ancient shrine to the goddess Mumba Devi and replaced it with a giant steel temple encased by a riot of crenelated neo-Gothic fantasy. Whiskered effigies of the company directors beamed benevolently from the rafters on the tumult below. But from chaos, order: the crowd, for all its heterodox color and noise, moved by the predetermined, civilized rhythm of the railway clock at the heart of the station. Beneath the clock was a giant marble statue of Queen Victoria. It rested almost exactly on the spot of Mumba Devi's ravished shrine.[37]

Something similar took place in the law, underscoring the vast gulf between theory and practice. The Charter Act of 1833, coming one year after the seminal Reform Bill of 1832 and described as "a watershed in the legal history of India," attempted to ship and reassemble reform in the most far-flung reaches of the empire. The East India Company, which had maintained dictatorial control for almost two centuries, was reconstructed along much narrower lines, and the governor-general of Bengal—a minor functionary—became the infinitely more powerful governor-general of India. "Regulations," a company term, were replaced by "laws." All colonial government was to be centralized under imperial authority, with the same body of laws applicable throughout the Raj. Indian judges were to be appointed to determine the common law, exactly as in Britain herself. In sum, as one historian describes it, "the gate was thrown open for the liberal spirit of the British Parliament to travel through the [Colonial] Secretary to India."[38]

The Charter Act was no mere reworking of company governance but a foundation for an entirely new legal relationship—to be placed alongside the Massachusetts Bay Company Charter of 1623 or even the "Great Charter" of 1215. The intent, M. P. Jain writes, was to create "a positive obligation on the government to provide for the protection of natives from insult and outrage in their persons, properties, religions and opinions"[39]—in other words, natural rights. Still, there were limitations. The charter theoretically abolished racial categorization, yet in 1853 the chairman of the Indian Law Commission noted resignedly that "during the last twenty years not a single native has been appointed to any office except such as were eligible before the statute." In response, the Indian Civil Service Act of 1853 introduced competitive examinations that were judged blind. Additional acts passed that same year formally established new penal, civil, and criminal procedural codes, which had been commissioned by the 1833 charter but then allowed to fall into desuetude.

Parliamentary reform could only do so much, however. The ultimate responsibility for the laws lay with local administration, where racial prejudice and outright cruelty continued unabated. Indian resentment at decades of broken promises, double-dealing, and cultural annihilation culminated in the Mutiny of 1857, which saw thousands of Indian militiamen turn on their British commanders and attempt, futilely, to restore independence. The revolt was short and bloody, and its suppression left a legacy of disillusionment and bitterness on both sides. Parliament did what it could. A general amnesty was declared in November 1858. That same month, Queen Victoria intervened personally on behalf of her captive subjects. Rejecting an earlier draft of a proclamation reestablishing royal authority in the dominions, the Queen warned the Colonial Office that it must "[bear] in mind that it is a female sovereign who speaks to more than a hundred million of Eastern people, on assuming direct government over them after a bloody war, giving them pledges, which her future reign is to redeem." She then made clear what those pledges entailed:

> Such a document should breathe feelings of generosity, benevolence and religious toleration, and point out the privileges which the Indians will receive in being placed on an equality with the subjects of the British Crown, and the prosperity following in the train of civilization.[10]

The result of this extraordinary command was the Queen's Proclamation of 1858, a singular document which functioned as a kind of Magna Carta for the Raj. In 1215, it was the barons that forced a reluctant King John to swear an oath upholding ancient rights and privileges; this time, the sovereign impressed such rights on her government and its officers. The provisions were startling, invoking both ancient natural law and modern (almost prescient) cultural awareness:

(g) We shall respect the rights, dignity and honour of our Native Princes as our own, and we desire that they as well as our own subjects, should enjoy that prosperity and that social advancement which can be secured by eternal peace and good government.

(h) We hold ourselves bound to the natives of our Indian territories by the same obligations of duty which bind us to all our other subjects.

(i) We disclaim alike the right and the desire to impose our religious convictions on any of our subjects. We will not interfere with the religious beliefs and modes of worship of our subjects....

(k) In framing and administering the law, due regard will be paid to the ancient rights, usages and customs of India.[41]

Had anyone but the queen advocated these reforms, they would instantly have been branded a heretic and possibly a traitor as well. The proclamation was a shocking refutation of civilization, in the received nineteenth-century understanding of the term. In contrast to Thomas Jones Barker's famous painting *The Secret of England's Greatness,* which depicted Victoria bestowing a Bible upon an amazed East African, here the sovereign in no uncertain terms rejected the missionary purpose that had long underlain Britain's colonization scheme. In the same breath she also granted local autonomy, due process of law, and—incredibly—deference to custom. This was a natural-rights document in the purest sense, an anomaly among the volumes of imperial legislation. "Its only fault indeed," historian Wilfrid Blunt remarked, "has been that it has never been carried out."[42]

That fault was universal. In London, earnest reformers could see for themselves the fruits of their labors, but in India and the empire all legislation—altruistic or otherwise—ultimately came down to local enforcement. When Mohandas Gandhi left India in 1893 to take a position at a law firm in Durban, South Africa, his first court appearance came to a sudden end when the presiding judge demanded he remove his turban. On the train to Pretoria he was ejected from first class, despite purchasing a ticket. A year later he was organizing an Indian Congress in Natal, and in 1914 he returned to India to continue the struggle for civil rights.[43] While Gandhi might never actually have said that Western civilization "would be a good idea," he certainly agreed with the sentiment.

The racism and class prejudice Gandhi observed was more systemic than the law itself. "The Hindu," one governor-general observed in 1814, "appears a being nearly limited to animal functions, and even in them indifferent."[44] The dapper colonial secretary of Victoria's later reign, Joseph Chamberlain, agreed. "You cannot make omelets without breaking eggs," he declared, "You cannot destroy the practices of barbarism, of slavery, of superstition...without the use of force."[45] Chamberlain's triad is revealing: barbarism, loosely defined as to apply to almost any offensive cultural practice; slavery, in direct reference to the roots of imperial reform; and superstition, which his listeners understood to mean all "pagan" faiths. It was as neat and concise a rejection of the queen's 1858 proclamation as could be found, yet by that time—1895—the question of cultural deference was largely moot.

Meanwhile, a counterrevolution had been quietly brewing in British political circles. Almost from its inception, Liberal imperialism was roundly critiqued by conservatives as idealistic and dangerous nonsense. Following Edmund Burke's denunciation of the French Revolution, they remained skeptical of holistic efforts to remake societies; better, they said, to let social institutions evolve organically—or, better still, remain unchanged. Inherently classist themselves, conservatives regarded India's caste system as a mark of civilization rather than backwardness. Thus men like Arthur Wellesley, Duke of Wellington, became unlikely cultural relativists. India's rich tapestry of cultures, beliefs, and practices enchanted rather than repulsed them, and as imperial overseers they favored a much more hands-off approach that encouraged profit over reform and gave greater legal authority to the *nawabs*. The Iron Duke famously opposed the India Bill of 1833, even its laudable intention of abolishing slavery throughout the empire. It was Britain's duty, he proclaimed, to "uphold the ancient laws, customs and religions of the country," even when doing so might be personally abhorrent.[46] This laissez-faire attitude was more reactionary than progressive; the duke also loathed that great engine of civilization, railways, as they "encouraged the lower classes to move about." He was referring to the British lower classes.

❖ ❖ ❖

Even those Englishmen who admitted, with Lord Rosebery, that their imperial model was "not without taint" still viewed it as a paragon compared with others. The German kaiser, arriving late in the game but with a show of force, unleashed the full might of the *Deutsches Heer* on a small tribe of West Africans that had resisted German expropriation of their land and cattle; 65,000 Herero people, or roughly three-fourths of the total population, were slaughtered between 1904 and 1907, an act which is often called the first genocide of the twentieth century. "The Kaiser went to playing the game without first mastering it," Mark Twain derided.

By the end of the century, the base hypocrisy of civilization was laid bare for all to see. Twain cannily described the difference between pretense and reality as between the cover and contents of a book. "Privately and confidentially," he wrote, "[civilization] is merely an outside cover, gay and pretty and attractive, displaying the special patterns of our Civilization which we reserve for Home Consumption, while inside the bale is the Actual Thing that the Customer Sitting in Darkness buys with his blood and tears and land and liberty. That Actual Thing is, indeed, Civilization, but it is only for Export. Is there a difference between the two brands? In some of the details, yes." What did the outside cover promise? "LOVE, JUSTICE, GENTLENESS, CHRISTIANITY, PROTECTION OF THE WEAK, LAW AND ORDER, LIBERTY, EQUALITY, HONORABLE DEALING, MERCY, EDUCATION, and so on." Inside, however, was nothing but tyranny and toil. Why, he wrote with heavy irony, was the civilization business falling into such disrepute? "It is because our Mr. McKinley, and Mr. Chamberlain, and the Kaiser, and the Czar and the French have been exporting the Actual Thing *with the outside cover left off.*"

Mark Twain's warning still resonates. The Victorians radically redefined understandings of rights, and we live in their shadow. At home, reform became Reform, as advocates for social justice and social welfare joined a growing chorus of political agitators demanding change. Some changes were incremental and benign, like Sunday holidays or safer working conditions. Others, advanced by Marx, Engels, and Proudhon, called for nothing less than a complete restructuring of society. Yet the cumulative effect was to drown natural rights in a deluge of new freedoms and privileges. Moreover, Marx's critique of traditional rights as ersatz egalitarianism began to resonate. Ordinary people, even those unpersuaded by the lure of socialism, nevertheless began to see rights not as something shared but something unique to each. One enjoyed their rights *as* a laborer, for example—distinctions of station determined which rights each individual should possess. The result was a universal clamor for recognition composed of a numberless crowd of diverse claimants.

Such is the case today. In the United States, we possess those rights guaranteed by the Constitution, which are mostly natural rights. Yet we may also advance additional claims unique to our status as a disabled person, or a person of color, or a Christian, or an LGBTQ individual, and so on. Many of these claims are simply for equal treatment under the law, but not all. Consider, for example, the plethora of religious exemption cases now working their way through the courts. Does baking a cake violate someone's rights "as a Christian"? Should adoption agencies be permitted to turn away LGBTQ applicants because of faith? The distinction here is that these individuals argue for *more* rights than others; special exceptions, not equality. Similarly, the nineteenth century introduced the idea of positive rights: standards of living the state is required to provide. Do we have a "right" to Social Security, welfare, health insurance, unemployment benefits? If some of these may still seem contentious, what about free education, fire departments, public transit, highways, or air traffic controllers? No one would seriously maintain that American citizens don't deserve the right to an education, but upon what basis is that right advanced?

Just as reform revolutionized rights at home, civilization did so abroad. The greatest legacy of imperialism is a deep distrust and cynicism by the non-Western world for any attempt to critique or alter cultural practices. One can hardly blame them. The "blessings of civilization" were shoddy wares, as Twain pithily describes. The laudable goal of ending slavery was wedded to the equally laudable goal of spreading universal human rights. But from there things went astray: "civilization" came to mean everything from Bibles to railroads to corsets. Worse still, these "advances" were not shared with captive peoples but impressed on them. Victoria Railway Station (now called Chhatrapati Shivaji Terminus) was a metaphor in more ways than one: forcing natives to conform to the dictates of the railway clock; placing the white, Western railway executives as demigods above the horde; dominating the cityscape with its distinctly Gothic presence; and, most telling of all, obliterating the local goddess and replacing her with a new statue to venerate—the goddess of Progress, standing atop the station's highest spire. So too did imperial law transform into something wholly different from the common law. Law was the principal conduit of civilization, the medium by which, as Chamberlain described it, old barbarisms and superstitions would be utterly erased. The core of legal universalism—that every human on earth is deserving of natural rights—came to be supplanted by a new concept: peoples could only enjoy their natural rights once they understood them. Understanding meant education, which meant conformity with Western norms.

In sum, the Victorians left us two tasks. First, we must distinguish negative and positive rights; more specifically, we need to draw distinctions between fundamental rights and other rights, liberties, and privileges. This does not mean abandoning the latter, at home or abroad. It does, however, mean establishing a core list of natural rights that we commit ourselves to defending regardless of circumstance. Second, and relatedly, we must find a way of articulating this language of rights that does not emerge from, or may be blamed on, imperialism. Rights have too often been a Trojan horse for interference and exploitation. When the United States articulates its vision of human rights in the next decade, it must pledge itself as Queen Victoria did to a basic recognition of cultural differences. And we need to "carry it out": ultimately our actions will demonstrate fidelity more than any protestations of intent. At present the world does not trust the West, and the West has given them little reason to.

The blessings of civilization were a curse on the colonizers as well as the colonized, and the curse is still with us.

— 4 —

THE GREAT ADVENTURE

In the second decade of the twentieth century the United States became the principal arbiter, defender, and proponent of human rights around the world, cloaking itself in a mantle of moral supremacy that it retained for a hundred years, until the presidency of Donald Trump.

It was not evident even ten years earlier that this would be the case. In the Victorian and Edwardian eras it was Britain, primarily and sometimes alone, that raised the tattered standard of universal justice on the world stage: abolishing the slave trade, spreading its message of Western law and morality throughout the empire, and critiquing other nations (with no small degree of self-satisfaction) for their deficiencies in the same. Among those nations was the United States, whose slave-owning South was an object of derision and bemusement. After the Civil War, the slaves were freed and the Union restored, but the republic itself was exhausted. It was not for several decades that Americans began to look outward, and even then rather timidly; colonial adventures in the Caribbean and South Pacific were almost afterthoughts. Even so, the juggernaut of American corporate wealth gathered steam. Fortunes born of the Civil War compounded and multiplied. By 1900, for example, industrialist J. Pierpont Morgan had amassed enough capital not only to establish a monopoly of American shipping but also to lay claim to British, French, Belgian, Dutch, and German lines as well.[1] American financial hegemony far outstripped its military or political prowess. Thus the new century opened with Great Britain at the fragile apex of its imperial power and the United States in a chrysalis between its bloody past and a new, possibly glorious, certainly very rich future.

Then the Great War came, and visions of universal human progress became quaint at best. By its conclusion, Britain and Europe had forfeited any claim to high ground. It was "the New World, with all its power and might," as Churchill later asserted in a similar context, that had stepped forth "to the rescue and liberation of the Old." The United States' belated entry on behalf of the Allies—not for territorial gain but "to make the world safe for democracy"—gave it political and moral credit. At the Paris peace talks, President Woodrow Wilson intended to expend that credit toward the creation of a new world order.

His failure was Shakespearean. Yet his legacy was more complex: despite the United States' refusal to join the League of Nations (caused in no small part by Wilson's rigidity during negotiations), the country somehow retained its status as international peacekeeper during the interwar years. Moreover, despite the futility and ultimate collapse of the league, the precedent was set for an international organization devoted to not only preserving peace but upholding human rights around the globe. That it would be an American organization in concept, design, and location was perhaps inevitable.

◆ ◆ ◆

Before there was genocide, ethnic cleansing, or war crimes, there were "crimes against humanity." It is impossible to say precisely when the term appeared, but until the mid-twentieth century its meaning was ambiguous: such "crimes" were not crimes at all, in the legal sense, but actions that shocked the conscience of the world. The accepted response was outrage, not legal sanction. The reason was simple: state sovereignty. State sovereignty meant that each nation and its government had absolute authority to enact all laws for citizenry and anyone else within its jurisdiction. Such laws might be mystifying, draconian, or even horrifying to others, but the state's right to enforce them was beyond dispute.

The long-established remedy for that challenge was revolution. A people might assert its rights and overthrow its own government; the people might even, as in the case of the American colonists, enlist the aid of other nations to do so. But there was no precedent for one nation to intervene unilaterally in the affairs of another, even to stop a mass atrocity. The unspoken understanding was that oppressed people, having suffered enough, would inevitably rise on their own. The possibility that these people might be a disenfranchised minority, lacking the numbers or resources to mount a revolt, was apparently not considered.

Yet by the beginning of the twentieth century this concept was beginning to seem antiquated, if not among governments then certainly in the court of public opinion. Consider the case of the Congo, at the time a personal fiefdom of King Leopold II of Belgium. For decades Leopold employed a policy of calculated brutality in the colony, enslaving its population and enforcing his will through institutionalized arson, rape, murder, and mutilation. Gradually, and despite the king's efforts at obfuscation, technological advances shed unwelcome light on these ugly truths. Photographers recorded images of maimed children, piles of corpses, and severed limbs; men tied to railroad tracks being whipped mercilessly by the *chicotte*. Journalists arriving on steamships and traveling inland by railroad sent back vivid accounts of the humanitarian crisis through another new medium, the wireless telegraph. Public outrage around the world was aroused. The British Parliament unanimously passed a resolution affirming that the Congolese "should be governed with humanity" and chided Leopold for his failure to do so. Newspapers demanded some form of international action to end the horror and ran editorial cartoons depicting Leopold as a malignant boa constrictor with an African victim in his coils.[2]

Yet response to the rape of the Congo and other atrocities also revealed the limits of what governments could legitimately do. They could protest, condemn, or—under rare circumstances—impose trade sanctions. Reformist sentiment in the United States and Britain, discussed extensively in the last chapter, fueled grassroots efforts pressuring governments to do yet more. But there was no mechanism to intervene, even in the most egregious cases. American secretary of state Elihu Root vented his frustration—not for Leopold, but for the American public:

"The very people who are most ardent against entangling alliances insist most fanatically upon our doing one hundred things a year on humanitarian grounds.... The Protestant Church and many good women were wild to have us stop the atrocities in the Congo.... People kept piling on the [State] Department demanding action."[3] But the limits of that action were cogently illustrated by a 1909 *Punch* cartoon titled "THE GUILT OF DELAY." It displayed a uniformed slaver brutally whipping a Congolese on the very steps of the "European Hall of Deliberation." *"I'm all right,"* says the slaver, *"they're still talking."*

Another atrocity, occurring almost simultaneously, is indicative. In 1903, following a mass killing of Jews in the Russian city of Kishinev, a delegation of American Jews asked the State Department to relay a petition to the tsar condemning the Kishinev pogrom. President Theodore Roosevelt was sympathetic. "Would it do any good for me to say a word on behalf of the Jews?" he asked his cabinet, "Or would it do harm?" Ruefully, he bowed to the realities of state sovereignty: "I suppose it would be very much like the Tsar spreading his horror of our lynching Negroes."[4] Ultimately the petition was not sent, though the American government registered its displeasure through the usual channels. The overriding message was clear.

Yet just as technology made it increasingly difficult for states to hide abuses committed within their borders or empires, it also facilitated the scale of such abuse. Not only railway lines and telegraphs but Maxim guns, repeating rifles, and other mechanical advances allowed for slaughter on an unprecedented scale. Terrible culmination came in the summer of 1914 with the beginning of the Great War. On the front lines, submarines attacked civilian vessels, howitzers leveled entire villages, and most notoriously poison gas was unleashed in the trenches. The war also facilitated the first genocide of the twentieth century: the deliberate destruction of the Armenian people by the Ottoman Empire.

Pogroms against the Armenians had flared for decades and were well known. In 1905, a British cartoon depicted the sultan seated on a divan with King Leopold, sharing a hookah. *"Silly fuss they're making about these so-called atrocities in my Congo property,"* Leopold laments. *"Only talk, my dear boy,"* the sultan assures him. *"They won't do anything."* However, in 1915 the Turks drastically escalated their efforts, confident that the confusion of war would conceal or at least excuse mass killings and forced relocations of alleged "fifth columnists." They were not wrong. Internal memoranda by their German allies described the genocide as "an internal matter" and even offered military instruction to the very officers tasked with the killings. But on the other side of the conflict there was shock and horror. In May 1915 the Allies released a joint statement decrying Turkish "crimes against humanity and civilization," further promising that perpetrators would be held "personally responsible." Criminal liability was implied, though not explicitly stated. That would prove useful later.[5]

The American position was more equivocal. A neutral nation until 1917, it could do little but register concern at the diplomatic level. The American ambassador to the Ottomans was Henry Morgenthau Sr., a career diplomat whose son, Henry Jr., would eventually become a leading advocate for justice against the Nazis. Henry Sr. was no less appalled by what he discovered in Constantinople. "Turkish authorities have definitely informed me that I have no right to interfere in their internal affairs," he cabled Washington in frustration, yet "there seems a systemic plan to crush the Armenian race." One of his interlocutors was even more brazen. "Why are you so interested in the Armenians, anyway?" he asked Morgenthau. "You are a Jew, these people are Christians.... We treat the Americans all right, too. I don't see why you should complain."[6]

Still international outrage continued, with the *New York Times* alone publishing 145 articles on the Armenian "crisis" in one year. Finally, at Versailles in 1919, the victorious Allies were poised to make good their promise to hold the Ottomans criminally accountable. Some nations, including Great Britain, were enthusiastic to do so. Yet it was the Americans—ironically, given what was to come—that ultimately balked. Secretary of State Robert Lansing, speaking for President Wilson, warned that international tribunals holding court over "internal matters" were not only unprecedented but dangerous. What was to prevent another tribunal from someday exercising its jurisdiction over the United States? (It was this very fear, incidentally, that has prevented the United States from joining the International Criminal Court, established in 1999.) Wilson was looking ahead: protracted Allied tribunals of German and Turkish war criminals would look like victors' justice and perpetuate animosities that hampered his ultimate goal of universal comity. Ultimately the Allies punted, handing the Turkish "defendants" over to the Turks themselves for trial. The result was a farce and a tragedy. As with the German war crimes tribunals at Leipzig, the Turks were universally acquitted. Worse still, the trials became a tool for the Ataturk government to foster its own dominant, nationalist narrative of the genocide—which the Turkish government holds to this day. "Who remembers the Armenians?" Adolf Hitler once scoffed, when the question of postwar reprisals was raised.[7]

This sorry outcome was foreordained. Several years earlier, former president Theodore Roosevelt rejected an invitation by a pro-Armenian protest committee to speak on its behalf. While he was entirely in accord with its aims, he told the committee, he had no faith whatsoever in its methods. His reply spoke not just to the futility of the Armenian crisis but to the basic inhumanity of state sovereignty itself:

> Mass meetings on behalf of the Armenians amount to nothing whatever if they are mere methods of giving sentimental but ineffective and safe outlet to the emotion of those engaged in them. Indeed they amount to less than nothing.... Until we put honor and duty first, and are willing to risk something in order to achieve righteousness both for ourselves and for others, we shall accomplish nothing; and we shall earn and deserve the contempt of the strong nations of mankind.[8]

The force of Roosevelt's argument lies in the fact that it could have been written yesterday, not over a century ago. Even as we grapple with issues of human rights now, there is a vast gulf between protest and policy; mass demonstrations often do little more than gratify the consciences of those engaged in them. But there was another, even more profound thread of argument: that states must, under certain circumstances, be willing to "risk something in order to achieve righteousness." The first cracks in the monolith of state sovereignty had begun to appear.

❖ ❖ ❖

Roosevelt would have found an unlikely ally in his Democratic successor. In the cold-eyed pantheon of Edwardian heads of state, Woodrow Wilson was an anomaly: a moralist. "We are but one of the champions of the rights of mankind," he famously stated, as he ushered his nation into war. "We shall be satisfied when those rights have been made as secure as the faith and the freedom of nations can make them."[9] Others wanted only victory; Wilson would accept nothing less than utopia. In another age, the president's inflexible idealism might have placed him favorably alongside men like John Winthrop; juxtaposed against the realpolitik ruthlessness of his peers, however, he appears naïve, even foolish. "Talking to Wilson is something like talking to Jesus Christ," Georges Clemenceau complained.[10] Historians have not been much kinder. Judged with the clear hindsight of two world wars and the failed League of Nations, chroniclers are apt to dwell on those aspects of Wilson's character that doomed his grand designs: rigidity, arrogance, self-righteousness, and a vindictive streak. Contemporaries noted these qualities and immortalized them. "I am coming to the conclusion," a British diplomat wrote, "that I do not personally like him. I do not know quite what it is that repels me: a certain hardness, coupled with vanity and an eye for effect."[11] His French colleague went even further. Given the right circumstances, he said, Wilson might "have been the greatest tyrant in the world, because he does not seem to have the slightest conception that he can ever be wrong."[12]

Such harsh judgments must be placed in context. Wilson's idealism and vision for the world were not entirely his own; rather, they reflected the progressivism of the United States at the dawn of the twentieth century. Wilson had emerged victorious from a three-way 1912 election where two candidates—he and Theodore Roosevelt—ran on near-identical progressive platforms. William Howard Taft, the Republican incumbent, received the fewest votes. The essence of progressive reform was a resolute belief that all things can be made perfect, and that all persons have a moral duty to try. It was a universalist worldview: at bedrock, all peoples' wants and desires are essentially the same. This was certainly the view of Wilson's first secretary of state, the irrepressible populist William Jennings Bryan. As one historian writes, "The precedents and minutiae of international law struck him as so many barnacles on the Bible. All men were brothers, were they not?"[13] In the tense spring of 1914, Bryan presented an astonished British ambassador with a sword hammered into a plowshare, inscribed with quotes from Isaiah and Bryan himself.

Balancing a progressive view of humanity with the realities of *weltpolitik* was no easy task. Heads of state had long learned to put aside their personal morality in international affairs and deal with persons whom, in any other circumstance, they would abhor. Theodore Roosevelt pungently described Venezuelan president Cipriano Castro as "an unspeakably villainous little monkey," yet did not hesitate to work with him in brokering a peace. Applying a morality test to international relations was, for men like Roosevelt, unworkable and absurd. It was tantamount to assuming all peoples and governments shared the same moral code.

It was precisely this understanding that Woodrow Wilson brought to international relations. Since not all people shared the same religion and culture, morality must transcend both. This belief was, in fact, a restatement of natural law. Wilson, a lawyer, historian, and Christian, understood this implicitly. The United States, he declared repeatedly, coveted no territory, wanted nothing from its neighbors but peace and equity. It had very definite political and economic interests yet would pursue them with the same morality that private citizens brought to their daily business. To those who thought "moral diplomacy" sounded like a contradiction in terms, Wilson had a stern reply. In a speech for the Railway Business Association in 1916, he lectured: "Gentlemen, there is something that the American people love better than peace. They love the principles upon which their political life is founded.... We cannot surrender our convictions. I would rather surrender territory than surrender those ideals which are the stuff of life, of the soul itself."[14]

Wilson's moral diplomacy was reciprocal; it expected other states to respond in kind. If they did not, the breach was not merely diplomatic but ethical. "And because we hold certain ideals," Wilson told the railroad men, "we have thought that it was right that we should hold them for others as well as ourselves." The theoretical implications were profound. Centuries earlier, Hugo Grotius posited that since states were nothing but collectives of moral beings, they likewise had morality themselves: a collection of like objects will share the intrinsic qualities of each object. Heads of state did not lose their morality by representing the collective but rather multiplied it millionfold. Consequently, heads of state who behaved immorally violated the trust placed in them by their people.

But what of other morally minded states, and their leaders? Should they suffer this aberration in their midst, even parlay with it? Until Woodrow Wilson, the answer was an unequivocal yes. Like Roosevelt, even the most upright statesmen followed the Jesuitical line that one might move amongst the unclean without sullying oneself. Wilson disagreed. Dealing with tyrants legitimized their rule, whereas in fact every nation had a contrary duty to uphold natural law principles wherever and whenever possible. "We hold," he declared in 1913, "as I am sure all thoughtful leaders of republican governments everywhere hold, that just government rests always upon the consent of the governed, and that there can be no freedom without order based upon law." There was nothing particularly radical in that statement, but what followed was truly revolutionary:

> We shall look to make these principles the basis of mutual intercourse, respect, and helpfulness between our sister republics and ourselves. We shall lend our influence of every kind to the realization of these principles in fact and practice, knowing that disorder, personal intrigues, and defiance of constitutional rights weaken and discredit government and injure none so much as the people who are unfortunate enough to have their common life and common affairs so tainted and disturbed.... We are friends of peace, but we know that there can be no lasting or stable peace in such circumstances.[15]

If his listeners could believe their ears, Wilson appeared to suggest that the United States might intervene, even militarily, to protect the rights of people around the globe. This was not merely a stark rejection of state sovereignty but a new and unique strain of American exceptionalism. The United States was the most virtuous of nations; if it must go to war, it would be guided by no craven territorial ambitions but something far nobler: "America has more than once given evidence of the generosity and disinterestedness of its love of liberty. It has been willing to fight for the liberty of others as well as its own liberty.... The world now knows... that a nation can sacrifice its own interests and its own blood for the sake of liberty and happiness of another people."[16]

In effect, Woodrow Wilson was applying natural law principles to international statecraft. All men might not be brothers, as Secretary Bryan had it, but they did exist within the same moral universe. Each had a responsibility to ensure the rights of others, regardless of state boundaries. Ironically, for all that Wilson loathed Old World imperialism, one might draw a direct line between his logic and theirs: both advocated the spread of Western values by force, if necessary. There was one crucial difference. Whereas imperialists underscored the need to raise other peoples to the same level of "enlightenment" as themselves, Wilson argued the opposite: all peoples *by their nature* already knew and sought their rights. If they did not enjoy them it could only be because an external force—namely, a tyrannical government—prevented it. In threatening military force or lesser measures to uphold natural rights, the United States was declaring recalcitrant governments not only illegitimate but criminal. By introducing morality to diplomacy, President Wilson provided the legal foundation for both international criminal law and, ultimately, human rights law as well.

In 1914, however, such potentialities seemed fantastical. The first tests of President Wilson's moral diplomacy came not from the Old World but the shallower waters of Latin America and the Caribbean. Weeks into his first term, Wilson added his own corollary to the Monroe Doctrine: "We can have no sympathy with those who seek to seize the power of government to advance their own personal interests or ambitions."[17] The president had the opportunity to exercise that principle in the spring of 1914, when revolution erupted in the Dominican Republic. Wilson initially supported the government of President Jose Bordas but withdrew after reports reached him of arbitrary executions and imprisonment. That August, just as events in Europe reached devastating climax, Wilson dispatched a commission to Santo Domingo with a plan, drafted by himself, demanding an immediate end to hostilities, establishment of a provisional government, and free and fair elections. The Wilson Plan—underscored by the threat of gunboat diplomacy—was sufficient to preserve the peace until 1916, when renewed conflict drove Wilson to order a full-scale military occupation.[18] Similar meddling in revolutionary Mexico provoked a storm of protest from all sides, including the American public. Stung, Wilson shot back:

> There is one thing I have got a great enthusiasm about, I might almost say a reckless enthusiasm, and that is human liberty.... I hold it as a fundamental principle, and so do you, that every people has the right to determine its own form of government;

and until this revolution in Mexico, until the end of the Diaz reign, eighty percent of the people never had a "look in" in determining who should be their governors or what their government should be. Now I am for the eighty percent![19]

Set against the cataclysm of the Great War, unfolding even as President Wilson spoke these words, the United States' hemispheric adventures seem almost quaint. Yet Wilson and his cabinet were not unmindful of events overseas. Since the beginning of the century, Wilson watched with alarm as Great Britain and Germany outpaced each other in dreadnoughts, armies, and munitions. As president, he believed his moral diplomacy offered an escape route for them as well. In 1913 Walter Hines Page, the American ambassador to the Court of St. James, came to the Asquith government with an extraordinary proposal: let all civilized nations put aside their animosities and use their armies instead to "clean up the tropics," presumably on the model of Wilson's gunboat diplomacy in the Caribbean. The beauty and simplicity of the plan was so self-evident that Page wondered how anyone could fail to see it. Give the armies and navies a job, he said, and "they'd quit sitting on their haunches, growling at one another." Instead of destroying the world, the great powers could save it once and for all.[20]

When the British expressed tepid interest, Wilson was emboldened. He dispatched his factotum, Colonel Edward M. House, to present the governments of Europe with an even more grandiose scheme. The United States, Britain, France, Germany—the wealthiest nations —would pool their resources and use them to invest in the underdeveloped world, literally building democracies from the ground up. The Great Adventure, he called it. Colonel House approached the British first and found them surprisingly receptive. It is difficult to speculate on what the Foreign Office actually made of this moonshine. Perhaps they regarded it as a potential American investment in the British Empire, or perhaps they simply didn't wish to seem like the aggressors in a conflict nearly everyone agreed was inevitable. It is even conceivable they believed—or hoped—some last-minute influx of American cash might succeed where decades of diplomacy had not. In any case, Colonel House left London convinced that the British would join the adventure, if the Germans did so as well. Go talk to the kaiser, House was advised.

Colonel House arrived in Berlin in late May of 1914 and was instantly disabused of all fantasies. Admiral von Tirpitz coldly informed him that the best way for Germany to ensure peace was to "put fear in the hearts of its enemies." When the colonel was finally granted an audience with Wilhelm II, he found the kaiser cordial but noncommittal. Troops drilled outside House's windows, and everyone seemed to be in uniform. Dejected, he wrote back to the president that in Germany "jingoism run[s] stark mad, [and] there is someday to be an awful cataclysm."[21]

When that cataclysm came, Wilson's response was a careful "watching and waiting and watching." American neutrality persisted even as the German government stepped up its aggressive campaign of submarine warfare, torpedoing vessels just off the US coast and, in May of 1915, sinking the British liner *Lusitania* at the cost of some 123 American lives. As late as 1917, Wilson still held out hope that the United States might broker a peace; the Great Adventure had been postponed but not canceled. Other voices were more strident. William Howard Taft, Theodore Roosevelt, and Henry Cabot Lodge, along with many other prominent Republicans, founded the League to Enforce Peace in 1916. Their aim was simple: create a postwar worldwide organization with a combined army greater than any one nation could possibly muster. "Probably it will be impossible to stop all wars," Lodge admitted, "but it certainly will be possible to stop some wars and to diminish their number."[22]

Such language seems astonishing from the very men who would later confound Wilson's dream of a League of Nations, but it also reflected popular sentiment. The Great War proved that the old system of alliances carved from the wreckage of the Napoleonic Wars was moribund; something new and radical was needed. Even before hostilities, English author H. G. Wells predicted that war would be endemic until some form of world government came into being. Wilson was initially dismissive of the League to Enforce Peace, composed as it was of political enemies whom he saw as jingoists. But he shared their vision. Surely, he declared in 1917, there must be a postwar international organization of such force that "no nation, no probable combination of nations could face or withstand it."[23] The difference lay not in the destination but the route: Roosevelt and Lodge believed America must wage war in order to determine the peace, while Wilson remained convinced—for the moment—that American neutrality made it an honest broker for the settlement to come.

It might therefore have been a matter of acute embarrassment for the president when German aggression finally provoked the United States into entering the war in 1917. Instead, Wilson sought to recast the United States' role in familiar terms. "The world must be made safe for democracy," he roared to a tumultuous Congress. "We desire no conquest, no dominion.... But the right is more precious than peace, and we shall fight for the things which we have always carried nearest our hearts—for democracy, for the right of those who submit to authority to have a voice in their own governments...for a universal dominion of right by such a concert of free peoples as shall bring peace and safety to all nations."[24]

On the one hand, this language was hardly original: Wilson had spoken in nearly identical terms in 1913 and reiterated his message of moral hegemony again and again throughout his presidency. America would wage war only to defend and preserve the rights of oppressed peoples. In fact, it had already done so. "The world sneered when we set out upon the liberation of Cuba," Wilson declared in 1916, "but the world sneers no longer."[25] That might not be strictly true, but—and this was the crucial point—it could be *made* true. For if the ideas themselves had not changed, their context certainly had. This was no backyard scuffle in Mexico or Haiti. By bringing American guns, men, and morality to turn the tide of the Great War, Woodrow Wilson was attempting an unprecedented act of political alchemy: transforming an amoral, meaningless, centuries-old dynastic squabble into a moral crusade for "a universal dominion of right." Having failed to lure the nations into his Great Adventure with diplomacy or cash, Wilson was now prepared to pay the price in blood. The Old World would be reshaped by the New, whether it liked it or not.

◆ ◆ ◆

For the remainder of the war, Wilson planned for the peace. In practical terms this meant transforming high-minded but vague rhetoric on peace, rights, and justice into a coherent plan. First and foremost was the establishment of an international organization tasked with preventing war, especially the catastrophic breakdown the Great War had become. On this point there was near unanimity of agreement among all the Allies and in the United States as well. Still mourning the death in battle of his youngest son, Quentin, Theodore Roosevelt gave a qualified endorsement. "Of course, fundamentally war and peace are matters of the heart rather than of organization, and any declaration or peace league which represents high-flown sentimentality of pacifists and doctrinaires is worse than useless," he began waspishly. One the other hand, "if, without in the smallest degree sacrificing our belief in a sound and intense national aim, we all join with the people of England, France and Italy... we may be able to make a real and much-needed advance in the international organization." He concluded, "The United States cannot again withdraw completely into its shell."[26]

Wilson agreed that, as war represented the ultimate collapse of civilization, preventing war must be any international organization's primary aim. But why stop there? At the risk of incurring Roosevelt's epithet of a woolly sentimentalist, he began to articulate a new and broader vision. "Shall there be a common standard of right and privilege for all peoples and nations, or shall the strong do as they will and the weak suffer without redress?" he demanded of the crowd on the steps of the Fourth Liberty Loan in September 1918. "Shall the assertion of right be haphazard and by casual alliance, or shall there be a common concert to oblige the observance of common rights?"[27] These rhetorical questions had very definite answers. A common standard of right and a common concert to oblige it meant a codified human rights law and an international organization with sufficient force to compel compliance. These aspirations were well beyond a League to Enforce Peace; in fact, Wilson appeared to advocate nothing less than world government.

The truth, however, was more nuanced. For all the derision of Woodrow Wilson as an impractical idealist, he understood only too well that utopia could not be constructed overnight. Writing privately to Colonel House, he admitted frankly, "The United States Senate would never ratify any treaty which put the force of the United States at the disposal of any such group or body." The wisest choice would be to secure the creation of a League of Nations based upon universal areas of agreement, then allow the institution to take on a life of its own. That, after all, was how all legal systems developed: a constitution or charter brought them into being, but it was humanity itself which added layer upon layer of precedent, transforming the law from brittle shell into a living entity. "My own conviction," he told House, "is that the administrative *constitution* of the League must *grow* and not be made…. Why begin at the impossible end when there is a possible end and it is feasible to plant a system which will slowly but surely ripen into fruition?"[28]

Wilson's Fourteen Points for Peace, released in January 1918, spoke of a "general covenant of nations…for the purpose of affording mutual guarantees of political independence,"[29] but said nothing of an international covenant of human rights. Arriving at the Paris peace talks in December of that year, his first public remarks sounded like platitudes. His audience could make of them what they liked:

> The triumph of freedom in this war means that spirits of that sort now dominate the world. There is a great wind of moral force moving through the world, and every man who opposes himself to that wind will go down in disgrace…. My conception of the League of Nations is just this, that it shall operate as the organized moral force of men throughout the world.[30]

What exactly was a "moral force?" Wilson did not elaborate. In all likelihood, human rights were not at the forefront of the president's mind. There were more pressing issues to be considered first: the French wanted German territory, the Italians coveted a share of the Balkans, and the Japanese sought Manchuria. Wilson, as self-appointed defender of the powerless, advocated self-determination for states and liberal terms for the vanquished. The majority of his time in Paris was consumed with territorial disputes and indemnities. This was enough to put him at odds with the French and British, whom he found hopelessly reactionary. Georges Clemenceau, he told House dismissively, was "an old man, too old to comprehend new ideas." David Lloyd George, almost ten years Wilson's junior, was merely a "second rate politician."[31] But at least in George he recognized someone with a comparable understanding of law and right. "An essential element in the peace settlement," George had written, "is the constitution of the League of Nations as the effective guardian of international right and international liberty throughout the world."[32]

When the time came to draft the founding covenant of the league, the practical limits of Wilson's vision—and his own faults as negotiator—became increasingly apparent. As chair, he was impatient with committee members, often terminating discussion midsentence. He also showed a curious reluctance for the use of force. Wilson himself had argued repeatedly that no international organization could preserve the peace or uphold human rights by word alone. Yet when the French delegate recommended the establishment of a league army, Wilson rejected it out of hand: "Unconstitutional and impossible."[33] He later admitted he was thinking of the Senate, which would never ratify a treaty that abrogated military authority to any other power. That was certainly true, but the lack of enforcement gutted the league's effectiveness and contributed to its ultimate failure.

As discussions dragged on, other uncomfortable issues bubbled to the surface. The Japanese delegation wished to add a seemingly innocuous paragraph to the covenant, which read as follows:

> The equality of nations being a basic principle of the League of Nations, the High Contracting Parties agree to accord, as soon as possible, to all alien nationals of States members of the League, equal and just treatment in every respect; making no distinction, either in law or in fact, on account of their race or nationality.[34]

It was hard to see at first how this could be controversial; the very foundation of natural law rights lay in their recognition of equality before the law. Yet the storm was immediate. The British, thinking of empire, objected at once. Others soon followed. "No government could live for a day in Australia if it tampered with a White Australia," one delegate declared. Sooner than agree to it, he would "walk into the Seine—or the Folies Bergere—with my clothes off." His colleague from New Zealand concurred. The ubiquitous Colonel House took Wilson aside and pressed a note into his hand. "The trouble is that if this Commission should pass it, it would surely raise the race issue throughout the world." Wilson, a

Virginian and avowed segregationist, did not need further elaboration. When the Japanese insisted upon a vote, much to his chagrin, the amendment passed by a small majority. Wilson abruptly declared from the chair that because there were strong objections to the language, it could not be included. This patent nonsense left the Japanese stunned, and the Tokyo press angrily derided "the so-called civilized world."[35]

Wilson believed he was bowing to greater realities. The league would not pass Congress with an army; it certainly would not pass if the Dixiecrats believed it enshrined desegregation. Nor would they be alone in their objections. Even as a distant aspiration, racial equality before the law threatened the very foundations upon which a great many societies rested, including the United States. Ultimately the league charter avoided any enumeration of rights and called instead for the creation of an international court of justice, provisions against slavery and human trafficking, and universal standards for working conditions.

This in itself was no small accomplishment. If the League of Nations was not exactly "the organized moral force of men throughout the world," it was at least a start. There is no evidence Wilson had abandoned his vision of international human rights; instead, he recognized the need to move incrementally, to build the house before furnishing it. He believed he had skillfully excised any language from the league covenant that his political enemies could object to; once it was ratified, the gates would swing shut behind them.

❖ ❖ ❖

It was said of Woodrow Wilson that he believed all men who opposed him were not only wrong but wicked.[36] He was also, one of his contemporaries noted, "a man who really knows how to hate." Miraculously, these failings had not prevented his steady ascension in public life until its climax, when he returned from the Paris talks in triumph with a draft treaty for the League of Nations ready to be signed.

There were warning signs. Unaccountably, Wilson had failed to bring a single Republican with him to Versailles, even men like William Howard Taft who shared his views. The president instead chose to surround himself with a cadre of sycophants who told him what he wanted to hear. Very little else reached him. A young Eleanor Roosevelt was astonished to discover that Wilson never read newspapers: his staff prepared briefs instead.[37] Having dealt handily, as he saw it, with the French, British, Italians, Japanese, and others, he had little fear of Congress. But when the first group of senators met with the president after his return, they came away mystified. "I feel as if I had been wandering with Alice in Wonderland and had tea with the Mad Hatter," one admitted.[38]

Wilson's confidence was not baseless. He was a successful wartime president who had also proved himself a shrewd negotiator. The American public wanted peace, and a league bearing the unmistakable stamp of American authority was an almost universally popular idea. Treaty ratification required a two-thirds majority of the Senate, but nearly that number had already expressed public support for the League of Nations, and others were open to being convinced. Even his archrival Henry Cabot Lodge privately admitted that ratification was a foregone conclusion.

But Wilson could not persuade; he could only preach. In an earlier speech he compared league opponents to Southern secessionists and came dangerously close to branding them traitors: "I look for the time when every man who now puts his counsel against the service of mankind under the League of Nations will be just as ashamed of it as he now regretted the union of the states."[39] Now addressing the Senate, he declared in ringing tones: "There can be no question of our ceasing to be a world power. The only question is whether we can refuse the moral leadership that is offered us, whether we shall accept or reject the confidence of the world."[40] The choice was between light or darkness, courage or cowardice. His argument could best be summed up by a Latin expression harkening back to his days as a university professor: *res ipsa loquitur,* the thing speaks for itself.

This was not enough for the Senate, which disliked being lectured to, and disliked even more having policy decisions presented to them in biblical terms. Article 10 of the Versailles Treaty stated, "The members of the league undertake to respect and preserve against external aggression the territorial integrity and existing political independence of all members of the league." To many this seemed impossibly vague. Even without an international army, would American boys be arbitrarily called upon to shed their blood all over the world, in conflicts they barely understood? Wilson tried to allay the senators' fears and succeeded in inflaming them. Senator William Borah asked him, "Mr. President, with reference to Article 10…in listening to the reading of your statement I got the impression that your view was that [it] was simply a moral obligation."

"Yes, sir," Wilson answered, "inasmuch as there is no sanction in the treaty."

Borah pressed, "But that would be a legal obligation so far as the United States was concerned if it should enter it; would it not?"

"I would not interpret it that way, Senator.… It is an attitude of comradeship and protection among the members of the league, which in its very nature is moral and not legal."[41]

Moral and not legal. Yet Wilson had spent much of his public life arguing they were one and the same. Sensing an opening, the Ohioan Warren G. Harding entered the fray: "Right there, Mr. President, if there is nothing more than a moral obligation on the part of any member of the league, what avail articles 10 and 11?"

The president affected astonishment. "Why, Senator, it is surprising that that question should be asked. If we undertake an obligation we are bound in the most solemn way to carry it out."[42]

There is a surreal quality to this exchange. Woodrow Wilson, righteous and indignant, was sparring with the man who would succeed him— whose own presidency would become synonymous with corruption and scandal. The immediate issue, ratification of the treaty, was subsumed by a philosophical conundrum that rang down the centuries: was there a universal standard of morality, and did all nations have an obligation to abide by it? If so, as Wilson argued, there could be no reason not to bind oneself to a document stating as much. Yet Harding, with a legal acumen few might have credited, raised the old ghosts of Demosthenes and Xenophon and seemed to hint at a form of cultural relativism that would appear long after both men were dead and gone:

> HARDING: Another question: That is surrendering the suggestion of a moral obligation for this Republic to the prejudices of the nations of the Old World, is it not?
>
> WILSON: I do not understand that we make such a surrender.…

> HARDING: Would it not be quite as moral for this Republic itself to determine its moral obligations?
>
> WILSON: Undoubtedly, Senator; but in the meantime the world would not have knowledge before it that there will be concerted action by all the responsible governments of the world in the protection of the peace of the world. The minute you do away that assurance to the world, you have reached the situation which produced the German war.[43]

The president's point was valid; in fact, it was the crux of the league itself. America alone might be moral, but America alone could not prevent the rise of another tyranny, another world war. There must instead be a shared moral standard, a legal covenant among nations akin to that which each state makes with its citizens. Wilson, who believed in natural law, saw nothing amiss in the assumption of a universal morality. Harding, on the other hand, saw "Old World prejudices" entangling the United States in their inextricable web. The gulf between their views would define American foreign policy for decades.

Faced with intransigence from the Senate, Wilson took his argument to the people. In the fall of 1919 he embarked on a cross-country tour, hoping a tsunami of public opinion would drown the naysayers. In San Francisco, he thundered, "We cannot desert humanity. We are the trustees of humanity, and we must see that we redeem the pledges which are always implicit in so great a trusteeship."[44] In Pueblo, he struck a note of confidence and inevitability:

> There is one thing that the American people always rise to and extend their hand to, and that is the truth of justice and of liberty and of peace. We have accepted that truth and we are going to be led by it, and it is going to lead us, and through the world, out into pastures of quietness and peace such as the world never dreamed of before.[45]

But the pastures of quietness were receding out of reach. Exhausted, desperately ill, Wilson was ultimately forced to cancel the remainder of the tour. Shortly after returning to the White House, he suffered a debilitating stroke that left him unable to speak or move unaided. The Senate, led by Henry Cabot Lodge, rejected membership in the League of Nations. The league itself would continue its half-life existence for another two decades, shorn of the moral mandate Wilson sought and sustained reluctantly by nations that had never shared his comprehensive vision. It is remembered now only for its failures: abortive attempts to quell aggression in Manchuria and Ethiopia, culminating in total collapse against the rise of Nazi Germany. Coupled with that failure is the even more maddening possibility of what might have been, if Wilson had prevailed. Yet the assumption that American membership alone might have prevented the Second World War also presumes universal adoption of Wilson's vision of moral diplomacy, and there is scant evidence to support that course of events. The objections of Borah, Harding, and Lodge mirrored a greater skepticism among other nations: for all their expressions of hope and optimism, few were truly committed to Wilson's new world order.

It is better to consider Wilson's legacy on its own merits. Though it rejected the league, the United States did not "withdraw completely into its shell," as Theodore Roosevelt feared. In 1922, Wilson's bête noir Harding hosted a conference resulting in the Washington Naval Treaty, ending an arms race among the great powers and committing them to peaceful competition. If America is—or ever was—"the leader of the free world," it owes that title entirely to Woodrow Wilson. The mantle of moral diplomacy would be taken up by every president that followed him, articulated most famously by Ronald Reagan in his vision of the United States as a "shining city on a hill." Wilson was the first president to advocate a natural law standard for international law, the first to suggest that nations had an equal duty to protect basic human rights around the globe. Even within the half-baked Great Adventure we might find the seedlings of such institutions as the World Bank and the International Monetary Fund. But most importantly, his vision of American exceptionalism—that America fights not for conquest or glory, but for the rights of the oppressed—became the touchstone of US foreign policy throughout the Second World War, Cold War, and the first decade of the twenty-first century.

Then it was abandoned. The Trump administration's isolationist "America First" policy may now be as moribund as the League of Nations, but its scars remain. That the United States was capable of so completely divorcing itself from the world, after decades of responsible stewardship, calls into doubt many of our most fundamental assumptions about ourselves and our role; doubts shared by other nations as well. In a radio address three months before his death, Woodrow Wilson bemoaned the "sullen and selfish isolation" of the United States, "which is deeply ignoble because manifestly cowardly and dishonorable." His last words hold sudden and terrible relevance as we craft anew our relationship with the global community:

> This must always be a source of deep mortification to us, and we shall inevitably be forced by the moral obligations of freedom and honor to retrieve that fatal error and assume once more the role of courage, self-respect, and helpfulness which every true American must wish to regard as our natural part in the affairs of the world.... Happily, the present situation in the world of affairs affords us the opportunity to retrieve the past and to render to mankind the inestimable service of proving that there is at least one great and powerful nation which can turn away from programs of self-interest and devote itself to practicing and establishing the highest ideals of disinterested service and the consistent standards of *conscience* and of *right*.[46]

— 5 —

THE PRESIDENT'S GHOST

One of the few luxuries Franklin Delano Roosevelt allowed himself during wartime was the private projection room arranged for him at the White House. Roosevelt loved movies. He was the first president to cultivate friendships with film stars and knew enough Hollywood gossip to ask Helen Gahagan Douglas what really happened with Anatole Litvak and Paulette Goddard under the table at Ciro's.[1] For a man who couldn't walk without braces or travel without a cavalcade, films were a rare form of escape.

But his selection one night in January 1945, was decidedly strange. With family and friends gathered around him, Roosevelt demanded a screening of Darryl Zanuck's new Technicolor biopic *Wilson*. As the former assistant secretary of the navy during the last war, FDR knew the plot better than most. When violins swell and Wilson declares to a recalcitrant Republican delegation, "America has but two choices, gentlemen. Accept the League of Nations or live with a gun in its hand," one can easily imagine FDR nodding in that characteristic manner of his, bringing his own hand down with an affirmative thump on the armrest. Yet his guests were anxious. They watched the president on the screen grow frail, isolated, ultimately undone by a paralytic stroke and his enemies in Congress. His grand dreams for a new world order were reduced to ruins. "By God, that isn't going to happen to *me,*" the current president muttered.[2]

It was happening. Roosevelt was dying. Everyone in the screening room knew it. Even Wilson's widow, Edith, took labor secretary Frances Perkins aside a few weeks later and said, "Oh, Mrs. Perkins, did you get a good look at the President? Oh, it frightened me. He looks exactly as my husband looked when he went into his decline."[3] Franklin Roosevelt lived with Wilson's ghost every single day. An almost inconceivable confluence of circumstances contrived to bring him in 1945 to exactly the same pivotal moment as his predecessor in 1918. A global war was coming to an end, and the United States would be called upon to help fashion the peace. Just as before, the American people—indeed, the peoples of the world—demanded of their leaders that the horrors they experienced should have some lasting, meaningful consequence. Justice must be done and measures taken to ensure that nothing like it could ever occur again. With a good portion of the world in ruins, it was a rare and fitting moment to lay the foundation of a new international law.

FDR might have seen his role in Shakespearean terms: the son avenging his father's disgrace. Or, as a great believer in destiny and divine providence, he might have thought that God had placed him there at that moment to do his work. There is a messianic zeal underlying his fight for the United Nations that one struggles to find in his other administrative endeavors. Indeed, it runs at crosscurrents with his perceived nature. Roosevelt was often cast as a pragmatist surrounded by dreamers. "I did not choose the tools with which I must work," he once explained wearily. "Had I been permitted to choose them I would have selected quite different ones."[4] He had little patience for ideologues. His creed was action, not theory; try something, and if it doesn't work, try something else. Even his secretary of war, Henry Stimson, said that following Roosevelt's thought processes was like chasing a beam of sunlight around an empty room.[5] Yet in 1945 FDR was the consummate idealist, preaching a form of world government more radical and far reaching than Wilson could have imagined. On few other subjects during his presidency was he less equivocal or more consistent. Thus one might begin to trace the reintroduction of natural law principles back into geopolitics simply by reviewing a record of Roosevelt's speeches from 1937 to 1945.

This requires a little explaining. At no time did Franklin Roosevelt explicitly reference natural law; instead he spoke of an "international morality" and universal human rights. It is sometimes suggested that human rights are a uniquely Western concept. That is not the case; the drafters of the Universal Declaration of Human Rights, for example, were primarily from non-Western countries.[6] But it is undeniable that human rights are the most contemporary iteration of natural law. The logic for this goes back to the earliest debates on the meaning of law itself. If there are no transcendent principles of justice, the sole and final arbiter of law is the state. It can sanction or proscribe as it wills. Its actions may be "immoral," as judged against conventional morality, but they cannot be criminal. Similarly, by this logic, human rights are not universal but privileges granted at the pleasure of the state. Just as each state has its own code of laws, each may decide what "rights" to grant its citizens.

On the other hand, if there is a natural law independent from states, it must supersede. Justice and right must be common to all, regardless of status or nationality. This argument, taken to its logical conclusion, allows (indeed mandates) recognition of universal human rights. It also provides the legal foundation to hold functionaries of the state criminally liable if their actions violate such rights. Thus both the Universal Declaration of Human Rights and the Nuremberg Tribunals rest on the same legal foundation of natural law.

While Franklin Roosevelt did not live to see either, no single person had a greater impact on their creation. If it seems unusual to frame the story of natural law and human rights in the twentieth century largely around one man, it is equally unusual for any individual—even a sovereign—to so completely and deliberately alter the law's trajectory. It is strange, therefore, that while FDR's role in the founding of the UN has been the subject of many books and articles, his equally vital role in human rights legislation seems overlooked. He is given proper credit for the Four Freedoms speech and the Atlantic Charter, but aside from these and a handful of other speeches, little is said. Few certainly would advance the claim that Roosevelt had a coherent *policy* on human rights.[7] His words, we are to understand, inspired others, particularly his wife. It was Eleanor who served as the first chairperson of the UN Human Rights Commission, and it was she who fulfilled the role of her husband's conscience while he lived. Crediting Roosevelt with the peacekeeping functions of the UN and Eleanor the HRC has a neat symmetry about it. It also jibes with what we perceive of their characters: the realpolitik pragmatist versus the idealist.[8] This is manifestly unfair to both. Eleanor believed her work on human rights continued her husband's labors, ensuring that his ideas were incorporated into the Universal Declaration. Moreover, Franklin Roosevelt might have been an indifferent law student and a reluctant attorney, but he was the only trained lawyer amongst the Big Three. When he spoke of the Four Freedoms, he knew he was advocating not just a political transformation but a legal one.

The story of natural law and human rights is, of course, much bigger than Franklin or Eleanor Roosevelt. Renaissance jurists and philosophers, and others after them, wrote of a future utopia when all the world might exist under a single, perfect law. They assumed, however, that, as law was a reflection of society, this happy state could only arrive when society itself had evolved to a similar perfection. The idea that such a law might appear after the most destructive conflict in human history, and as a direct result of the atrocities inflicted during that conflict, was inconceivable. When Enlightenment scholars spoke of the rights of man, they acknowledged that every sovereign had the duty to grant (or not impede) those rights for their subjects. It was even presumed that a people might overthrow their sovereign if such rights were not given. Yet few contemplated the possibility that one state might hold the leaders of another criminally liable for breach, or that an international body might one day establish and impose universal legal norms. State law was still exclusively the domain of state actors.[9]

In the aftermath of the Great War, that narrative changed. Inspired by Woodrow Wilson's efforts to establish the League of Nations, a small but motivated group of activists and academics saw the league's potential to evolve into something more: world government. Collective security was a necessary first step, but only the beginning. Particular attention was given to Wilson's attempt to include language in the league charter offering protection for minority groups.[10] Of note also were the ongoing efforts of the International Labor Organization (ILO) in encouraging the community of nations to establish basic standards of living.[11] Yet neither the league nor the ILO could properly be understood as a foundation of universal human rights, any more than could the pleasant but vague language of the era, such as the Kellogg-Briand Pact's stated intention, in 1928, "to promote the welfare of mankind."[12]

One obvious problem with establishing a universal law was that each group—religious, social, political—in each nation had its own conception of what "basic" human rights consisted of. In the United States alone there was a plethora. Religious leaders saw it as "God's law"; patriotic Americans (especially in Congress) saw it as the Bill of Rights; socialists saw it as the welfare of the worker; etc., etc. Only a small coterie of academics saw universal human rights as a species of natural law—but they became crucial later, as we shall see.

It was Franklin Roosevelt who gave both shape and direction to this amorphous public sentiment, leading to an entirely novel understanding of natural law. First, he reduced the concept of right from its innumerable possibilities down to four basic freedoms. Second, he used the power of his office to promote recognition of those freedoms at home and abroad. Third, he employed diplomacy to engineer the creation of an international organization whose mandate included protection of human rights, with the United States occupying a principal role. Fourth, and most importantly, he cast aside forever the idea that the welfare of each individual was solely the province of their state. From the very beginning of his political career, Roosevelt spoke of a global community whose members were responsible for one other. This community was not a future possibility but an existing fact. It was in this conception that we find most clearly an awareness of natural law, of a desire to see "a new moral order" arise everywhere in the world.

❖ ❖ ❖

As assistant secretary of the navy, Roosevelt was a late and reluctant convert to the concept of the League of Nations. "Last spring," he declared in his first major address on the subject in March of 1919, "I thought the League of Nations merely a beautiful dream, a Utopia."[13] Yet there is some evidence that even in 1919 Roosevelt saw its potential to evolve. In July of that year he gave a speech before the League to Enforce Peace that offered an interesting analogy:

> When the federal constitution was adopted it was called impractical and illegal. Yet it was adopted with faith in its authors. Should we not have equal faith in the authors of this treaty of peace with its clause for the League of Nations? If it is adopted we will have given the world something besides Magna Carta and the federal constitution. It will be a document that will make the world a safe place to live for ages to come.[14]

The comparison is a strange one. The Magna Carta and the US Constitution were not treaties, but foundations of law. By placing the league within this pantheon, Roosevelt appears to be suggesting it too will serve as a legal foundation. But for what, exactly? Making "the world a safe place to live" implies more than merely preventing war. Stranger still is the implication that the league is somehow perceived as "illegal." By whose law? And what would be illegal about the maintenance of peace? A possible answer to these conundrums is that Roosevelt saw the league as the beginning of a new international law.[15] There is other evidence for this contention. In all, FDR gave nearly eight hundred speeches in support of the league; much of the language was boilerplate, but occasionally he grapples with something larger. Accepting his party's nomination for vice president in 1920, he lectured:

> We must open our eyes and see that modern civilization has become so complex and the lives of civilized men so interwoven with the lives of other men in other countries as to make it impossible to be in this world and not of it…. We cannot anchor our ship of state in this world tempest nor can we return to the placid harbor of long ago. We must go forward or founder.[16]

On the one hand this was an attack on isolationism, yet the focus of this passage is not on the interconnectedness of governments or trading partners but rather "the lives of civilized men." Reducing vast societal forces down to the ordinariness of daily life would later become a hallmark of FDR's fireside chats, but there is interesting ambiguity here. Are the "other men in other countries" also civilized? If so, what is the nature of this civilization that binds them? If not, is it the responsibility of the civilized men to make them so, as this passage seems to imply? Either way, it is impossible not to read within this excerpt some undercurrents of natural law philosophy, in either its classical or nineteenth-century form.

Progress, Roosevelt is saying, is a collective effort. Likewise there is a haunting echo in this speech of the very last one Roosevelt wrote, which lay on his desk in Warm Springs, Georgia, as its author expired upstairs: "The only limit to our realization of tomorrow will be our doubts of today. Let us move forward with a strong and active faith."[17]

Progress and faith. In Roosevelt's mind they were inextricably linked and might have occupied much of the landscape of the "thickly forested interior" within his soul that he revealed to almost no one. "His religious faith," speechwriter Robert Sherwood wrote, "was the strongest, most mysterious force within him."[18] Mysterious perhaps, but not unknowable. At Groton School young Franklin fell under the tutelage of Reverend Endicott Peabody, a staunch advocate of "muscular Christianity." By this Victorian creed all life's struggles were sent by God to test man's ability to master them, and himself.[19] For Franklin, the lesson stuck. "He believed in God and in his guidance," Eleanor Roosevelt would write. "He felt that human beings were given tasks to perform and with those tasks the ability and strength to put them through."[20] The president would later credit Endicott Peabody as the most important man in his life besides his own father.

The core of Rooseveltian philosophy lay in his belief that humanity evolved toward a greater end, directed by its own essential goodness and intelligence—hence his reminder to have "faith in the authors" of the league—and by a divine hand. In a 1943 speech, for example, Roosevelt pitched the United Nations as a means whereby "mankind may enjoy in peace and in freedom the unprecedented blessings which Divine Providence through the progress of civilization has put within reach."[21] Whether or not he read Cicero or Aquinas (though, with the benefit of a Harvard education and legal training from Columbia, he probably did), Roosevelt intuited the fundamental precept of Aquinian natural law: that God instilled in humankind an instinct for justice, which if allowed to fully develop would lead ultimately to utopia.[22] Again and again (to borrow his own phrase) Roosevelt reaffirmed this correlation between faith, progress, and civilization. In his last inaugural address, delivered just weeks after Dr. Peabody's death, Roosevelt expressed it succinctly: "I remember that my old schoolmaster, Dr. Peabody, said in days that seemed to us then to be secure and untroubled, 'Things in life will not always run smoothly. Sometimes we will be rising toward the heights—then all will seem to reverse itself and start downward. The great fact to remember is that the trend of civilization itself is forever upward; that a line drawn through the middle of the peaks and the valleys of the centuries always has an upward trend."[23]

Just as fervent as Franklin Roosevelt's faith in human progress was his conviction that the United States had a unique role in that "upward trend." In a 1920 stump speech in Mitchell, South Dakota, Roosevelt declared, "The United States has an opportunity to write the title of the ensuing chapter of history either as 'America leads the world toward a New Era' or 'America abandons her Faith.'"[24] For FDR the fight for the league became something greater than wrangling over a peace treaty: it was about a vision of the future and the United States' role in hastening that vision into reality. "The younger nations are looking to the United States for justice and liberty, and ours is the task to see that the safety of these nations is wrapped up."[25] Justice and liberty, of course, are legal concepts, and the United States' role in safeguarding them in other nations was left vague. In a speech entitled "The National Emergency of Peace Times" he was more explicit: "We have taken on for all time a new relationship, recognized by the fact of our entry into the war for civilization, the duty we owe to other peoples and nations and which they owe to us."[26]

Thus, as early as 1919 these crucial elements may be found in Roosevelt's character and speeches: 1) a recognition of the interrelatedness of all "civilized" persons; 2) an acceptance of the responsibility for states, especially the United States, to foster that interrelationship and, by extension, civilization itself; 3) a genuine belief in American exceptionalism; 4) a staunch belief in universal human progress buttressed by his own "strong and active" personal faith. Combined, these elements would form the moral foundation of FDR's push for the United Nations and universal human rights.

In later years, some would accuse Roosevelt of pressing for the UN out of revenge for Wilson's humiliation. They were not entirely wrong. At the 1920 Democratic Convention in San Francisco, a demonstration in favor of the departing president was met with stony silence by the New York delegation until Roosevelt himself wrested the banner from Tammany hands and led an insurgent parade up the aisles.[27] His boss at the Department of the Navy, Josephus Daniels, noted years later that among FDR's most prized possessions as president was the desk on which Wilson had written the first draft of his league covenant.[28] Yet Roosevelt the pragmatist was also conscious of Wilson's failings. When asked years later about the failure of the league, he answered glibly, "That needs a politician like me."[29] Someone, in other words, who could do the things Wilson could not: obfuscate, compromise, wait on events, and hide his true intentions until a favorable climate matured.

For all his earlier fervor, Roosevelt allowed the league to recede from his thoughts until a second world crisis once again brought it forward. But there were glimmerings. In 1923, responding to a contest in the *Saturday Evening Post* for the best essay on international cooperation (with a cash prize of $100,000), Roosevelt drafted a proposed "Society of Nations" that looked remarkably like the existing league, with a few technical alterations.[30] The whole project, in fact, might have been a form of recuperative therapy: he had been diagnosed with polio months before, and Eleanor later admitted that "the writing of the peace plan was proposed largely as something to keep alive his interest in outside affairs during the first years of adjustment, when it would have been easy for him to become a self-centered invalid."[31] The futility of the project was underscored by the fact that, since Eleanor herself served on the prize committee, her husband's contribution was necessarily void. Of more interest than his proposal was the letter he wrote to publisher Edward Bok, who sponsored the contest. Despite his own entry, Roosevelt had publicly scoffed at the idea that any plan—even his—could be a "short cut to Eutopia" (given the Eurocentric nature of the league, this might or might not have been a typo).[32] Yet in his private letter to Bok, Roosevelt admitted to "malice aforethought" in this declaration. "Public opinion must be educated to expect necessarily complicated machinery," he wrote, instead of "the mere establishment of a formula."[33] Cognizance of public opinion, and the willing manipulation of it, would be hallmarks of FDR's own attempts to create a second, successful league.

Judging from his own words, however, it was decades before the thought entered Roosevelt's mind once again. In this he was in the majority. The trajectory of events by the mid-1930s had moved so completely

away from Wilson's promised "utopia" as to make any serious proponent of democratic world government naïve at best. Despite his earlier
musings about the comity between "civilized men," when confronted
with mounting evidence of brutality within the Nazi state, Roosevelt's
response was initially muted. He liked to keep lines of communication
open, and filing meaningless protests bound to fall on deaf ears was not
his style of politics (again in contrast to his mentor, Wilson). Immersed
in its own problems since the start of the Great Depression, the United
States had little interest in assuming the role of global nanny.[34] Moreover,
even if Roosevelt had wished to intervene, there were few practicable
avenues. King Leopold II's horrors in the Congo led to demands that
he be tried for "crimes against humanity," but outcry remained limited
to newspaper editors and Leopold died in his bed.[35] Similar cries had
come at the end of the First World War, insisting Kaiser Wilhelm II
be charged with a host of offenses. The delegates at Versailles adopted
a Napoleonic approach instead and sent him into exile. There was simply no precedent for policing the internal affairs of another nation or
holding its leaders criminally accountable. As the Nazi state grew and
consolidated, the Roosevelt administration initially employed a cautious
policy of watching and waiting. But that was to change.

◆ ◆ ◆

As early as 1937, Franklin Roosevelt evinced a remarkably clear-eyed
understanding of the dangers Nazism posed, not merely to global security but to the upward trajectory of human progress described by Dr.
Peabody—an evolution whose benchmarks were measured in adherence
to natural law. In a Chicago speech given on October 5 of that year, he
warned: "The landmarks and traditions which have marked the progress of civilization toward a condition of law, order and justice are being
wiped away," and called upon Americans to join with other nations to
"work together for the triumph of law and moral principles in order that
peace, justice and confidence may prevail in the world."[36] This was no
empty rhetoric. The "Quarantine" speech, as it came to be known, laid
the foundations of an argument Roosevelt would return to many times
in the coming years. Interdependent economies, fluid borders, and even

technological advances like airplanes and railroads meant that no nation could live in isolation from its peers. States were bound by invisible cords in a vast, intricate network; when one cord strained or snapped it disturbed the whole. Thus any turbulence—even if confined within the borders of a single nation—was as relevant to the American citizen as the price of corn in Iowa: "There can be no stability or peace either within nations or between nations except under laws and moral standards adhered to by all.... It is, therefore, a matter of vital interest and concern to the people of the United States that the sanctity of international treaties and the maintenance of international morality be restored."

Roosevelt's conception of law was both new and ancient. Its novelty lay in challenging the oldest precept of diplomacy: that every state had absolute sovereignty over laws and policies within its borders. The president was not (yet) suggesting the United States might intervene militarily or otherwise to stop an atrocity, but rather that it exert whatever influence it could to induce all nations to adopt a universal standard of law to prevent such atrocities before they occurred. Equally novel was the presumption that this was not a new departure but recognition of an existing reality. In the president's depiction, trade and travel had succeeded where the league failed: a global community already existed.

What this community lacked, however, was a universal standard by which to function. In supplying that standard, the president reached past centuries of realpolitik, all the way to the Renaissance. Placing "law and moral principles" in an overall rubric of "international morality," Roosevelt resurrected humanist visions of a holistic code of justice based on natural law. Further, by drawing a direct line between a single domestic disturbance and the collective harmony of nations, the Quarantine speech raised ancient echoes of the "King's Peace." In medieval England the sovereign was responsible for preserving the peace; disturbance of that peace upset the delicate balance and harmony within the kingdom. Therefore, any crime was considered not merely an assault on the victim but on the "King's Peace" and thus the community as a whole.[37] Roosevelt had, almost offhandedly, extended the King's Peace to cover the entire world.

If the president's call for an "international morality" seems naïve, it must be understood in context. Until the twentieth century, the basic precepts of natural law had never been so thoroughly subverted; indeed, one of the most sinister aspects of Nazism was its ability to cloak unconscionable acts in the raiment of familiar legal language. Article 4 of the infamous Nuremberg Laws of 1935, for example, states: "Jews are forbidden to fly the Reich or national flag or display Reich colors; They are, on the other hand, permitted to display the Jewish colors. The exercise of this right is protected by the state."[38] While expressly denying Jews a vital element of participation in the Reich (at a time when displaying the swastika on storefronts, houses, or upon one's person was all but required), the law appears to be making a "separate but equal" distinction. Naturally, display of "Jewish colors" would further distinguish the Jews, making them easier to identify. But the most revealing passage comes at the end. In the Nazi state there were no rights under law but rather privileges granted by the state and conditional on the individual's continued, active display of fealty. Voting, citizenship, marriage, worship, education, employment—any and all participation in society—were privileges, not rights.[39] Hence, when we find language suggesting that the "right" to display Jewish colors shall be "protected by the state," it is impossible not to conclude that the purpose of this language was to placate the reader into a false sense of security with the deliberate use of natural law language.

Roosevelt was not alone is seeing past this subterfuge. Journalists, diplomats, and even tourists had long warned that the seeming orderliness of the Third Reich concealed a callous disregard for the rule of law.[40] While Nazi "ideology" was chaotic and contradictory, its legal philosophy was brutally simple; it was, in fact, the embodiment of Xenophon's precept that whatever the state wills is law. Legal theorists had long pondered the ethical implications of that idea, yet assumed that other factors—the benevolence of the ruler, volatility of the governed, or the basic goodness of humankind—would ultimately restrain the state and its leaders from their worst impulses. Even Cicero had counseled against resisting an unjust magistrate; since human nature was inherently good, he argued, evil must be an aberration. Therefore the wisest counsel was to have patience and wait for the natural balance to be restored. Nazism proved the fallacy of this belief. Under the Reich, the will of the state was omnipresent, immovable, and unrestrained.

Indeed, the counterexample of Nazism seemed to bring the original beauty of natural law into stark relief by contrast. Writing for the *Notre Dame Law Review* in 1939, Professor Brendan F. Brown guided his readers through an examination of "Natural Law and the Law-Making Function in American Jurisprudence" before ultimately revealing his true purpose at the conclusion. Casting aside the veneer of academic detachment, his article became a jeremiad:

> The chaotic stage through which the whole world seems to be passing at the present time, largely as a result of rejecting natural law philosophy in international relations, the complete breakdown of the natural law mode of thought as the basis of international law, the rejection of the natural law category in the totalitarian countries...in short the elimination of natural law philosophy from both the international and national orders, with results which are obviously disastrous to the happiness of man...must be apparent to all American jurists. The lesson learned from this should be utilized now—the lesson that the annihilation of the *jus natural*...must place men on a purely animal or physical plane, wherein the savagery of the jungle will be imitated with consummate astuteness.[41]

The implication here, as with the Quarantine speech, is that the current state cannot persist indefinitely. There could be no coexistence between Nazi law and natural law, since one was the logical and political negation of the other. They could not occupy the same era, much less the same hemisphere, without coming into conflict. For Dr. Brown and many others, the nature of that conflict was Manichaean: civilization on one side and "the savagery of the jungle" on the other.

Ironically, just as the specter of Nazism brought forth a spirited defense of natural law, the darkened political landscape also awakened dreams of a new world order. On the eve of conflict in 1939, a book titled *Union Now* suddenly skyrocketed to the top of the best-seller lists. Clarence Streit, a *New York Times* reporter who had spent much of his career covering the League of Nations, offered a clinical autopsy of its failure. The league was weak, inadequate, and poorly structured, and thus incapable of responding to German aggression—the very purpose for which it was created. Yet in contrast to the majority of the league's critics who called for disbandment, Streit argued instead that it be strengthened.

The league must become a federation with a single currency, postal service, economy, defense force, and most importantly, law. Streit likened his proposed reform to the transition from Articles of Confederation to the US Constitution. Just as the Constitution allowed the United States to consolidate itself under a single federal government and present a united front to the world, so too would the reorganized league strengthen each of the member nations through their participation in the collective.[42]

Although Roosevelt probably never read *Union Now* or Dr. Brown's article, both are indicative of the public debate that underlay his State of the Union speech delivered on January 6, 1941. The war, rapidly assuming its ultimate dimensions as a global struggle between democracy and totalitarianism, all but necessitated consideration of the world that would come after. Instead of the vague "future," people now spoke of the "postwar world." The same week as Roosevelt drafted his address, Eleanor finished reading Henry Jesson's *And Beacons Burn Again: Letters from an English Soldier,* which framed the European war as a coming triumph of liberalism over tyranny. "Justice for all," Eleanor wrote approvingly in her column, "security in certain living standards, a recognition of the dignity and the right of an individual human being without regard to his race, creed or color—these are the things for which vast numbers of our citizens will willingly sacrifice themselves."[43]

Her husband's thoughts were similarly occupied as he drafted his address. It is worth noting that Roosevelt's speeches were collaborative efforts. While the president approved and contributed to every speech, it is not always possible to discern which language is uniquely his own. The 1941 State of the Union had been through several drafts, much of it concerning taxes and armaments. During their last planning session, speechwriter Sam Rosenman recalled, Roosevelt suddenly went quiet. He stared for a moment at the ceiling, then began to dictate what he called his "peroration."[44] The words appeared in the final text virtually unchanged. "In the future days," he declared, "which we seek to make secure, we look forward to a world founded on four essential freedoms."[45] These were freedom of speech, freedom of worship, freedom from want, and freedom from fear. How exactly he arrived at these four is a matter of debate. Some point whimsically to a cluster of statuary at the 1939 World's Fair that featured four allegorical freedoms, including speech and worship (want and fear, however, replaced by assembly and the press). These were also cornerstones of the US Bill of Rights. The other two are somewhat murkier. Freedom from want likely drew its inspiration from the New Deal, though in his speech Roosevelt refers vaguely to "economic understandings" between nations. Freedom from fear was the most expressly political: Roosevelt refers not to the fear individuals might have of their governments but rather to the fear of invasion by a conquering nation. It is unique among the freedoms in that it does not refer to the relationship between the citizen and their government but rather the citizens of one nation with those of another.[46]

The Four Freedoms were not legal definitions and were not meant to be so. But they were not empty words either. For all its vagaries, the January 6 speech marks the first time a head of state publicly committed his nation to promoting universal human rights. Roosevelt left no doubt on that point. Each freedom closed with the same ringing coda: "Everywhere in the world!" The exclamation point can be heard in sound recordings of the address. Roosevelt nearly shouts the phrase, as if underscoring a promise made.

Historians largely regard the Four Freedoms speech as a mixture of high idealism and shrewd politics: by offering his own vision of a postwar world, Roosevelt was attempting to convince the American public (which still, as late as 1941, overwhelmingly favored neutrality) that its interests were inextricably bound with the global conflict.[47] This is certainly true, but there are other currents within the speech. Earlier in his address, Roosevelt castigates the Axis powers for "their new one-way international law, which lacks mutuality in its observance, and, therefore, becomes an instrument of oppression." The Four Freedoms, drawn expressly from natural law philosophy and applied universally, amount to an alternative international law that would be, in contrast, mutual and an instrument of liberation.

That the United States should take the lead in shaping the postwar moral order was foreordained: "Just as our national policy in internal affairs has been based upon a decent respect for the rights and the dignity of all our fellow men within our gates, so our national policy in foreign affairs has been based on a decent respect for the rights and dignity of all nations, large and small. And the justice of morality must and will win in the end." Left unsaid, however, was that America had faced this test before and failed. Three weeks before Pearl Harbor, Undersecretary of State Sumner Welles gave an address at a memorial for President Wilson and took the opportunity to drive the point home in sentiments that his boss, another old Wilsonian internationalist, indubitably endorsed: "The heart-wrenching question which every American citizen must ask himself on this day of commemoration is whether the world in which we have to live would have come to this desperate pass had the United States been willing in those years which followed 1919 to play its full part in striving to bring about a new world order based on justice."[48]

Roosevelt was determined not to let past become present. This is made explicit in the conclusion of his speech, remarkable both for the breadth of its pledge and lack of ambiguity:

> That is no vision of a distant millennium. It is a definite basis for a kind of world attainable in our own time and generation. That kind of world is the very antithesis of the so-called new order of tyranny which the dictators seek to create with the crash of a bomb. To that new order we oppose the greater conception—the moral order.... This nation has placed its destiny in the hands and heads and hearts of its millions of free men and women; and its faith in freedom under the guidance of God. Freedom means the supremacy of human rights everywhere.

It was consistent with President Roosevelt's optimistic nature to see calamity as opportunity. In contrast to earlier speeches, where he spoke vaguely of hopes for the future, the Four Freedoms speech adds a crucial time line: victory in Europe would doom the "new order of tyranny," and an equally new "moral order" would emerge. This transformation seems almost mystical. The triumph of democracy over fascism is symbolically linked to the triumph of "faith in freedom under the guidance of God" over godless tyranny. The faithful, therefore, would inherit the task of reshaping the world by the grace of God after his design.

This was FDR's version of a natural law argument. While legal scholars have long maintained that natural law may exist without the presence of God, for Roosevelt that was not the case. Perhaps as a legacy of Dr. Peabody, the president construed morality in Judeo-Christian terms. Thus the concluding paragraph reads like a logical proof from Aquinas: the right to freedom, being given by God, must be universal. Therefore any state that denies human rights defies God's will. This idea was not original to Roosevelt. A similar view was propounded by William Henry Seward in his famous 1850 antislavery speech before the Senate. The Constitution was the ultimate source of American law, and the Constitution allowed slavery. "But there is a higher law than the Constitution," Seward told his listeners, "which regulates our authority over the domain, and devotes it to the same noble purposes. The territory is a part, no inconsiderable part, of the common heritage of mankind, bestowed upon them by the Creator of the universe. We are his stewards, and must so discharge our trust as to secure in the highest attainable degree their happiness."[49] Roosevelt would have understood and agreed with these sentiments.

It is telling that among the first major groups to respond to FDR's call for action was the Federal Council of Churches, which incorporated the Four Freedoms into its thirteen "Guiding Principles" for a new world order. Soon after, representatives of the Catholic and Jewish faiths likewise lent their support.[50] Their endorsement was encouraging but also potentially problematic. Some listeners might interpret FDR's frequent invocation of the divine and "international morality" as advocacy of a postwar world governed by a form of biblical law; certainly he did nothing to discourage this reading. As one author notes, such groups "had now received a mandate to press with holy fervor" and did so.[51]

A notable example was the Commission to Study the Bases of a Just and Durable Peace, representing twenty-five Protestant denominations and over ten million parishioners. John Foster Dulles, future secretary of state under President Eisenhower, served in 1942 as its chairman. While not a zealot, Dulles was a man of deep faith who regarded the present war in spiritual terms as the ultimate struggle between the forces of God and Satan.[52] Victory for the Allies was victory for God; naturally, the postwar world would be refashioned under God's law. Along with American League of Nations director Clark Eichelberger, Dulles produced a thirteen-part radio series on NBC in the summer of 1943, bringing this view to the American public. *Justice and Human Rights* reached some four million households. For those without a radio, Dulles and Eichelberger distributed a printed pamphlet, *Winning the War on the Spiritual Front*, encouraging Americans to form local organizations in support of human rights and, of course, write their representatives in Congress. Their efforts ultimately bore fruit. In June 1943 Dulles met personally with the president and presented him with a "Statement of Political Propositions," including "the right of individuals everywhere to religious and intellectual liberty."[53] He left convinced that Roosevelt was in complete sympathy with his biblical view of universal law. That might have been the case, but it was also true that Roosevelt had a gift for making every supplicant in his office feel the same.

Having dedicated his own nation to the cause of human rights, FDR then took the first tentative steps toward gaining international support. Elements of the Four Freedoms resurfaced in the Atlantic Charter issued jointly with Winston Churchill on August 11, 1941.[54] The two leaders pledged to "respect the right of all peoples to choose the form of government under which they will live" and "afford assurance that all the men in all lands may live out their lives in freedom from fear and want."[55] In his message to Congress ten days later, Roosevelt added: "It is also unnecessary for me to point out that the declaration of principles includes of necessity the world need for freedom of religion and freedom of information. No society of the world organized under the announced principles could survive without these freedoms which are a part of the whole freedom for which we strive."[56] On January 1, 1942, similar language was incorporated into the Declaration by the United Nations. Drafted by Roosevelt and Churchill, endorsed by all the Allies and eventually over forty other nations, the declaration would become the basis for the UN and its foundational charter. It declared that the purpose of the Allies was "to defend life, liberty, independence and religious freedom, and to preserve human rights and justice in their own lands as well as in other lands." The declaration, scarcely a page long, nevertheless formally bound all its signatories to uphold for themselves and the global community the basic principles of natural law.[57]

Though the Atlantic Charter and the Declaration of the United Nations were scarcely five months apart, the symbolic weight behind their words is radically different. America's entry into the war transformed the conversation on human rights. Until then, Roosevelt had to trust in God's will and (even less reliably) British acquiescence to see his Four Freedoms become a universal standard of law. Now, as dominant partner, the United States would have a powerful role in reshaping the postwar world.[58] Among the first to realize the potential of this mandate was Secretary of State Cordell Hull. In a speech delivered to a worldwide radio audience titled "The War and Human Freedom," Hull predicted that after victory, with much of the world lying in ruins, it would be the job of the Allies—especially the Americans—to reconstruct the "political, economic and spiritual foundations" of each defeated nation and of society as a whole. Like Roosevelt, Hull saw opportunity in calamity. Not since the empires of the last century had any nation attempted to refashion the legal landscape of the world in its own image; what the imperialists did by force the Americans would do out of altruism—and necessity.[59]

Religious leaders saw a postwar world governed by biblical law; Secretary Hull balanced this with the Bill of Rights. After the war, he declared, "there will lie before all countries the great constructive task of building human freedom and Christian morality on firmer and broader foundations than ever before. This task, too, will of necessity call for national and international action."[60] If listeners momentarily boggled at the thought of China or Saudi Arabia being rebuilt on the basis of Christian morality, Hull went on to reveal where his own preference lay:

> Within each nation, liberty under law is an essential requirement of progress. The spirit of liberty, when deeply embedded in the minds and hearts of the people, is the most powerful remedy for racial animosities, religious intolerance, ignorance, and all the other evils which prevent men from uniting in a brotherhood of truly civilized existence.

It might be wondered what an African American listening in South Carolina made of Hull's assurance that the spirit of liberty remedied racial animosities, but that was not the audience the secretary had in mind. A civilized world, Hull insisted, could only be one in which "there is acceptance of human rights and human freedoms" by every nation. The United States pledged itself to ensuring that every person on earth should live by the same freedoms as its own citizens. This sounded good enough, but the implication was clear: American rights were human rights, and vice versa. Though well intentioned, this kind of thinking was hardly distinguishable from those earnest moralists in the British Empire (a few of whom, in 1942, might still have been above ground) who saw their solemn duty to spread English common law throughout the world.

If Secretary Hull conflated human rights with American values, he was in accord not only with the majority of the American public but his boss as well. It was Roosevelt who declared in 1920 that the "younger nations are looking to the United States for justice and liberty" and reinforced that sentiment in his third inaugural address with the assertion that "democracy alone, of all forms of government, enlists the full force of men's enlightened will.... Democracy alone has constructed an unlimited civilization capable of infinite progress in the improvement of human life...for it is the most humane, the most advanced, and in the end the most unconquerable of all forms of human society."[61] This was, of course, what his audience wanted to hear. Roosevelt needed the public to abandon its hidebound isolationism and embrace a new globalist role for the United States. If Christian faith moved them to support human rights, so be it. If patriotism worked, that was fine by him too. Lest this seem cynical, it is worth remembering that just as Roosevelt shared a Judeo-Christian worldview with men like John Foster Dulles, he was no less sincere in his belief in American exceptionalism. For him democracy, liberty, and right were not only symbiotic but synonymous. The "upward trend" of human progress was, necessarily, a democratic one. Therefore, as the world's most powerful democracy, America was also the most advanced along that path to perfection:

> The democratic aspiration is no mere recent phase in human history. It is human history. It permeated the ancient life of early peoples. It blazed anew in the Middle Ages. It was written in Magna Carta.... Its vitality was written into our own Mayflower Compact, into the Declaration of Independence, into the Constitution of the United States, into the Gettysburg Address. Those who first came here to carry out the longings of their spirit, and the millions who followed, and the stock that sprang from them—all have moved forward constantly and consistently toward an ideal which in itself has gained stature and clarity with each generation.

Shortly after America's entry into the conflict, Roosevelt ordered Hull to supervise the drafting of an international bill of rights. This would, he hoped, serve as the foundation for a worldwide organization committed to upholding those rights. It was also the first time any head of state had made international human rights law a national policy. The State Department responded enthusiastically, incorporating the project within its overall postwar planning division. Secretary Hull had closed his address by calling upon "parents, and teachers, and clergymen, and all those within each nation that provide spiritual, moral and intellectual guidance" to determine, as he loftily described it, "the fundamental policies which will chart for mankind a wise course based on enduring spiritual values." Yet the men and women actually engaged in this task were determined that it reflect US law as closely as possible. Hull conscripted a number of prominent academics and jurists, including Adolf Berle, one of FDR's former "brain trust," and Green Hackworth, who would eventually become the first American judge on the International Court of Justice.[62] In early 1942, the Council on Foreign Relations proposed a new postwar league that would "encourage, in every feasible way, adherence to a charter of individual rights."[63] The newly formed and pithily titled Subcommittee on Political Problems began work on the document itself.

Framers drew from predictable sources: the American Constitution, Magna Carta, sundry European civil codes, the 1689 English Bill of Rights, Blackstone and Coke, the 1789 French Declaration of the Rights of Man, and of course the Four Freedoms and Atlantic Charter. This was a formidable list, though the dearth of non-Western texts is regrettable. Each committee member also added his or her own contributions: philosophical, economic, and political. Worse yet, when the project became publicly known, the committee was inundated with suggestions. Law professor Percy Bordwell wrote a personal letter to the president proposing a "Constitution for the United Nations" that borrowed heavily from the American model and from Streit's *Union Now*. (Roosevelt, who doubtless remembered his own pipe-dream plan of 1923, responded politely.)[64] As a result, early drafts were vast, unwieldy compendiums, some running up to thirty pages in length. Nor was there any attempt to differentiate between types of rights: Locke and Rousseau rubbed shoulders metaphorically with John L. Lewis and

Albert Schweitzer. In nearly every case of conflict, however, deference to existing US law prevailed.

The final result was a disappointment. As Rowland Brucken writes, it was little more than a restatement of the American Bill of Rights with odious, hedging language designed to excuse America's ongoing abuses against African Americans and roughly 100,000 Asian Americans confined to internment camps.[65] An early draft had called for an international tribunal to adjudicate human rights abuses; this was struck down as being too controversial. The committee was wary of the so-called Dixiecrats, Southern Democratic members of Congress whose support was crucial to FDR and who regarded any outside interference with segregation much the same as their antebellum predecessors had with slavery. Their influence—or, more accurately, intransigence—seemed to permeate the entire State Department. Independent of the Subcommittee on Political Problems, a second group created by Secretary Hull in advance of the 1943 Quebec Conference produced a much shorter draft titled "Staff Charter of the United Nations," which committed signatory nations to "agree to give legislative effect" to a Declaration of Human Rights. Its language proscribing "discrimination as to nationality, language, race, political opinion or other belief," however, was undercut by addenda pledging that nothing in the charter would "interfere with the laws of some of our states for the segregation of races."[66] If nothing else, the collective efforts of both committees revealed the enormous difficulties inherent in drafting a universal bill of rights.

Endless squabbles over which provisions should be included—with religion and politics staking their respective claims—obscured a fundamental truth. At its core, the question of what constitutes a universal human right was the same question scholars had asked for millennia: what constitutes a natural law? The answer would have momentous consequences for the law and for society itself.

One man who understood the stakes was international law professor Quincy Wright. In an article entitled "Human Rights and the World Order," published in April 1943, Wright built a powerful case for the international bill of rights by placing it in its proper historical and legal context. He began by quoting Undersecretary of State Sumner Welles: "This is a war which cannot be regarded as won until the fundamental rights of the peoples of the earth are secured." Given this declaration, Wright posed the following questions: 1) What commitments has the United Nations made for securing human rights after victory? 2) Is it important that the world order concern itself with human rights? 3) What specific human rights should be recognized by the world order? 4) How can the world order protect human rights? As to the first, Wright analyzed the speeches of Roosevelt, Vice President Henry Wallace, and others, determining that these amounted to a definite commitment that could only be fulfilled by a world organization. As to the second, he was affirmative: "Recognition that the individual is a subject of international law…has become in the modern world an essential condition…of social and political stability and of human welfare and progress."[67] Intended or not, this was an erudite restatement of Roosevelt's own view of the international community.

But it is Wright's analysis of the third query that merits particular attention. He posited two parallel trajectories: first, the development of natural law from antiquity to the present; second, the gradually evolving interdependence of nations Roosevelt frequently referenced in his own speeches. It was no longer possible, Wright concluded, for an individual to exist solely as a citizen of his or her own nation; they also belonged to the world. As such, they existed under two distinct yet complementary legal systems, similar to the American distinction between state and federal law. In advocating universal human rights, Roosevelt was in effect transposing natural law onto the world stage. Therefore the "rights" of each individual should be those that centuries of inquiry on natural law had winnowed down: life, liberty, property.

Professor Wright was more than a detached academic. As early as 1939 he, Clark Eichelberger, and Columbia law professor James T. Shotwell formed the Commission to Study the Organization of Peace, which was endorsed by both Roosevelt and Secretary Hull and reported directly to the State Department. Wright's article became the basis of the commission's final plan. Although Professor Wright's insights appear to have made little impact on the Subcommittee for Political Problems, his presence would be felt in time. By the war's end, Wright emerged as among the most prominent and respected advocates for human rights law. In 1945 he had the unique honor of serving both as an adviser to

Justice Robert Jackson at the Nuremberg Tribunals and as a delegate to the San Francisco conference that founded the United Nations. In both arenas, as shall be seen, he was an ardent and successful advocate for natural law.[68]

Perhaps one reason for the State Department's indifferent response was that by late 1943 its own work had become something of a political land mine. Even as Roosevelt's Four Freedoms gained more adherents at home and around the world, countervailing forces mobilized in response. Squawking Dixiecrats were only the beginning. As Franklin Roosevelt began laying the groundwork for the United Nations, his machinations for an "international morality" entered their most delicate and dangerous phase.

❖ ❖ ❖

It was clear to President Roosevelt and his advisers that universal human rights required a postwar international organization for enforcement. Consequently his foreign policy aims in this regard were twofold: gain domestic and international support for the United Nations and likewise for its mandate to protect basic rights. These goals were intertwined and, ultimately, conflicting.

The seeds of discord were sown in Argentina in 1941. The original Atlantic Charter, drafted by British aide Alexander Cadogan at Churchill's request, called for an "effective international organization" to sustain the peace postwar. Surprisingly, Roosevelt demurred. The American people, he said, would bristle at anything that sounded too much like the League of Nations.[69] This was a valid point, but it is likely Roosevelt was more concerned that what Churchill meant by an "international organization" was along the lines of Clarence Streit's Anglo-American dominion—one that kept the British Empire intact. This became clear when the two men traveled together through the Virginia countryside in January 1942. In the front seat of the president's Packard, Churchill declared expansively, "After the war we've got to form an Anglo-American alliance to meet the problems of the world!" Roosevelt characteristically nodded and answered, "Yes! Yes! Yes!" Overhearing this exchange, Eleanor was horrified. Any postwar world with the British Empire intact was anathema to her, and to most Americans. "You know, Winston," she interjected, "when Franklin says yes, yes, yes it doesn't mean he agrees with you. It means he's listening."[70]

A month later Clark Eichelberger, then serving as chairman of the Commission to Study the Organization of Peace (the same commission cofounded by Quincy Wright), sought an audience with the president. The commission wished to present Roosevelt with a "blueprint of the future on the basis of the Atlantic Charter and United Nations," with specific proposals for protecting human rights. Roosevelt refused to meet and dictated a curt reply: "Tell him I would like to see him some day and for heaven's sake not to do anything specific at this time…as things are changing every day."[71] They were indeed. Preliminary negotiations with the Soviets revealed their deep suspicion of any form of international organization whatsoever; discussion of human rights would be not only futile but nullifying. Even in Washington, familiar obstacles appeared. When Chairman Hackworth presented a draft of the international bill of rights to Undersecretary of State Welles, the response was chilling: "[He] could not foresee this Government's ever agreeing to enter into any international obligation which would let other governments determine what its relationship with its citizens should be."[72] By "citizens," Welles meant "nonwhite citizens."

Britain would agree to nothing that compromised sovereignty over its empire; Congress would accept nothing that interfered with segregation; the Soviet Union wouldn't accept anything at all. Yet the president was undiscouraged. In April 1943, William Hassett recorded in his diary an interesting exchange. "We got to talking about future organization of the United Nations to maintain the peace of the world…. No one ever mentions these days the possibility of resurrecting the League of Nations. It seems dead for keeps." Roosevelt disagreed. "The President said the policy of policing the world [was] not insurmountable…. The League must be judged for what it did not attempt—for sidestepping every responsibility and moral obligation." It was a familiar theme of the president: the league failed because it lacked an "international morality"—it was an organization without a soul. Clearly Roosevelt would not allow the same for the United Nations. The very next exchange revealed just how expansive his vision was. "The President [was] nettled today over Mark

Sullivan's article today warning against postwar planning.... Plain to see he [Roosevelt] has old-age security in mind for the whole world."[73]

Throughout 1943 and 1944, Roosevelt charted a careful course: employing every diplomatic tool at his disposal to line up support of the United Nations, while referring to it primarily as a peacekeeping organization. In December 1943 Roosevelt demanded from the State Department its latest UN plans, including an international court of justice. A human rights commission, however, was considered "politically unacceptable"; rights were relegated to an "agency for co-operation in... social activities," which made them sound like sporting matches.[74] This raised the ire of Professor Wright, who proposed instead an international commission of jurists to oversee human rights violations. This too was rejected. Roosevelt also enlisted Cordell Hull to play the familiar role of heavy. One month after the president pledged the United States to uphold "moral security in a family of nations," Hull released a statement to reassert that nothing in the United Nations would compromise national sovereignty. As a result, one author writes, "colonial powers and American white supremacists did not need to fear investigation, condemnation, or invalidation of their repressive systems."[75]

Roosevelt himself sometimes seemed alarmed by the depth of the wellspring he had tapped into. Having launched a crusade, he was frequently compelled to restrain his crusaders from charging on ahead into (as he saw it) political disaster. Ironically, this would lead scholars to question the fervency of his own commitment. In *FDR and the Creation of the U.N.,* authors Townsend Hoopes and Douglas Brinkley provide a comprehensive account of the machinations leading to the 1945 San Francisco UN conference, with only a cursory mention of human rights.[76] The implication is that it was largely absent from the deliberations, and indeed from Roosevelt's mind. Rowland Brucken expresses a more nuanced appraisal, writing that Roosevelt's approach consisted of "the issuing of grand statements of humanitarian war aims such as the Four Freedoms and the Atlantic Charter, and the preparation of early proposals for a postwar community that lacked reference to such principles."[77] In fact, Brucken argues, FDR quashed any State Department proposal that made specific reference to human rights or international law beyond peacekeeping. The accepted truth is that this is yet another example of Roosevelt's guile; or, more charitably, the dichotomy between the idealist and the politician.

These arguments are not without merit. FDR spoke in grand generalizations about human rights but often appeared ambivalent about the specifics. To some extent this posture was necessary: the president had to sway multiple audiences, many of them hostile. He needed to remain flexible and not be chained to any categorical absolutes—even those he drafted himself. The 1941 Atlantic Charter, the language of which expressly framed the war as a struggle for civilization and committed the Allies to upholding international human rights after victory, was dismissed by the president at a press conference in 1944 as "a mere memorandum." He even went so far as to employ the old lawyer's dodge of saying it couldn't be a binding contract since none of the parties actually signed. At the Yalta Conference in February 1945, Churchill offered his own aphorism: "The Atlantic Charter is not a law," he said. "It is a star."[78] Nevertheless, even as Roosevelt remained annoyingly (and necessarily) vague, he could take comfort from the knowledge that his State Department was hard at work drafting an international bill of rights.

In the end, Roosevelt's caution paid dividends. Arthur Vandenberg, the senior senator from Michigan, had once been both an ardent isolationist and one of FDR's severest critics. Suddenly and shockingly he experienced a change of heart, endorsing the United Nations and becoming an invaluable conduit between the administration and isolationist members of Congress.[79] More encouraging news came in October 1943, when negotiations between Secretary Hull and Soviet foreign minister V. M. Molotov produced the Moscow Declaration, which called for "the necessity of establishing at the earliest practicable date a general international organization…for the maintenance of international peace and security."[80]

This rapprochement went only so far. Roosevelt knew he risked losing congressional support—especially from the Dixiecrats—if there was even a suggestion that the UN might meddle in domestic policies. At a press conference on May 30, 1944, he made light of the idea. The UN was for "general world peace," he said, not "decid[ing] whether we were to build a new dam on the Conestoga Creek."[81] It would not compromise "the integrity of the United States in any shape, manner or form." If the

Dixiecrats were wary of this vague assurance, the Soviets were more so. They even disliked the term "United Nations," preferring "International Security Organization."[82] At the Dumbarton Oaks Conference, convened in August 1944, the Russian delegation arrived with a clear mandate. "The primary and indeed only task" of the United Nations would be peacekeeping and security. Referencing a recent article in a Leningrad newspaper, they added that it "will be much easier to observe the success or failure of an organization for security if it is not burdened with an endless number of superfluous functions."[83] Among these, of course, were human rights.

But the American delegation had its instructions as well. Roosevelt planned to move incrementally, garnering support for the United Nations as a peacekeeping organization while at the same time gently prodding the issue of human rights from periphery to center. The Atlantic Charter and Declaration of the United Nations had been the first steps; the "Proposal for the Establishment of a General International Organization," agreed upon at Dumbarton Oaks, was another. Edward Stettinius, acting on instructions from the president, lobbied hard at the conference for human rights to be included among the primary purposes of the United Nations. Britain and the USSR jointly refused, but finally consented to their inclusion among so-called economic and social questions. Stettinius confided to his diary that the president "seemed gratified by these developments and felt the inclusion of the human rights sentence was extremely vital. He seems rather surprised that the Soviets had yielded on this point."[84]

The modest success of Dumbarton Oaks left Roosevelt buoyant. Shortly after the conference concluded, the president addressed a vast crowd at Soldier Field in Chicago, on one of the coldest October nights ever recorded. "Some people," he told them, "have sneered...at the ideals of the Atlantic Charter, the ideals of the Four Freedoms. They have said they were the dreams of starry-eyed New Dealers, that it is silly to talk of them because we cannot attain these ideals tomorrow or the next day. The American people have greater faith than that."[85]

Roosevelt was returning to an old theme: the inevitability of human progress and America's role in its advancement. By the end of 1944, his political intuition told him that public opinion had come to accept the idea of international human rights. Having stonewalled the academics for months, he now gratefully accepted Quincy Wright's suggested addition to the UN charter calling for a declaration of human rights. He also personally read the American Law Institute's proposed international bill of rights, forwarded to him by his press secretary, Stephen Early. Proponents of natural law pressed their advantage. On February 4, Wright's Commission to Study the Organization of Peace bought time on CBS to announce its endorsement of a human rights commission; the statement—signed by 150 academics, activists, and jurists—was read by former Democratic presidential candidate John W. Davis. From the opposite end of the political spectrum came a similar proposal from none other than Herbert Hoover.[86] Quincy Wright even managed to apply a donnish form of academic pressure, agreeing to review a collection of former undersecretary of state Sumner Welles's speeches, which had been published in 1943 in book form as *The World of the Four Freedoms*. Praising Welles as "a liberal in the Wilsonian tradition," he went on to subtly bind the present administration to the promises of its former representative:

> These addresses are the words of a diplomat, not of an economist or a political scientist, but they provide the elements of a coherent policy linking American ideals with a realistic comprehension of world conditions. In the main, they point to objectives. Some of them, however, include practical proposals which Mr. Welles, on behalf of the United States government, made before inter-American conferences, thus indicating his realization of the kind of implementation necessary to realize these objectives.[87]

Professor Wright, for one, was prepared to regard the Four Freedoms (and their subsequent reiteration) as a binding pledge to natural law. Much of the international community shared this view and evinced a desire to take their own part in achieving universal human rights. The Inter-American Conference on Problems of War and Peace, convened in Mexico City in February 1945, affirmed the principles of the Atlantic Charter and drafted its own code of human rights, which would eventually become the American Declaration of the Rights and Duties of Man. In the months leading up to the first UN conference, scheduled for April

25 in San Francisco, dozens of nations contributed memoranda affirming their commitment to universal human rights postwar. Egypt and New Zealand jointly called for "respect for human rights and freedoms," while Poland, Denmark, and Norway insisted that both the Atlantic Charter and the 1942 United Nations Declaration be incorporated within the proposed UN charter.[88]

Naturally there were difficulties. The British continued to worry about their empire: India and South Africa were intent on sending separate delegations to San Francisco. The USSR was already committed to being as obstructionist as possible on every point. Even those countries favorable to the idea of universal human rights would inevitably have differing ideas of what such rights comprised. In his State of the Union message delivered on January 6, 1945, Franklin Roosevelt acknowledged these differences: "Nations, like individuals, do not always see alike or think alike, and international cooperation and progress are not helped by any nation assuming that it has a monopoly of wisdom or of virtue."[89] After the frustrating and exhausting Yalta conference, he was even more circumspect. Addressing Congress for the last time on March 1, he admitted that the framework for the United Nations was far from finished. "It cannot be a structure complete. It cannot be what some people think—a structure of complete perfection at first." The last two words were vintage Roosevelt: patient but optimistic.

Imperfections and delays were only to be expected from a project so new in world history, so vast in scope. "No plan is perfect. Whatever is adopted at San Francisco will doubtless have to be amended time and again over the years, just as our own Constitution has been." But of the final outcome he had no doubt. The postwar world would be "based on the sound and just principles of the Atlantic Charter, on the conception and dignity of the human being, and on the guarantees of tolerance and freedom of religious worship."90

By this time there was no need to awaken the American public to their international responsibilities, nor motivate them to support the Allied cause. In reminding Congress of his pledge for universal human rights, he could have no motive other than to speak the truth as he saw it. Roosevelt closed his address to Congress by enjoining all Americans to "begin to build, under God, that better world in which our children and grandchildren—yours and mine, the children and grandchildren of the whole world—must live, and can live." The ellipses were an improvisation. At the very last, Roosevelt transformed a typical bromide about "our children's future" into something else: recasting America's responsibility not only to its own citizens but to all the citizens of the world, born and unborn.

A few weeks later President Roosevelt departed for Warm Springs, Georgia. The last cabinet member to see him was labor secretary Frances Perkins. She found the president "lively and full of pep," excited about going south. But it transpired that his excitement was twofold. "All I am going to do while I'm there," FDR told her of Warm Springs, "is work on my speech for the United Nations. Then I'm going to fly out there and make that speech—but I'm not going to stay, Frances, I'm not going to stay. I am going to make the speech…meet the delegates, and then I am going to come right back."

"But why not stay a while?"

"No," Roosevelt answered, "I want this thing done without me. It's all fixed, it's all arranged and it will be much better if I did not take part in it and sort of bully it through."[91]

The exchange is revealing. By the spring of 1945, Roosevelt believed he had successfully laid the foundation for a new international law and was prepared to gradually step aside. That was not to say he wanted no further role; his instructions to the American delegation were extensive. First, the promotion of human rights would be included as a central purpose of the United Nations—no longer peripheral, as it had been at Dumbarton Oaks. Second, they were to insist upon the creation of a Human Rights Commission with authority to receive and respond to individual claims of abuse. Third, the General Assembly would, at the earliest possible time, enact a universal declaration of human rights that would serve the same function for the world as the Bill of Rights did for the United States.[92] Edward Stettinius, who had replaced Cordell Hull as secretary of state, would carry with him to San Francisco the staff charter of the United Nations (which had presumably sat dormant in a filing cabinet since 1943) as a useful guide.[93]

Nevertheless, Roosevelt recognized that while he had given form to the idea of universal human rights with his Four Freedoms and Atlantic

Charter, the task ahead would be the work of committees, not individuals. Plus, he was tired. In her diary, longtime friend Daisy Suckley recorded a conversation with Dr. Bruenn, the president's physician. It was clear, she told him, that FDR's "one really great wish is to get this international organization for peace started … nothing else counts next to that." Could not someone say to him, "You want to carry out the United Nations plan? Well, without your health you will not be able to do it. Therefore— take care of yourself."[94] This advice, if it was ever tendered, came too late. Roosevelt arrived in Warm Springs on March 30. He immediately surrounded himself with drafts of previous speeches, State Department memoranda on the United Nations, even a proposed seating chart for delegates and a detailed map of San Francisco.[95] On the night of April 6, Suckley wrote that Roosevelt talked "seriously about the San Francisco Conference, and his part in World Peace," yet confided that he would "probably resign sometime next year, when the peace organization—the United Nations—is well started."[96]

Less than a week later, he was dead. His last official act was to direct aide William Hassett to inform the postmaster general that the president, an avid philatelist, would like to purchase the first issue of a new stamp to be released that week. It displayed a laurel branch against a royal blue background with the words: "Towards a United Nations, April 25, 1945."[97]

❖ ❖ ❖

"Franklin Roosevelt at rest in Hyde Park," a writer for the *New Republic* declared, "is a more powerful force for America's participation in a world organization than was President Roosevelt in the White House."[98] Certainly the president's ghost loomed large over the San Francisco conference, convened just eleven days after the funeral. Addressing delegates over the wireless, President Harry Truman eulogized the man most responsible for gathering them there:

> In the name of a great humanitarian—one who surely is with us today in spirit—I earnestly appeal to each and every one of you to rise above personal interests, and adhere to those lofty principles, which benefit all mankind.

> Franklin D. Roosevelt gave his life while trying to perpetuate these high ideals. This Conference owes its existence, in a large part, to the vision, foresight, and determination of Franklin Roosevelt.[99]

In fact, Roosevelt's spirit was as present in Truman's speech as at the conference itself. The new president began in his very first line by employing a favorite phrase of his predecessor to describe natural law: "The world has experienced a revival of an old faith in the everlasting moral force of justice." The similarity is not to be wondered at. Truman's address was written primarily by Sam Rosenman, the same speechwriter who was present when Roosevelt dictated his Four Freedoms. Rosenman had served FDR since the latter was governor of New York. Few men better knew Roosevelt's mind, and there is no question that when he began drafting the San Francisco speech, Rosenman intuited exactly what his old boss wanted to say.[100] Something of Roosevelt's rhythm and cadence burrowed itself into Rosenman's writing, which sounded oddly stilted as it emerged from the wireless in a flat Missouri monotone. Reading the text instead of hearing it, it is easy to imagine Roosevelt's voice rising with the words: "We must build a new world—a far better world—one in which the eternal dignity of man is respected." In every sense, this was the speech Franklin Roosevelt would have given, had he lived.

It is fitting, then, to consider this as a coda to Roosevelt's efforts on behalf of human rights and, by extension, natural law. Certainly the results of the conference were all he could have hoped. The charter of the United Nations pledged in its preamble "to reaffirm faith in fundamental human rights, in the dignity and worth of the human person, and in the equal rights of men and women of nations large and small."[101] Cordell Hull, who had supervised the drafting of the very first international bill of rights, channeled Roosevelt's own philosophy to describe the charter as "one of the great milestones in man's upward climb toward a truly civilized existence," while Harry Truman hailed the UN's forthcoming bill of rights as soon to "be as much a part of international life as our own Bill of Rights is part of our Constitution."[102]

But the *New Republic* was wrong: Franklin Roosevelt in the White House had every bit as much of an impact on human rights as his posthumous spirit. It was he who had set the great diplomatic and bureaucratic machine in motion, and he who monitored it as it gathered steam. Roosevelt conditioned a reluctant American public to accept a postwar world in which the United States had a permanent commitment to universal law. If his conception of an "international morality" seemed vague, it had to be. Religious leaders read it one way, politicians another, academics another still. Roosevelt encouraged them all but committed himself to none. In this manner he was able to garner broad support for a truly radical idea—the internationalization of natural law—by framing it within familiar religious and political contexts.

How much of this was deliberate policy versus his own convictions is impossible to know. Roosevelt genuinely believed in God's law and in the American system of rights. But he was also a trained lawyer, advised by some of the greatest legal minds of the day. Judging by his own words, he very likely saw divine law, natural law, and the Bill of Rights as essentially synonymous—all part of mankind's "upward trend." His call for universal rights struck a chord with a global community that was engaged in an epic struggle with tyranny; much as emancipation gave moral and spiritual validation to the Union cause during the Civil War, Roosevelt's vision of a free, democratic, and just postwar world transformed the Second World War into a crusade.[103] Thus the Four Freedoms were echoed by scores of other nations and embraced by a heterodox cross section of American society. They were even immortalized in a series of illustrations by the artist Norman Rockwell in the *Saturday Evening Post,* appearing between February 20 and March 25, 1943; millions of Americans promptly demanded reprints to display in their own homes.[104]

Convincing the Allies to accept universal human rights as both an inevitable and necessary war aim required an even greater diplomatic balance. Here his audience was no less skeptical than the isolationists and segregationists in Congress. Neither Britain nor the Soviet Union would consent to any document that compromised even fractionally their legal dominion over their territories. Consequently the president employed his frequent strategy of moving in two directions at once: issuing soaring proclamations of a postwar world based on essential freedoms while privately tamping down expectations and employing Secretary Hull to assure his fellow statesmen that the only real purpose of the United Nations was security. Prevarications like these have led historians to look at actions rather than words: discounting the political philosophy of the Four Freedoms in favor of a minute examination of the boardroom and back-room politicking between the Big Three and their plenipotentiaries.

Another reading of the evidence, however, suggests that in judging Roosevelt's words and actions toward the end of his life, we should give equal weight to both. He understood, as few could, the power of speech. Having brought his voice into the homes of millions of Americans, he meticulously reviewed every address before delivering it. In plain terms, he knew what he was saying, and he knew people expected him to deliver. Moreover, a crucial element of Roosevelt's political acumen was his ability to learn from mistakes: his own and others'. Woodrow Wilson failed with his League of Nations because, like most academics, he believed the rightness of his argument spoke for itself, *quod erat demonstrandum*. FDR harbored no such delusions. "It's a terrible thing to look over your shoulder when you're trying to lead," he once said, "and find no-one there."[105] He had to move incrementally, sometimes even in reverse, in order to placate and reassure those who might otherwise thwart his ambitions.

Nor can we appreciate the significance of Roosevelt's reintroduction of natural law absent the unique historical circumstances surrounding it. His efforts coincided with—indeed responded to—the greatest atrocities ever perpetrated by a state. The causal relationship between them is crucial. While jurists had long dreamed of a global community governed by universal principles of justice, it may be truly said that natural law only triumphed when the consequences of its inverse were made horrifically plain. As Justice Robert Jackson declared at the Nuremberg Tribunals, "The wrongs which we seek to condemn and punish have been so calculated, so malignant, and so devastating, that civilization cannot tolerate their being ignored, because it cannot survive their being repeated."[106]

Roosevelt saw opportunity in calamity. Confronted with the barbarity and lawlessness of Nazism, he was among the first to recognize that the postwar world would need "a revival of an old faith in the everlasting moral force of justice." Roosevelt began laying plans for that revival several years before the first American boots touched European soil. As president, he was able to call upon the entire State Department to give tangible form to his ideas and provide a blueprint for the postwar "moral order" he envisioned. They, in turn, enlisted the services of numerous legal scholars, many of whom—including Quincy Wright—would later serve as key functionaries in the United Nations. The result of their collective labors was the first international bill of rights ever conceived. Flawed and limited though it was, as a precursor to the Universal Declaration of Human Rights this document stands alongside Roosevelt's speeches and diplomacy as an extraordinary example of the melding of natural law and statecraft.

There is evidence that Roosevelt himself understood the magnitude of what he was attempting. In October 1944, he gave an address at the Waldorf-Astoria in New York City. It was a smaller crowd than usual and the president felt relaxed, even chatty. He riffed. His subject was American foreign policy—past, present, and future. Of the past, he was rueful and self-aware: "After the last war—in the political campaign of 1920—the isolationist Old Guard professed to be enthusiastic about international cooperation. And I remember very well, because I was running on the issue at that time."[107] Of the present, he was cautiously hopeful. The greatest mistake America could make in the present war was ignoring the lessons of the last, most particularly on human rights: "A quarter of a century ago we helped to save our freedom, but we failed to organize the kind of world in which future generations could live— with freedom. Opportunity knocks again. There is no guarantee that opportunity will knock a third time." In a meandering thirty-minute address he bounced from topic to topic, from isolationists in Congress to the guilt of the German people. Of the latter, he offered a defense that not only foreshadowed Justice Jackson's address at Nuremberg but also clearly displayed an awareness and acceptance of natural law: "I should be false to the very foundations of my religious and political convictions if I should ever relinquish the hope—or even the faith—that in all peoples, without exception, there live some instinct for truth, some attraction toward justice, some passion for peace—buried as they may be in the German case under a brutal regime."

Yet in his conclusion Franklin Roosevelt looked to the future, and revealed something truly remarkable. Absent was the soaring optimism of the Four Freedoms speech, where universal human rights were "no vision of a distant millennium" but "a definite basis for a kind of world attainable in our own time and generation." Absent too was the chest-thumping patriotism of the third inaugural, where he hailed American democracy as the author of "an unlimited civilization capable of infinite progress in the improvement of human life." The man in the Waldorf was more circumspect. He knew that universal justice would not be the work of one lifetime. He knew too that even as he called for a world free from intolerance, want, and fear, those qualities were still very much present in his own country. For all his faith in the upward slope of humankind, experience taught him it was a long, even endless, slog. At the historic moment when natural law became the basis for worldwide human rights, its chief proponent offered a candid view of the struggle that still resonates today:

> We are not fighting for and we shall not attain a Utopia. Indeed, in our own land, the work to be done is never finished. We have yet to realize the full and equal enjoyment of our freedom. So, in embarking on the building of a world fellowship, we have set ourselves a long and arduous task, which will challenge our patience, our intelligence, our imagination as well as our faith.... We shall bear our full responsibility, exercise our full influence, and bring our full help and encouragement to all who aspire to peace and freedom. We now are, and we shall continue to be, strong brothers in the family of mankind—the family of the children of God.

— 6 —

THE ADVANTAGE OF THE STRONGER

A criminal trial in common law is an alternate universe. It rests on a fiction and a paradox. The fiction is that when proceedings begin, reality itself is suspended. Not all reality, to be sure—the president is still president; it may still be raining outside; and the daily round of births, marriages, and deaths continues unabated—but rather the much narrower reality that surrounds the events in question. For these the trial creates an invisible frame, extends it to the furthest parameters of all evidence, and erases everything within. There was no crime, no victim, no perpetrator. There is nothing at all except that which is ultimately proved within the trial proceedings. Thus the crime is recast as the "indictment," the criminal as the "accused." A fixture of common law is that every person is presumed innocent until proven guilty. In order to create a universe in which this is possible, or even conceivable, every other "fact" must be expunged until it can be reestablished within the trial itself. Evidence is introduced, the frame is gradually filled in. But not until final judgment is the image unveiled. For that brief window of time, from opening statements to concluding arguments, the defendant is the only truly innocent person in the room. His or her denials are given equal weight to the voices of their accusers—greater, in fact, since the burden of proof requires more of the prosecution than defense.

The paradox is that by suspending reality, a new reality is created. This is the verdict. The verdict establishes once and for all the dominant narrative of events and culpability. It does not, however, alter the truth. We may, for example, still believe that a certain celebrity murdered his wife, but the dominant narrative declares that he did not. Even if we disagree with this version of reality, it cannot be altered. That is both the majesty and terrible power of the law.

One must comprehend this concept of a trial in order to fully appreciate the challenges of the Nuremberg Tribunal. Before its planners could even approach debate over evidentiary issues, sovereign immunity, relative guilt, or *nulla poena sine lege,* there remained a philosophical objection—perhaps even a moral one. Applying the common law's tabula rasa at Nuremberg meant that when the opening gavel came down in November 1945, there would be no war, no broken treaties, no ravaged countries, no casualties, and most importantly (for posterity, if not the prosecutors) no Holocaust. No one could seriously deny the facts or the culpability of the defendants; to do so insulted not only common sense but the victims. And yet justice required precisely this formulation. "You must put no man on trial before anything that is called a court," Supreme Court justice (and future Nuremberg prosecutor) Robert Jackson declared in a speech given one day after President Roosevelt's death, "under the forms of judicial proceedings, unless you are willing to see him freed if he is not proven guilty."[1]

At the opening of the Nuremberg Tribunals, Jackson provided his own answer: "That four great nations, flushed with victory and stung with injury, stayed the hand of vengeance…is the greatest tribute Power has paid to Reason."

I first encountered these words as a law student. They made no particular impression on me at the time. I found them again many years later in audible form: a recording of Justice Robert Jackson's address for the prosecution at the Nuremberg Tribunals, November 21, 1945. The voice on the tape is strong and commanding, the slightly mid-Atlantic accent reminiscent of the recently deceased president. As are the words themselves. There is no newsreel footage of this moment, but one photograph shows a slight man with a bookish demeanor, thinning hair unflatteringly lit by klieg light, glasses perched on the end of his nose.

One hand is raised in the Ciceronian manner emphasizing a point. His podium is nearly consumed by a mountain of binders and loose papers stacked on the table before it. Behind him a small crowd is seated in various attitudes of discomfort and apparent boredom. Jackson alone is bathed in light; the courtroom recedes rapidly into shadow. Other than this chiaroscuro, the scene has all the drama of a planning committee hearing in Akron.

Studying the photograph, listening to the recording, one would not imagine Jackson was knowingly stepping out onto a tightrope. Yet his speech, and the tribunal itself, was the legal equivalent of Philippe Petit's high-wire walk between the twin towers of the World Trade Center. The confidence in Jackson's voice masks profound uncertainty; the disquiet of his listeners was not boredom but real fear.

Reconsider this image. The wainscoting and marble surrounds of the courtroom look impressive, but color photographs reveal the stain to be streaked and thin, the marble cracked. The furniture is cheap. This was Room 600 in the Nuremberg *Justizpalatz,* or Palace of Justice. In the city where the infamous anti-Semitic Nuremberg Laws were promulgated in 1935, this was the building—the very room—where they were enforced. Jews and other minorities were stripped of their rights, humiliated, criminalized. In returning the courtroom to a semblance of its former self, the tribunal was raising a ghost to exorcise it.

Beyond the courtroom lay a wasteland. The church where King Wenceslas IV was baptized in 1361 was nothing more than a hollow shell. The Army Corps of Engineers had been tasked with clearing paths through the rubble; prosecutors' cars passed through canyons of bricks and beams, studded with heartrending items like warped bicycles and children's dolls. In a single hour on January 2, 1945, Allied bombing destroyed over 90 percent of the medieval quarter and left a hundred thousand homeless. In the last days of the war, Nuremberg was one the final cities to surrender, with battles raging along every street and often house to house. Nuremberg was a city of ruins and grief.

There were even starker dichotomies. At the left of the courtroom two benches had been erected for the defendants. The seats were deliberately truncated, forcing the men to huddle together and stumble over one another as they took their seats. Military officers wore plain tunics stripped of insignia; others wore business suits that grew rumpled and frowsy as the trial went on. Some had dark glasses shielding their eyes from the bright lights. Behind them stood a row of white-helmeted military police, as if these paunchy middle-aged bureaucrats might suddenly break loose and resist. But there was little resistance left in them. "Twenty-odd broken men," was how Robert Jackson described them. "It is hard now to perceive in these men as captives the power by which as Nazi leaders they once dominated much of the world and terrified most of it." But their ranks included such nightmarish figures as SS *Obergruppenfuhrer* Ernst Kaltenbrunner, who personally oversaw operations at a handful of concentration camps, including Mauthausen. Tall and gangling, his face deeply scarred from duels, he sat expressionless as Jackson spoke. Near him slouched *Reichsmarschall* Hermann Goering, chief of the Luftwaffe and a member of Hitler's inner circle. So famously fat and self-indulgent that he was routinely caricatured in everything from Warner Brothers cartoons to Charlie Chaplin movies, Goering shed over sixty pounds in captivity and now looked alert, intelligent, and menacing.

The defendants saw the wire beneath Jackson's feet as clearly as he did. The Nazi state, the most systematically barbarous in human history, was, in law, blameless. There had never been a successful prosecution of a head of state or state functionary for actions committed in that capacity. On the contrary, sovereign immunity dictated that governments had absolute and unlimited prerogative to fashion their own laws and carry out their own policies, however unconscionable. The imperial German government itself referred to the 1915 Turkish genocide of millions of Armenians as "an internal matter."[2] Not many years earlier, King Leopold II of Belgium waged a decades-long campaign of terror, mutilation, and murder in the Congo. Yet neither the Turks nor Leopold ever faced justice for their actions, nor anyone before them. Criminal law was unique to each nation; international criminal law existed in the minds of scholars, but nowhere else. For centuries jurists and philosophers spoke of a "natural law" that transcended state law, yet not one man or woman had ever been convicted of a crime against natural law. "The refuge of the defendants," Jackson warned the court, "can be only their hope that international law will lag so far behind the moral sense of mankind that conduct which is crime in the moral sense must be regarded as innocent in law."

That was a real conundrum. Just as the Nuremberg courtroom was fundamentally ersatz, a stage set for an elaborate play, the legal foundations of the tribunal were also quicksilver. The common law upon which the tribunal rested was constructed entirely of precedent. With no legal precedent to draw from, Jackson and the prosecution team were forced to cobble together an indictment from philosophical constructs that, while not unknown, had never been tested in law. The concept of war crimes dated to Renaissance theories of just and unjust war, yet aside from a failed attempt at Leipzig in 1919 it had never constituted a criminal charge. Crimes against humanity and crimes against peace were even more esoteric: actions that "shocked the conscience" of all humanity. What that meant in law was anyone's guess. Was a Malawi tribesman reading of Nazi atrocities as much a "victim" as an individual who perished in the death camps or fell on the battlefield? Jackson said he was. "The real complaining party at your bar is Civilization," he told the court. "Civilization asks whether law is so laggard as to be utterly helpless to deal with crimes of this magnitude by criminals of this order of importance."

It was a neat bit of logic, yet the defendants still had cause to smile. The full weight of history argued against the novelty of a trial. Even if they were convicted and executed, the tribunal itself could never be remembered as anything but ritualized murder. Martyrdom was not acquittal, but it had its advantages. "In fifty or sixty years," Goering told his jailers, "there will be statues of Hermann Goering all over Germany. Little statues, maybe, but one in every German home."[3] The truth of Goering's claim would rest on the tribunal and its legacy.

"This Tribunal," Jackson declared, "while it is novel and experimental, is not the product of abstract speculations nor is it created to vindicate legalistic theories." But of course it was. The fundamental problem was philosophical. Was law essentially the will of the state or a universal principle of justice? High-minded academics favored the latter, but the full sweep of sociopolitical history reinforced the former. One could argue that Nazism was the final and inevitable result of that positivist philosophy. The Nazis took state prerogative to its furthest extremes and thus brought humanity to the depths of utter barbarism. Jackson and others under-stood that if the positivist view of law prevailed, law as a construct would have no viable meaning: not justice or right or equity, but the point of a sword. That was what Jackson meant by including "civilization" among the victims: for humanity to continue, some reckoning had to be made.

Hence the Nuremberg Tribunal represented a wholesale rejection of legal positivism in favor of a universalist understanding derived from ancient principles of natural law. It stands today as a watershed moment in human history, when abstract theories debated by scholars for millennia suddenly became the foundations for a new and radically different world. The success of Nuremberg emboldened contemporaries to envision a global community operating under fixed, immutable natural law and right. They saw this not as an impenetrable future but something that could be achieved in their own lifetimes.

◆ ◆ ◆

At the beginning, there was a powerful argument against having a tribunal at all. Compared with the unimaginable magnitude of Nazi atrocity, the image of "twenty-odd broken men" gathered in a drafty courtroom, listening with bored expressions to a translation of their crimes fed into headsets that looked like rabbit ears, seemed a feeble response. "The guilt of such individuals is so black that they fall outside and go beyond the scope of any judicial process,"[4] British foreign secretary Anthony Eden wrote in 1942—a time, it should be noted, before the worst horrors of the Nazi state had occurred. Even the solemn specter of punishment was insufficient. Commenting on the Nuremberg Tribunals much as she would later at the Eichmann trial, Hannah Arendt wrote, "For these crimes, no punishment is severe enough. It may well be essential to hang Goering, but it is totally inadequate. That is, this guilt, in contrast to all criminal guilt, oversteps and shatters any and all legal systems."[5]

The argument that Nazi guilt eclipsed the moral and physical parameters of a criminal trial was not without merit. It referenced not merely the scope of the offense but the number of perpetrators. Indeed, over seventy years after the end of the Second World War, we are still identifying and prosecuting them. How could the crimes of thousands, perhaps millions, be fixed on twenty men? What of the others? And was that even fair to those particular defendants? A common complaint was that the men at Nuremberg were, in the words of one prosecutor, "junior varsity." The leaders—Himmler, Goebbels, Hitler himself—were dead. Moreover, Axis guilt extended well beyond Germany's borders. What of the Italians, or Japanese, or all the Pétains and quislings who offered themselves to the occupiers? The guilt of the Third Reich and its allies was so vast that it may never be fully known, and it certainly lay beyond the power of a single court to render justice.[6]

Yet there was an equally compelling response: that such guilt *demanded* the countervailing effects of a trial. Writing to President Harry Truman to advocate the tribunal, Robert Jackson invoked a theme that his good friend Franklin Roosevelt often employed: "Our test of what is legally [a] crime gives recognition to those things which fundamentally outraged the conscience of the American people and brought them finally to the conviction that their own liberty and civilization could not persist in the same world with the Nazi power."[7] There were two powerful ideas expressed in this single sentence. First, criminality was defined as that which offends the conscience, a natural law conception that pointedly avoided issues of state sovereignty in favor of a universal norm. Second, it was the very denial of this universal law by the Nazis that demanded an American response. Neither system could live, in other words, while the other survived.

But it was much more than American conscience or conviction that was threatened by the Reich. By the war's end, the full catalog of atrocity was so enormous that it challenged the very concept of civilization. Axiomatic to the evolution of society and law was inevitable progress, yet how could anyone in 1945 seriously believe that humanity still followed Dr. Peabody's upward trend? "Civilization seems to have lost control of itself," Jackson admitted. "Certainly here is lawlessness which challenges not only the lawyer but the law itself."[8]

Justice Jackson returned to this theme repeatedly during the tribunal. "The real complaining party at the bar," he told the tribunal in his opening address, "is Civilization."[9] This was not bombast, but rather a reckoning with the enormity of what the Nazis had done and what had been done in response. Just as Americans had finally realized their values could not coexist in a world with Nazism, "at length bestiality and bad faith reached such excess that they aroused the sleeping strength of imperiled Civilization." The image Jackson implicitly invoked was of a balance scale, akin to that dangling from the arm of the goddess Justitia. Every crime, however small, was an imbalance to the social order; the law existed to restore that balance. Nazi crimes had weighted down one side of the scale to such an extent that it threatened to topple over entirely. For the social order to be preserved, for humankind's faith in its own progress to be restored, the law needed to act as a counterweight. Thus the trial was not only proper but vital. It did not need to be as sweeping or dramatic as the crimes it judged; in fact, its very banality was the bedrock of its strength. Harold Nicholson witnessed the tribunal and came away impressed: "In the courtroom at Nuremberg something more important is happening than the trial of a few captured prisoners. The inhumane is being confronted with the humane, ruthlessness with equity, lawlessness with patient justice, and barbarism with civilization."[10] In his memoirs, Airey Neave offered an even more compelling image that deserves to be quoted in full:

> The central figure at the Nuremberg Trial, from beginning to end, was not Goering. It was not Hess or Keitel, nor any of the defendants. It was Lord Justice Lawrence. This benign, balding figure dominated the proceedings for nearly twelve months. He was a staunch, enduring man, who upheld the traditions respected by the world, in those far-off days, of British justice.... Lawrence embodied in his wing collar and bowler hat the principle of a fair trial.[11]

Conceptualizing the Nuremberg Tribunal as humanity's attempt to restore faith in itself brings it squarely within long-standing debates about natural law. Recall the ancient dichotomy between Demosthenes and Xenophon. Demosthenes writes of the law as a moral truth, "a discovery and gift of the gods, and at the same time a decision of wise men, and a righting of transgressions." Countless scholars from Cicero to Aquinas to Coke reiterated and reinforced this image. Yet Demosthenes' contemporary Xenophon, a student of Socrates, saw the law very differently: "Whatsoever the ruling part of the State, after deliberating as to what ought to be done, shall enact, is law." Law is essentially amoral, the articulated and enforced will of the state. This view too has a long and distinguished history, from Plato to the positivists. "Everywhere justice is the same thing," says Thrasymachus in Plato's *Republic,* "the advantage of the stronger."[12]

An enthusiastic proponent of legal positivism was Adolf Hitler. Between 1933 and 1945, centuries of German law were arbitrarily swept aside by *Gemeinschaftsdenken,* "communal thinking." Laws passed unanimously through the Reichstag, which now existed purely as a rubber stamp, or were issued as *Maßnahmen,* "arbitrary measures," and *Führerprinzip,* "Führer's orders." The Nazis called upon judges to "overcome narrow normatism" through a process euphemistically described as unrestrained interpretation. The result, as one historian writes, was "that the judiciary, because of its positivist orientation, [was] helpless in the face of a legislator freed from all constraints."[13] It is tempting to see Nazi law as raw articulated power absent any ideological or ethical buttressing, consistent with a Nazi "philosophy" that was both inchoate and contradictory. Yet if Nazi law had existed for the sole purpose of extending and reinforcing the state's tyrannical grip and implementing its policies, it would be hardly unique. In fact there was a legal philosophy of sorts underpinning it, the very antithesis of natural law. As Hitler explained to the president of the Danzig senate: "Conscience is a Jewish invention. It is a blemish, like circumcision.... I am freeing men from the dirty and degrading self-mortification of a chimera called conscience and morality."[14]

A debate among scholars dating back millennia had suddenly, in 1945, assumed the dimensions of an existential crisis for humanity itself. Put simply, the Nazi state was the fullest expression of Xenophon's principle. If there was no transcendent justice, there could be no higher authority than the will of the state. Consequently it would be up to the state to determine criminality, and it could not, by definition, be criminal itself. No state or group of states could impose their form of law on another by anything except force. Even if the Allies lined the Nazi elite up against a wall and shot them (as nearly everyone in the British, Soviet, and American governments wished at some point to do), that action would be political rather than moral. The entire political history of the world up to that point reinforced the truism that acts of state could not be criminal. Yet if that principle was allowed to stand, Nazism as an idea would triumph though the Nazis themselves had fallen.

For there to be any kind of justice, a natural law perspective had to prevail. Justice Jackson illustrated the dilemma at Nuremberg through an apt Shakespearean quotation. In his concluding address, he said of the defendants:

> They stand before the record of this trial as bloodstained Gloucester stood by the body of his slain King. He begged of the widow, as they beg of you: "Say I slew them not." And the Queen replied, "Then say they were not slain. But dead they are." If you were to say of these men that they are not guilty, it would be as true to say that there has been no war, there are no slain, there has been no crime.

The catalog of decisions that determined the course of the Nuremberg Tribunal, most importantly the decision to hold it in the first place, collectively represents an endorsement of natural law principles by the community of nations. While it cannot be said to end the debate between naturalists and positivists, it radically altered the trajectory of international law and provided the foundation, legal and ethical, for all subsequent human rights legislation. But that ultimate decision was not foreordained, and indeed for much of the war it seemed unlikely at best. It is crucial to consider, therefore, how consensus for the tribunal was reached, and the role which natural law and its proponents played in the process.

❖ ❖ ❖

The concept of individual responsibility under a universal code of justice was not unknown before Nuremberg, but its history was one of almost perfect failure studded with tiny glimmers of hope, glittering like mica in slag. When Nuremberg planners spoke of the "St. Helena precedent," they referred to the singular case of Emperor Napoleon Bonaparte, whose decades-long wars made him a figure of hatred such as few conquerors in history had known before Hitler. After Waterloo, the British government moved to brand not only Bonaparte himself but also his most devoted followers as "conspirators." The idea was designed to appeal to lawyers. It went like this: From the fall of the Bourbon monarchy to the final defeat of the Bonapartists in 1815, there existed what amounted to an illegal state. The proper government was that of King Louis XVI, which passed intact to his heirs upon his death and had never ceased to exist. Everyone, therefore, who took up arms against this rightful monarch or served any false usurper—from Robespierre to Napoleon—was part of a vast treason against France, a criminal conspiracy. It was no state at all, and therefore its members could not claim the privilege of sovereign immunity. This applied equally to the emperor, his ministers, and his officers. British prime minister Robert Jenkinson, Lord Liverpool, wrote in 1814: "It appears quite indispensable that in the event of the restoration of Louis XVIII a severe example should be made of those commanding officers … who deserted the King and went over to Bonaparte."[15]

This would later become something of a mania for him. He began referring to Napoleon as "the USURPER," a term which enjoyed limited currency during the wars but now became increasingly ubiquitous. Soon many within government came to share the view that the "emperor" was nothing more than a brigand who had unlawfully seized the reins of government and should meet the same fate as any traitor. After Waterloo, with Napoleon under house arrest, Liverpool drew up a proscription list with several dozen names, insisting that the only way to establish order was through bloodletting: "One can never feel that the King is secure upon his throne till he has dared to spill traitors' blood. It is not that many examples would be necessary, but the *daring* to make a few will alone manifest any strength in the government."[16]

Lord Liverpool's solution, which read startlingly like the statements once issued by the Committee of Public Safety, was quashed by an unlikely figure: the Duke of Wellington. Now the hero of Waterloo and the most popular man in Britain, Wellington saw his former nemesis as a fellow warrior and entitled to be treated with dignity. Executing him like a common criminal might please the masses (which, for the aristocratic duke, was suspect in itself), but it was unconscionable policy. "Such an act," he declared, "would hand our names down to history stained by a crime, and posterity would say of us that we did not deserve to be the conquerors of Napoleon."[17] The word of the duke was enough to quash Liverpool's schemes, though there were mutters in Whitehall that Wellington was motivated less by valor than vainglory: as the man who actually did conquer Napoleon, he preferred to see his adversary as an equal rather than a mad dog. In any event, the problem of the emperor was solved, illegally but successfully, by exiling him to St. Helena and quietly poisoning him some years later.

Declaring Napoleon Bonaparte a criminal conspirator neatly avoided troubling questions of natural law: he had violated the laws of France, and France (with Britain's help) could judge him. Such was not the case in 1918. Kaiser Wilhelm II was heir to a throne that by tangled skeins dated itself back to the Holy Roman Empire. In other ways, however, the two sovereigns were similar. Both bore the guilt of war on their shoulders—especially in the eyes of outraged Britons. Both, moreover, had inflamed public opinion against them and were the darlings of political cartoonists. Napoleon was depicted in scatological terms squatting ominously over Europe, Kaiser Wilhelm as a voracious animal devouring the continent. "Hang the Kaiser!" became a wartime rallying cry, simpler and more satisfying than Wilson's vague musings about making the world safe for democracy. But how, exactly, was the kaiser a criminal?

Even before the war's end, the British government took up the task of answering this question. Attorney General Frederick Smith suggested: "We should…take the risk of saying that in this quarrel we, the Allies, taking our stand upon the universally admitted principles of moral law, take our own standards of right and commit the trial of them [the Kaiser and his General Staff] to our own tribunals."[18] Note how Smith describes the invocation of natural law for international tribunals as a "risk." The risk was actually threefold. Such a tribunal had never been done or even tried before, invited countercharges against Britain herself, and set a dangerous precedent for all states in the future. Little of this mattered to President Wilson, whose idealism ran in a purer vein. In his "War Address" to Congress in 1917, referencing numerous attacks against civilian shipping including the *Lusitania* disaster, he declared: "We are at the beginning of an age in which it will be insisted that the same standards of conduct and of responsibility for wrong shall be observed among nations and their governments that are observed among the individual citizens of civilized states."[19]

The legal formulation of Smith's and Wilson's positions was a derivative of the conspiracy charge. Just as brigands remain brigands even if they seize control of the state, so too might otherwise legitimate heads of state lose their status if they committed acts that offend the conscience of humanity. After the torpedoing of the *Lusitania* by a German submarine, former president Theodore Roosevelt and many others labeled it an "act of piracy." Pirates were *hostis humani generi*, enemies of the human race, and it was the legal duty of every state and citizen to crush them by any means necessary. At the root of "Hang the Kaiser" was not just bloodlust but a revolutionary (in both senses) concept: that there could be such a thing as criminal guilt for sovereigns, and that it could be used to distinguish the relative culpability of state actors from their people as a whole. The basis of this guilt was an offense against natural law.

Nevertheless, despite urging from Great Britain, prosecution of the kaiser languished. Ironically it was the Wilson government that balked, shelving its own idealism in favor of hastening a postwar utopia freed of Old World enmities. "I am not wholly convinced that the Kaiser was personally responsible for the war or the prosecution of it,"[20] Wilson told reporters. He instructed his secretary of state, Robert Lansing, to make this clear to the British and French. Lansing, a successful attorney and expert on international law, was horrified by the unprecedented nature of what the Lloyd George government proposed. "Restrained by a reverence for law which is inseparable from that high sense of justice which is essential to social order," he began loftily, the United States government could not countenance a breach of the kaiser's "immunity from suit and prosecution...according to the municipal law of every civilized country and also according to the Common Law of Nations."[21]

In the end Kaiser Wilhelm was exiled to Doorn in the Netherlands, his own St. Helena. Germany was given the task of trying her own officers for war crimes at Leipzig. It quickly became a farce. The Turkish government, which massacred one and a half million of its Armenian citizens under cover of war, never admitted its guilt and refused to supply British prosecutors with records or divulge the whereabouts of any suspects. Three pashas who helped orchestrate the killings were convicted in absentia and then the Allied courts-martial in Constantinople officially disbanded. The Armenians took matters into their own hands; two out of three were later assassinated.

It is hard to read this catalog of failures and discern much useful precedent, but in fact there were three. First, it was possible to exempt certain heads of state from sovereign immunity if it could be convincingly shown that they usurped power illegally. They would then be guilty of treason and conspiracy in addition to whatever crimes they committed during war. The Napoleonic precedent failed not because Napoleon was an unsuitable candidate but rather due to the aristocratic intervention of the Iron Duke.[22]

Second, it was theoretically possible for heads of state to lose their immunity if their actions in time of war shocked the conscience of humanity. The example of the kaiser was reinforced by a Hague Convention signed by numerous heads of state—including Wilhelm—in 1907. Signatories bound themselves to "serve the interests of humanity and the ever-progressive needs of civilization," even in wartime. Accordingly, "inhabitants and belligerents remain under the protection and governance of the principles of the law of nations, derived from the usages established among civilized peoples, from the laws of humanity, and from the dictates of public conscience."[23] By signing this convention, Wilhelm voluntarily submitted his subsequent actions to the judgment of the law of nations. Not surprisingly it would be invoked during the abortive effort to place him on trial. The limiting language was "in time of war." There was still no mechanism or precedent to hold heads of state accountable for actions taken in peacetime against their own people.

Third, it was clear by 1918 that any successful prosecution for war crimes or other crimes relating to state action required a foundation, as the Hague Convention termed it, in the law of nations, the laws of humanity, and the public conscience. In other words, a transcendent notion of justice derived from morality. It was not sufficient simply to rely on broken treaties; a treaty was a contract between nations, and thus breach meant nullification but not criminal liability. For that one needed natural law.

Taken together, the ideas of conspiracy, loss of immunity, and the "public conscience" would become cornerstones of the Nuremberg prosecution. Yet there were other legacies of St. Helena and Leipzig. The

British, who had taken the lead both times, approached the issue of Nazi criminality warily, scarred by past failures. Many within the Roosevelt administration, including the president himself, had once been members of the Wilson administration that doused any plan of legal action against the kaiser. And in 1945 the issue of assigning blame would be infinitely more complex than in 1815 or 1918.

◆ ◆ ◆

The first official response to Nazi atrocity came in January 1942, when representatives of nine occupied nations—Belgium, France, Czechoslovakia, Greece, Luxembourg, Norway, Poland, Yugoslavia, and the Netherlands—met in London and released the "St. James Declaration." It condemned the savagery of Axis rule and declared that "the sense of justice of the civilized world" mandated that the Allies "place among their principal war aims the punishment, through the channel of organized justice, of those guilty of or responsible for these crimes, whether they have ordered them, perpetrated them or participated in them."[24] The legal and political weight of the declaration was exactly what one might expect from a document signed by nine governments in exile at the nadir of the Allied cause.

But occupied Europe was not alone in clamoring for postwar justice. Religious groups, Catholics and Jews especially, lobbied in Britain and the United States to raise awareness of Nazi crimes and demand retribution after victory. Their effect, however, was negligible. A more significant effort was undertaken by the United Nations War Crimes Commission, formed in October 1942 to make specific recommendations on how to deal with the Nazi leadership after the war. Despite its official-sounding title, it was an advisory group only and derided by historians as weak and politically compromised. An illustrative example was the American delegate, Congressman Herbert C. Pell. Pell seemed an ideal candidate: he had already served as ambassador to Hungary and Portugal, was an old Bull Moose progressive, and belonged to the same Brahmin class of New Yorkers as the president, his close friend. Pell was also an enthusiastic proponent of the tribunal idea, even advocating charges against the Nazi state for crimes committed against its own nationals. He had previously been active on the War Refugee Board, trying to open the floodgates of American immigration to as many Jews as possible.[25]

This action earned him the enmity of the State Department, especially Assistant Secretary Breckinridge Long (another Brahmin friend of FDR's but of Southern stock). Under Long, the State Department became a bastion of anti-Semitism and obstruction; its policy was to thwart as much Jewish immigration as possible under the thin excuse that Nazi spies might infiltrate the United States as fifth columnists. Regarding Pell as both a political and ideological enemy, the State Department delayed his departure to London for over a year, until December 1943. Upon arrival, Pell immediately drafted a proposal recommending that "crimes committed against…any persons because of their race or religion" should be punishable as war crimes. In an extraordinary rebuke, the State Department informed the British Foreign Office that Pell (an alumnus of Harvard, Columbia, and NYU) was "ignorant of law" and "difficult."[26] President Roosevelt, as was his custom, sided with neither Long nor Pell but kept both men in place. The UNWCC would continue to meet until January 1945, but its recommendations had little effect on actual policy.

One reason for this was that there was no clear Allied policy on postwar justice, nor would there be, until nearly the war's end. Each ally had divergent views, and even within governments there was little consensus. This produced a string of discordant pronouncements, underpinned by even more inconsistent diplomacy. In October 1942, Roosevelt declared that perpetrators of mass crimes would "answer for them before courts of law."[27] He added that "it is not the intention of this Government or the Governments associated with us to resort to mass reprisals." This pronouncement was seemingly reinforced by the Soviet Union, which declared that same month its abhorrence for the "abominable crimes" of the Third Reich and its commitment to postwar "courts of the special international tribunal."[28] One month later, Ivan Maisky, Soviet ambassador to Britain, conveyed the view of the general secretary that such a tribunal must be convened for "major war criminals."[29] Most significantly, the Moscow Declaration of November 1943 pledged the Allies to acting "without prejudice to the case of the major war criminals whose offenses have no particular geographic location and who will be punished by joint decision of the Governments of the Allies."[30] Note that the declaration speaks of punishment, not trial. More specific language dealt with persons who had confined their crimes to a defined geographic location (for example a general on the battlefield, or a *gauleiter* of an occupied territory). These "will be sent back to the countries in which their abominable deeds were done in order that they may be judged according to the laws of these liberated countries."

Yet discussions amongst the Big Three—Churchill, Stalin, and Roosevelt—took on a very different cast. Churchill's government had rejected Maisky's request in 1942 as "premature," in effect buying itself time to consider the matter.[31] There was also reason to doubt Soviet sincerity. At the Tehran conference in 1943, Stalin recommended arbitrarily shooting fifty thousand German officers and state functionaries.[32] Churchill predictably exploded (indeed, that might have been the Soviet premier's intention). It became plain that the "tribunals" Stalin envisioned would be show trials, modeled on those made infamous throughout the USSR wherein Stalin had purged his own officer corps and other branches of government.

The British position was more nuanced. Outraged as he was by wholesale slaughter and kangaroo courts, Churchill favored a compromise policy drafted by his foreign secretary, Anthony Eden. "Judicial procedure would seem inappropriate for dealing with Hitler and Mussolini," Eden wrote, "and with a limited number of important enemy leaders such as Goering, Goebbels and Himmler.... [Trials] based on the laws of war would be reserved for the crimes committed by enemy nationals other than outstanding leaders."[33] The implication was that Hitler and his immediate circle would be executed; lesser functionaries might be tried. Churchill himself had witnessed the singular failures of Leipzig and Constantinople. It was he, as former first lord of the admiralty, who had advocated military tribunals for WWI U-boat commanders. The memory of these legal disasters effectively stymied the British response; as the most logical and likely advocates for universal justice, they balked and were even more reluctant than the Soviets to endorse the tribunal concept for the surviving Nazi leadership.

The American position was even less defined; in effect, it was not a policy at all. In 1943, Secretary of State Cordell Hull articulated the view that "if I had my way I would take Hitler and Mussolini and Tojo and their accomplices and bring them before a drumhead court-martial and at sunrise on the following day there would be an historic incident."[34] It is impossible to know whether this was policy or wishful thinking. Such vagaries permeated the departments of state and war, even the White House. Despite his fervor for postwar international organization, Roosevelt seemed curiously indifferent, initially, to postwar justice. Even the revelations of Nazi atrocity, while alarming, didn't move him. The president would controversially veto several plans to bomb railroad lines into concentration camps and even the camps themselves, repeating that the only way to end Nazi brutality was to win the war as quickly as possible.

By 1943, the only person in government who had devoted a great deal of time and thought to postwar justice was Secretary of the Treasury Henry Morgenthau Jr. As a Jew, Morgenthau was one of few sympathetic audiences when Jewish refugees arrived in Washington and tried to raise awareness of the swiftly escalating crisis that became the Holocaust. It was Morgenthau, moreover, who endorsed and circulated Raphael Lemkin's controversial book, *Axis Rule*. Lemkin, a Polish-Jewish lawyer and refugee, laid bare the full horror of the Nazi state by providing a compendium of its laws. Lemkin would later coin the term "genocide" and take a lead role in drafting the first UN Convention on Genocide.[35]

Unlike most of his colleagues, Morgenthau was only too willing to believe the worst of Nazi savagery. His father, Henry Sr., had served as American ambassador to the Ottoman Empire from 1913 to 1916 and was thus a key witness to the Armenian genocide. His office in Constantinople became overwhelmed with pleas and affidavits from victims seeking protection. Morgenthau, shocked and horrified, took the extraordinary step of advocating American intervention to halt the killings. When this was refused, he resigned. "I found intolerable my further daily association with men, however gracious and accommodating …. who were still reeking with the blood of nearly a million human beings."[36] In a further breach of protocol, Morgenthau went public with his outrage, publishing an account of the atrocity in 1919.

Now it was his son's office that was flooded with stories of unspeakable horror, and Secretary Morgenthau—an affable, ardent New Dealer and old crony of the president—hardened into a zealot. His influence on Roosevelt would be hard to overstate. Eleanor once called him "Franklin's conscience"—a role she would often play herself—and referred to their relationship as one between brothers.[37] Morgenthau was so concerned for the president's safety during wartime that he ordered construction of a bunker beneath the Treasury. "Henry," Roosevelt said, "I will not go down into the shelter unless you allow me to play poker with all the gold in your vaults."[38]

Thus, when Morgenthau in 1944 began advocating a plan for postwar Germany that envisioned destruction of nearly all productive capacity, the so-called "Ruhr plan" or "Morgenthau plan," he found a receptive audience. Famously declaring that he wanted Germans to never again be able to build anything more dangerous than cuckoo clocks, the otherwise kindly secretary of the treasury remained unmoved at the human cost this entailed: "Why the hell should I care what happens to their people?"[39] Morgenthau also called for wholesale execution of the Nazi leadership. "A list of the arch criminals of this war whose obvious guilt has generally been recognized by the United Nations shall be drawn up as soon as possible," he wrote. "They shall be apprehended as soon as possible and identified.... When such identification has been made the person identified shall be put to death forthwith by firing squads made up of soldiers of the United Nations." [40]

The clinical tone of the document contrasting with advocacy of extralegal slaughter makes it difficult reading today; indeed, it sounds all too much like the kind of memoranda emerging from Berlin at the time. It is only possible to understand Morgenthau's policy if one recognizes a man whose conscience was so outraged by the full scope of the horror—of which only he amongst Roosevelt's cabinet was fully aware—that he truly believed it had gone beyond the law. Indeed, one extraordinary exchange suggests even the legacy of the Armenian genocide had become twisted in his mind. Beyond the execution of high-ranking Nazis there remained the problem of what to do with the rank and file. Morgenthau's answer could have been copied verbatim from Nazi debates over the "Jewish question," most particularly the so-called Madagascar solution. "When you get right down to it," he told the president, "it may be a question of taking this whole S.S. group—because you can't keep them in concentration camps forever and deporting them somewhere—out of Germany to some other part of the world. Just take them bodily. And I wouldn't be afraid to make the suggestion just as ruthlessly as it is necessary to accomplish the act."[41]

Defending this policy to his colleagues—the term "ethnic cleansing" did not exist in 1944—Morgenthau invoked a grotesque comparison that speaks volumes of the depths of his rage and what it had done to his soul:

> I will give you people an example which I lived through in the eyes of my father. One morning the Turks woke up and said, "We don't want a Greek in Turkey".... Now, whether it is one million, ten million, twenty million, it still has got to be done. A whole population was moved.... If you can move a million, you can move twenty million. It seems a terrific task, it seems inhuman; it seems cruel. We didn't ask for this war; we didn't put millions of people through the gas chambers. We didn't do any of these things. They have asked for it.[42]

Initially, the Morgenthau plan found general favor in the administration. Even Eleanor Roosevelt, according to Morgenthau's notes, approved. "It doesn't bother her at all," he recorded. "She said, 'Put the thing under lock and key and shut it down completely.'"[43] As late as August 1944, secretary of war Henry Stimson noted in his diary after a meeting with the president that "if shooting is required it must be done immediate, not postwar."[44] Momentum for the Morgenthau plan continued to build, reaching its climax at the Quebec Conference in September 1944, which resulted in a solid endorsement of the policy by both Roosevelt and Churchill. In fact, British policy had remained unchanged since 1941; it was Roosevelt who had seemingly evolved from insisting on postwar tribunals to allowing summary executions. One cannot fault Morgenthau entirely for this. Like the treasury secretary, the president also received intelligence on the catalog of horrors committed by the Nazis. It is quite likely that he too saw justice as well as expediency in the firing squad. Churchill's initial opposition to the Morgenthau plan was not for its treatment of the Nazi elite, but rather ordinary citizens. It would be, he said, like "chaining ourselves to a dead German." Morgenthau admitted, "I have never had such a tongue lashing in my life."[45] But in the end, the prime minister acquiesced.

The central figure in the ensuing drama was Stimson. Hollywood typecasting could not have come up with a figure more diametrically opposite to Morgenthau. Aside from their first names, New York roots, and prominent positions in the Roosevelt administration, the men had nothing in common. Stimson was a Republican who despised the New Deal, a close friend of both the late Theodore Roosevelt and William Taft, and had served as both secretary of war and secretary of state under Republican presidents. Prim, contained, correct, and rather cold, Stimson was a Harvard-educated lawyer who thought like a judge. Unlike Morgenthau, he was not a friend of the current president. Stimson came to respect Roosevelt but remained critical of his abilities and motives. In his diary he frequently derided the president as "impulsive" and "lacking steadiness and balance."[46]

The secretary of war's response to Nazi atrocity was markedly different. While writing frequently of war crimes (a subject Morgenthau rarely touched upon), there is scant reference in his copious diaries to the plight of Europe's Jewry. He had allied with the State Department in opposing Jewish immigration and regarded most social issues of race, class, religion, and civil rights as so much wasted time. On the question of desegregating the armed forces and allowing African Americans to become commissioned officers, he wrote in his diary: "Leadership is not embedded in the Negro race.... I hope for heaven's sake they won't mix the white and colored troops together in the same units for then we shall certainly have disaster."[47]

It is possible, even likely, that Stimson's opposition to the Morgenthau plan stemmed in part from his animus to Morgenthau personally and Jews generally. Calling the plan "Carthaginian"—a neat and very Ivy League allusion to the Roman destruction of Carthage—Stimson concluded brutally: "It is Semitism gone wild."[48] Indeed, studying the characters of Stimson and Morgenthau and their respective stances on international tribunals, one is reminded of the famous depiction of the Puritan Roundheads and Royalist Cavaliers in the historical satire *1066 and All That:* Roundheads were "Right But Repulsive," while Cavaliers were "Wrong But Wromantic."

Naturally there was more to it than that. Stimson's detachment from the horrors of the Holocaust (indeed from most human passions) allowed him to frame the issue of Nazi guilt as a legal rather than strictly moral one, and thus kept him free from the morass of relative barbarism that had mired Morgenthau. Only a mind of prodigious sangfroid could assess the full panoply of Nazi atrocity and see a parallel to antitrust suits against American sugar manufacturers. "In many respects," Stimson wrote, "the task which we have to cope with now in the development of the Nazi scheme of terrorism is much like the development of big business."[49] The key word was "scheme." He believed that the whole story of the Nazi state could be rewritten as a vast criminal conspiracy—just like the trusts. As anachronistic as this might sound, it had the advantage of placing Nazi crimes within the framework of existing law. In other words, the scope of the Nazi conspiracy might be unprecedented, but the crime itself was not.

There were limits to dry legalistic thinking.[50] Whereas Morgenthau built his case for retribution on the Holocaust, Stimson doubted whether such crimes could be brought to trial at all: "I have great difficulty in finding any means whereby military commissions may try and convict those responsible for excesses committed within Germany both before and during the war which have no relation to the conduct of the war."[51] Labeling the Final Solution as "excesses" was certain to make Morgenthau's blood boil, but Stimson's reasoning was not as callous as it sounds. There was no need, he thought, to add additional charges to the indictment; Nazi guilt could be proved tenfold on the basis of war crimes alone. By framing the indictment around conspiracy and war crimes, Stimson was also placing it on relatively solid ground under the law of nations. Recall that the examples of Napoleon and Kaiser Wilhelm II, though failures, nevertheless introduced the twin concepts of conspiracy and individual responsibility for heads of state. The secretary of war, well versed in international law (and an eyewitness to the failed attempts at justice in 1919), implicitly referenced these precedents in his proposed tribunal.

Stimson was also genuinely appalled at the prospect of American soldiers murdering persons in cold blood. The enthusiasm of the Soviets for this policy was another mark against it.[52] Finally, crucially, he sought counsel from many of the same legal scholars who had been pressing President Roosevelt for a charter of human rights and international tribunals; two sides, as they saw it, of the same coin—namely, the restoration of the rule of law under universal principles. Among these were Professor Quincy Wright and Myron Cramer, the judge advocate general. The result was to embolden Stimson's legalist position and flesh it out with a wealth of precedent steeped in natural law. In the end, Stimson came to regard the tribunals as a reflection of not only universal justice but the United States' singular role in fostering that justice through action and example. He wrote to the president:

> Under the plan proposed by Mr. Morgenthau, the so-called arch-criminals shall be put to death by the military without any provision for any trial and upon mere identification after apprehension. The method of dealing with these and other criminals requires careful thought and a well-defined procedure. Such procedure must embody, in my judgment, at least the rudimentary aspects of the Bill of Rights.[53]

Stimson was shrewd. By invoking the Constitution he was implicitly reminding Roosevelt of the president's own frequently stated desire to restructure the postwar world on the legal model of the United States. Here, Stimson appears to say, is their chance. Moreover, as the Bill of Rights itself was predicated on Enlightenment concepts of natural law (which were themselves derived from Renaissance and classical models, and so on), the secretary effectively placed the tribunal alongside other historical landmarks of jurisprudence. If it was the first of its kind, that did not mean it broke entirely new ground—not if one presupposed an immutable standard of justice. "There was, somewhere in our distant past, a first case of murder," Stimson argued, "a first case where the tribe replaced the victim's family as a judge of the offender.... New decisions do not become *ex post facto* law merely because until the punishment comes, a man's only warning that he offends is in the general sense and feeling of his fellow men."[54]

Stimson was not alone in advocating a natural law solution. Nuremberg prosecutor Telford Taylor would later describe the tribunal's earliest proponents as "a group of New York lawyers,"[55] and he was not wrong. Aside from Stimson, and eventually Justice Robert C. Jackson, the two most significant members of the New York cabal were Murray Bernays and Sam Rosenman. Bernays, a Lithuanian Jew and successful trial lawyer, had, as one author described, "a streak of mysticism in him" and "adopted the belief that the Nazis represented a barbarian reaction and were attempting to destroy the structure of the western world."[56] Bernays occupied a curious ideological position halfway between Stimson and Morgenthau. Like the latter, he too had read an advance copy of Lemkin's *Axis Rule* and felt deep outrage—as a Jew and as a human being—at Nazi perversion of law. Yet like Stimson, he saw the trial as a means of reestablishing order: not just retribution, but the salvation of civilization itself. Bernays developed Stimson's idea of conspiracy well beyond sugar trusts. If one could argue that the Nazis had been a criminal organization *prior* to 1939, then the clock of its criminal culpability could begin before the war—in fact it would begin the moment the Nazis seized power. He drafted a proposal along these lines in September 1944 titled "Trial of European War Criminals" and submitted it to Stimson, who forwarded it with his recommendations to Attorney General Francis Biddle.[57] Biddle, in turn, put his seal of approval on the plan and sent it to the president.

The timing of the memorandum was significant. The Quebec Conference had occurred that same month, committing Britain and the United States to the Morgenthau plan. But details of the plan leaked and public opinion soured. Despite a general desire to exact vengeance on the Nazis ("Torture them to a slow and awful death," one letter to the White House advised), the American people were less inclined to inculpate the German people as a whole. FDR never explicitly revoked the Morgenthau Plan—he rarely explicitly changed course on anything—but rather let it wither on the vine. In January 1945, he wrote to Secretary of State Edward Stettinius:

> Please send me a brief report on the state of the proceedings before the War Crimes Commission, and particularly the attitude of the U.S. representative on offenses to be brought against Hitler and the chief Nazi war criminals. The charges should include an indictment for waging aggressive war, in violation of the Kellogg Pact. Perhaps these and other charges might be joined in a conspiracy indictment.[58]

This would be Roosevelt's only written instruction on the Nuremberg Tribunal. The "US representative" was of course Herbert Pell, who had languished in the political wilderness for almost two years. Until now, as far as Roosevelt was concerned, neither Pell nor the UNWCC even existed; suddenly he was being asked to make specific recommendations for the indictment. The reference to the Kellogg Pact (the Kellogg-Briand Pact of 1928, which outlawed aggressive war) and charges of conspiracy make it clear that both Bernays's and Stimson's recommendations had reached FDR's desk. The memo was likely written at the instigation of presidential adviser Sam Rosenman, the same ubiquitous figure who drafted most of FDR's speeches and had been a key advocate for human rights. Rosenman was also a judge and by December 1944 had become the president's point man on all issues relating to war crimes and postwar justice. Despite his Jewish heritage, he was vehemently opposed to the Morgenthau plan and became a crucial ally of Stimson and Bernays. It was Rosenman who would eventually approach Supreme Court justice Robert Jackson and formally invite him to lead the prosecution at Nuremberg. Mindful of the disasters of the First World War, FDR told Rosenman, "This time let's get the trials started quickly and have the procedures all worked out in advance. Make the punishment of the guilty swift."[59]

Two weeks after his letter to Stettinius, Roosevelt received a response signed by the secretary of state and attorney general Francis Biddle. Biddle, whose support had likewise been crucial in the formative months of the tribunal proposal, would serve as the American judge on the Nuremberg panel. The memorandum was clear and concise, representing the combined views of Stimson, Bernays, Rosenman, Biddle, and Jackson—the New York cabal: "After Germany's unconditional surrender the United Nations could, if they elected, put to death the most notorious Nazi criminals, such as Hitler or Himmler, without trial or hearing. We do not favor this method.... We think that the just and effective solution lies in the use of the judicial method."[60]

Roosevelt agreed and pressed this view at the final conference of the Big Three at Yalta. Eventually both the British and the Soviets reluctantly signed on; the liberated French would join as well. By April 1945, the Allies had committed themselves to the first international tribunal under natural law.

❖ ❖ ❖

The complete record of the Nuremberg Tribunal is over a hundred thousand pages long. Even one prosecutor's "comprehensive" account runs two volumes and nearly sixteen hundred pages. In both documents philosophy is largely eschewed in favor of a more workmanlike civil procedure. Yet the presence of natural law permeates the whole, most especially in how each of the principal characters, from the prosecution to the judges, conceived the trial.

Robert Jackson had been an enthusiastic proponent of the tribunal long before he was asked to serve as prosecutor. In 1941 he opened an address to the American Bar Association with a prayer: "Grant us grace fearlessly to contend against evil, and to make no peace with oppression; and, that we may reverently use our freedom, help us to employ it in the maintenance of justice among men and nations." In this early address, Jackson evinces a prescient understanding that the crimes of the Nazi state could be addressed only by invoking natural law. "Lodged deeply in the culture of the world, unaffected by the transitory political structures above it, is a bedrock belief in a system of higher law." Yet its presence did not guarantee its use. The American people were too complacent and trusting, in his view, that their ideals would naturally triumph—even absent any effort on their part. Jackson wasn't so sure. Quoting Oliver Wendell Holmes, he reminded his audience that the proper test of the law was whether it dealt justly and efficiently not with the moral man but rather the bad. "The world is in war today chiefly because its civilization had not been so organized as to impress the 'bad man' with the advisability of keeping the peace," he warned. "Five years of this sort of thing the world now witnesses and twenty centuries of civilization will not be worth a damn."[61]

In the struggle to save civilization, lawyers' quibbles over *nulla poena sine lege* ("no punishment without law," or no retroactive criminal prosecution) seemed pettifogging. Yet the problem remained. Jackson, well in advance of Bernays or Stimson, addressed this issue in a second speech, given in Havana. Natural law as understood in common law societies meant constant evolution expressed through cases. The law was never static, and each case, while resting on the principles of its forebears, was nevertheless original. If the common law outstripped its own mechanisms of adjudication, that simply meant the mechanisms needed to be brought up to speed: "In the evolution of the law we advance more rapidly with our concepts of substantive rights than with our machinery for their determination. Rough justice is done by communities long before they are able to set up formal governments."[62] The international community had lagged in creating a mechanism necessary to deal with Nazi crimes. But that did not, *could* not mean it was prohibited from doing so. Jackson's understanding of the law of nations thus freed it from what Telford Taylor described as "a slavish positivism that would emasculate international law."[63] If basic principles of justice had been violated, the law required that they be addressed, even if it meant creating a court anew.

Justice Jackson addressed this point emphatically in his opening address for the prosecution. To the charge that the tribunal was invalid since nothing like it had existed before, he answered:

> It is true of course, that we have no judicial precedent for the Charter. But international law is more than a scholarly collection of abstract and immutable principles. It is an outgrowth of treaties and agreements between nations and of accepted customs. Yet every custom has its origin in some single act, and every agreement has to be initiated by the action of some state. Unless we are prepared to abandon every principle of growth for international law, we cannot deny that our own day has the right to institute customs and to conclude agreements that will themselves become sources of a newer and strengthened international law.... The fact is that when the law evolves by the case method, as did the common law and as international law must do if it is to advance at all, it advances at the expense of those who wrongly guessed the law and learned too late their error.[64]

Jackson thus presents the law of nations as an organic construct, evolving in tandem with the common law because they are both derived from the same immutable natural law principles. High in the rafters of the Palace of Justice, one of the silent stone auditors would have been well satisfied. Construction crews sent in to restore the building in preparation for the tribunal noticed that while shrapnel had destroyed nearly all the classical statues that once lined the lintel above the great stone archway, one remained: Hugo Grotius.[65]

Aside from the novelty of the tribunal, there remained the novelty of the law. This was a thornier problem. The cornerstone of the Nazi defense was that their "crimes" under international law were not crimes at all, as no such law existed when they were committed. Jackson's initial response was withering: "It may be said that this is new law, not authoritatively declared at the time they did the acts it condemns, and that this declaration of the law has taken them by surprise. I cannot, of course, deny that these men are surprised that this is the law; they really are surprised that there is any such thing as law."[66]

Yet the conundrum remained. If the tribunal was to be an exemplar of justice under the common law, it had to respect and follow the whole of that law's injunctions; prosecutors could not cherry-pick which to hold sacrosanct. One of those principles was that no defendant could be charged with a crime ex post facto. How could the tribunal claim to be following ancient rules of justice yet willingly flout sovereign immunity and put men on trial for "crimes" that no one had ever been charged with before (war crimes, crimes against humanity, crimes against peace) under "laws" that were little more than a loose collection of international covenants?

"Of course," Jackson answered, "it was, under the law of all civilized peoples, a crime for one man with his bare knuckles to assault another. How did it come that multiplying this crime by a million, and adding fire arms to bare knuckles, made it a legally innocent act?"[67] Expanding on this theme, he referenced the ancient debate of whether sovereigns were under the law. A positivist reading would argue the negative: if the state creates the law, it cannot be itself beneath the law. A universalist understanding, however, bound both sovereign and subject to the same code of justice. Just as John Locke reasoned that kings could break faith with their people by disobeying the natural law, Robert Jackson applied the same argument to the Nazis—using the same historical example: "The Charter of this Tribunal evidences a faith that the law is not only to govern the conduct of little men, but that even rulers are, as Lord Chief Justice Coke put it to King James, 'under God and the law.'"[68]

That was fine, but neither Locke nor Coke had ever suggested or envisioned that *another* state would intervene to hold the sovereign accountable. Yes, that was novel, Jackson admitted, but it was also necessary. Leipzig had shown that the vanquished could not always be relied upon to judge themselves. Moreover, the scope of Nazi criminality meant that there were virtually no neutrals left. The position of the English people vis-à-vis King James II, or the barons and King John, was directly comparable to that of the whole of humanity and the Nazis. The Reich's actions had transcended the barriers of state, placing themselves on one side of the scales of justice and all of civilization on the other:

> But if it be thought that the Charter, whose declarations concededly bind us all, does contain new law I still do not shrink from demanding its strict application by this Tribunal. The rule of law in the world, flouted by the lawlessness incited by these defendants, had to be restored at the cost to my country of over a million casualties, not to mention those of other nations. I cannot subscribe to the perverted reasoning that society may advance and strengthen the rule of law by the expenditure of morally innocent lives but that progress in the law may never be made at the price of morally guilty lives.[69]

Yet reliance on common-law understandings of justice was not without its pitfalls. Pointing disparagingly at the sullen figures in the dock, Jackson said of them: "Merely as individuals their fate is of little consequence to the world. What makes this inquest significant is that these prisoners represent sinister influences that will lurk in the world long after their bodies have returned to dust. We will show them to be living symbols of racial hatreds, of terrorism and violence, and of the arrogance and cruelty of power."[70] But trials determine the guilt of persons, not symbols. This was precisely Hannah Arendt's critique of Nuremberg and even more emphatically of the 1961 Adolf Eichmann trial in Jerusalem. If the defendant represents something greater than himself, it is no longer possible to grant him presumption of innocence. He must on the contrary be judged as an individual and only answer for those crimes that he himself has committed. Reducing Nazi culpability down to a handful of defendants, however high their rank, risked absolving countless others whose guilt was almost if not equally great. Moreover, investing each of the Nuremberg defendants with symbolic status risked turning the entire tribunal into a show trial—precisely what the Nazis themselves claimed. This critique would come to haunt nearly every subsequent tribunal for crimes under international law, up to the present day.

Perhaps cognizant of the scores of academics and jurists whose efforts had led to the creation of the tribunal, and anxious that it not be seen as simply a deus ex machina for natural law proponents like Quincy Wright, Justice Jackson opened his address by pointedly distancing himself from them. Yet natural law was referenced in nearly every account of the trial by those that helped create and administer it. Professor Wright himself, who served as chief adviser to the American judge, Francis Biddle, and is credited with educating him on the intricacies of international law, summarized it thus:

> Opinion is coming to realize that international law cannot survive in the shrinking world...if sanctioned only by the good faith and self help of governments. Sanctions to be effective must operate on individuals rather than on states. But regularly enforced world criminal law applicable to individuals necessarily makes inroads upon national sovereignty.... The United Nations in the Charter of the International Military Tribunal, as in the Charter of the United Nations, performed an act of faith in, and commitment to, a law governed world and the principles which must be accepted and applied if there is to be such a world.[71]

Wright's conception of Nuremberg was reinforced by the participants themselves. "The fundamental purpose of the trial," wrote Chief Justice Sir Geoffrey Lawrence, "was not only the punishment of those who were guilty but the establishment of the supremacy of international law over national law." In other words, natural over state law. The prosecution team was even more sweeping in its conception of the trial's impact. "A landmark for the progress of man," American prosecutor Thomas J. Dodd described it.[72] "A desire of mankind for progress and to prevent recurrence of calamities suffered,"[73] declared Soviet prosecutor general Roman Rudenko. "It gives warning for the future, to dictators and tyrants masquerading as a state that if...they debase the sanctity of man in their own country they act at their peril, for they affront the international law of mankind,"[74] said British prosecutor Sir Hartley Shawcross. There could be no question that the trial represented a commitment to reestablishing humanity on the "upward trend" toward utopia, under a universal natural law.

Jackson himself recognized this. "It is common to think of our own time as standing at the apex of civilization," he told the court. "The reality is that in the long perspective of history the present century will not hold an admirable position, unless its second half is to redeem the first.... The refuge of the defendants can be only their hope that international law will lag so far behind the moral sense of mankind that conduct which is crime in the moral sense must be regarded as innocent in law."[75]

❖ ❖ ❖

It was an accident of history that the United Nations Charter and that which created the Nuremberg Tribunal should both emerge from the San Francisco conference, the same one Franklin Roosevelt spent the last few hours of his life planning. But in another sense the confluence of circumstances was foreordained. Justice Robert Jackson's son William, a formidable legal mind in his own right, put it best: "It is perhaps not commonly apprehended that the principles of Nuremberg...go hand in hand with the organization of the United Nations as the twin foundations of an international society ordered by law." Without Nuremberg, as we shall explore in the next chapter, there would have been no impetus or consensus on human rights. Without the New York cabal and their dogged emphasis on natural law, there would have been no Nuremberg.

— 7 —

THE CAROUSEL OF PROGRESS

On the shores of the Pool of Industry, at the intersection of the Avenue of Commerce and the Court of the Universe, was Progressland. A collaborative effort between Walt Disney and General Electric, it quickly became one of the most celebrated pavilions at the 1964 World's Fair. Guests entered a saucer-shaped structure that looked vaguely like a hubcap and were briskly guided through a series of turnstiles before arriving at its heart—the Carousel of Progress. The concept was novel: a theater placed on a revolving turntable like a giant record player, moving audiences past audio-animatronic scenes of daily life from past, present, and future. Here technology and democracy, symbiotically linked, advanced mankind toward utopia. Disney commissioned the Sherman brothers, fresh off their triumph in *Mary Poppins*, to provide an appropriate song. The result was so catchy, so emblematic of the age, that it became Walt Disney's personal theme and plays even now throughout his vast entertainment empire:

> *"Oh there's a great, big, beautiful tomorrow,*
> *shining at the end of every day,*
> *Yes there's a great, big, beautiful tomorrow,*
> *just a dream away!"*

It is unlikely that many visitors to Progressland paused to consider the architectural absurdity of a pavilion devoted to forward-moving progress that revolved instead in an endless repetitive gyre, thus borne back, like the metaphorical boats in *The Great Gatsby*, ceaselessly into the past. Disney himself certainly never did: the attraction proved so popular that it was moved first to Disneyland and eventually to Walt Disney World, where it remains—creakily intact despite annual threats of closure—to this day. Like a time capsule, it perfectly captures that volatile admixture of optimism, vainglory, and myopia that animated the fair itself and the entire postwar world.[1] It was this same spirit that produced the Universal Declaration of Human Rights.

The impetus toward some form of international bill of rights had been gathering steam since the end of the Second World War. The Nuremberg Principles, enacted in August 1945, codified the crimes of the tribunal and pledged the international community to uphold them sine die. But these applied only to atrocities committed during war. For months, religious organizations and NGOs had been pressuring the State Department to include protection for human rights into the draft charter of the United Nations. Ultimately they were successful, albeit to a limited degree. The UN charter pledged to "reaffirm our faith in fundamental human rights, in the dignity and worth of the human person, in the equal rights of men and women and of nations large and small."[2] But such high-sounding language was so vague as to be practically meaningless.

Events began to shift when President Truman appointed Eleanor Roosevelt as a delegate to the first meeting of the UN General Assembly in London in January 1946. She was to serve as the first chair of the newly created Human Rights Commission. The commission, like holding the chair, was likely meant to be a sinecure; Secretary of State Edward Stettinius had little interest in human rights. But if Stettinius or Truman expected Eleanor to regard the post in the same symbolic light, they misjudged badly. Despite feeling unqualified for the role of diplomat, Eleanor embraced the commission as an opportunity to consolidate her husband's legacy.[3] The General Assembly met in the Methodist Central Hall of Westminster, a symbolic vortex of Protestant dissent and natural law philosophy. Drawing inspiration from her surroundings, Mrs. Roosevelt pressured the assembly to commission a new bill of rights.

As she put it, "Many of us thought the lack of standards for human rights the world over was one of the greatest causes of friction among the nations, and that recognition of human rights might become one of the cornerstones on which peace could eventually be based."[4] Counting the number of conditional tenses in the preceding statement gives one a fairly accurate idea of the scale of the project. Bland, opaque platitudes about human dignity were easy enough; to create an actual list of rights was quite another matter. Which rights, whose rights, and how should they be enforced? These became the paramount questions of the Human Rights Commission.

The work began with laudable circumspection. The commission was determined not to replicate the disastrous wartime bill of rights produced by the State Department—a document, as will be recalled, that was little more than a restatement of the US Bill of Rights. Universal rights had to be universal and therefore multinational; anything less would be justly condemned as imposing an American *lex imperatoria* on the entire world. To that end, the commission sent a questionnaire out to the foremost legal minds of dozens of nations, soliciting their views. The response was enthusiastic.[5] Nearly every respondent affirmed their culture's recognition of basic human rights, but it soon became clear that "right" had a subjective meaning. Philosopher Chung-Shung Lo affirmed that "the idea of human rights developed very early in China, and the right of the people to revolt against oppressive rulers was very early established," but demurred from the Western conception of law as the protection of individual rights. "The basic ethical concept of Chinese social political relations," he wrote, "is the fulfillment of the duty to one's neighbor, rather than the claiming of rights."[6] Mohandas Gandhi agreed. "I learned from my illiterate but wise mother that all rights to be deserved and preserved came from duty well done. Thus the very right to live accrues to us only when we do the duty of citizenship of the world."[7]

Fulfilling one's role within a community entitled one to rights, not the other way around. Implicit within this construction was not only a rejection of Western legal norms but of several centuries' colonial domination. Echoing a much earlier argument about Queen Victoria's proposed bill of rights for India, Bengali poet Humayun Kabir wrote pithily that the "fundamental flaw in the Western conception of human rights" was the

West's failure to live up to them. "In practice [human rights] often applied only to Europeans, and sometimes only to some Europeans."[8]

This polite but pointed clapback hinted at a much larger phenomenon taking shape beyond the walls. The Philippines had already gained its independence from the United States; Indonesia was on the cusp of breaking off from the cash-strapped Netherlands. Within the British Empire, Transjordan had been freed, and negotiations were underway for the momentous dissolution of the Raj. Before the end of the decade, India, Pakistan, Israel, Burma, and Ceylon would join the growing list of independent nations. This explosion of independent states set the stage for the cataclysms of the 1950s and 1960s, when decolonization spread throughout the world and the last vestiges of European domination were swiftly, often violently, overthrown. Though the Human Rights Commission could not have known it, Kabir's critique would come to dominate the language of postcolonial resistance to human rights.

Even within the committee itself there were fractures. The communist delegation, voiced by Yugoslav representative Vladislav Ribnikar, rejected any form of individualism in favor of the collective. Human liberty, said Ribnikar, is "the perfect harmony between the individual and the community," whose best and only guarantor was—not surprisingly—the state. "The psychology of individualism has been used by the ruling class in most countries to preserve its own privileges; a modern declaration of rights should not only consider the rights of the ruling classes."[9] Beneath the Marxist-Leninist dogma was an arguable point: Western rights were both political and negative, enjoining the state from certain actions against the individual. The century-long impact of socialism had introduced a counterpoint: actions that the state was required to ensure, including the right to work and a decent standard of living. But the obvious danger was of a state pursuing these goals at the expense of natural rights—as the Soviets had done since 1917. This provoked an outraged response from French jurist Rene Cassin: "The deepest danger of the age," he warned, was a collectivist state that demanded "the extinction of the human person as such in his own individuality and inviolability."[10]

It was inevitable that Cassin, with his encyclopedic knowledge of French law from the rights of man to the *Code Napoléon*, should emerge at the conference as the most ardent proponent of natural law. His draft for a preamble, which eventually became Article I of the declaration, included a familiar restatement of the Ciceronian credo: "All men are endowed by nature with reason and conscience and should act towards one another in a spirit of brotherhood." Then the storm broke. The Catholic element, voiced by Brazil, vehemently demanded that the secular language be replaced with "all human beings are created in the image and likeness of God."[11] The Soviet response was apoplectic. Chinese delegate P. C. Chang warmly endorsed the brotherhood aspect as reflective of both Confucian and Enlightenment thought but suggested that any reference to nature or God was too culturally specific. It was enough, he said, to recognize that each person was endowed with reason; the agency was immaterial. Eleanor Roosevelt, who had hitherto remained largely silent on the matter, agreed. As she later explained:

> Now, I happen to believe that we are born free and equal in dignity and rights because there is a divine Creator, and there is a divine spark in men. But there were other people around the table who wanted it expressed in such a way that…left it to each of us to put in our own reason, as we say, for that end.[12]

There is an aura of unreality to these exchanges. Western and Eastern notions of right and justice, Grotius and Confucius, Judeo-Christian natural law and nineteenth-century socialism all collided and combined, embodied in the delegates seated around the table at Lake Success, New York. Probably not since the Synods of Antioch had so many divergent and combustible views been aired within a single room. This heterogeneity came to be reflected in the list of rights ultimately chosen. The delegates had two choices before them: include only those rights upon which universal agreement could be found, or include everything but the kitchen sink. From the outset it became clear how difficult the former option would be. In January 1947, Eleanor invited Lebanese delegate Charles Malik, Canadian John P. Humphrey, and P. C. Chang to her Washington Square apartment for tea. Dr. Humphrey had been tasked with drawing up a preliminary list of rights; Malik suggested he need look no further than the precepts of natural law. Dr. Chang swiftly objected, as Mrs. Roosevelt relates:

> The Declaration, he said, should reflect more than simply Western ideas and Dr. Humphrey would have to be eclectic in his approach. His remark, though addressed to Dr. Humphrey, was really directed at Dr. Malik, from whom it drew a prompt retort as he expounded at some length the philosophy of Thomas Aquinas.... I remember that at one point Dr. Chang suggested the Secretariat might well spend a few months studying the fundamentals of Confucianism![13]

Teatime wrangles were just the beginning. Months of debate produced little consensus, but rather a hardening of respective positions. The original forty articles in the Universal Declaration of Human Rights were reduced by only ten. The final product was thus not one list of rights but two. Articles 1–21 were a grab bag of Western legal and political theory, mandating everything from democratic government (Article 21) to the presumption of innocence (Article 11)—this last despite the fact that only common-law nations like the United Kingdom and the United States had it in their legal systems. The language of the articles revealed obvious linkages to everything from the Magna Carta to FDR's Four Freedoms. Articles 22–29 were expressly social (and, in some cases, socialist), and many commentators would question whether many, like Article 24, had ever been considered "rights" at all: "Everyone has the right to rest and leisure, including reasonable limitation of working hours and periodic holidays with pay." There was nothing in the document to indicate which rights were most fundamental (except possibly that political rights came numerically first, and there were twice as many of them) or what would happen if two or more articles conflicted. There was no mechanism for enforcement. This was a particular grievance of Mrs. Hansa Mehta, the Indian representative. A Brahmin and prominent jurist in her own right, she had spent decades challenging Britain's illegal detention of Indian subjects and confiscation of their property.[14] The British themselves denounced the list as "highly unsatisfactory" on related grounds; how, they wondered, was the international community supposed to compel a state to grant its citizens paid vacation?

One might argue that consensus among the delegates was impossible, and therefore a "kitchen sink" list of rights was the only practicable outcome. P. C. Chang, addressing the General Assembly on the day of ratification, acknowledged this problem. "Preoccupations of a political nature" and "uncompromising dogmatism," he admitted, meant that any list of rights that did not include the controversial political elements—democratic and socialist—could be upheld by the UN only with the use of force. "But however violent the methods used, equilibrium achieved in that way could never last."[15] The failure of the declaration, however, was already apparent even as the document was being drafted: with so many rights, and no differentiation between them, each state would choose for itself which articles to follow and ignore the rest. Thus the Universal Declaration was not so much a blueprint for the future as a reflection of the moment, particularly the divergent ideological poles of democratic and socialist nations. It was neither binding nor enforceable; not a single state was in compliance with all its provisions or wished to be. That being the case, one has to wonder what, exactly, the delegates and Mrs. Roosevelt hoped to accomplish.

In a word: progress. Examining the cold record of committee discussions and disagreements today is to reckon without the incandescent optimism that infused the proceedings. That quicksilver sense of limitless possibility was everywhere. Utopianism seems to come in historical waves; one can find evidence of a swelling of enthusiasm in the sixteenth, eighteenth, and late-nineteenth centuries. Now its cause was clear: war had completely devastated the structural, social, and political order. A new world would have to be built. Emergent nations had already begun clamoring for some form of international human rights law to protect them from aggressors. The Organization of American States (OAS), representing Latin America, produced its own 1948 American Declaration of Rights and Duties that in many ways mirrored the optimistic language of the Universal Declaration. All over the world new constitutions were being drafted with economic and social liberties jointly enshrined. For the briefest of moments, from 1945 to the early 1950s, it truly seemed as if a new world order was not only possible, but necessary. The Human Rights Committee—and Eleanor Roosevelt in particular—believed they stood at a moment of historic flux. But overconfidence bred hubris. The consensus among historians and political scientists is that the committee overreached: in attempting to hasten utopia, they crafted a document that was too broad and too weak.[16] It would be unfair to blame or credit

Mrs. Roosevelt with a declaration that was the collaborative effort of dozens of brilliant legal minds. It is inarguable, however, that the finished product would not have pleased her late husband as much as it did her. FDR, the consummate realist, would have seen at once the fatal flaws within a document of so many conflicting and controversial provisions. His own vision of postwar human rights was no less radical but considerably more focused. Nor would he have countenanced a bill of rights without any enforcement mechanisms. The record of his views and actions suggests, on balance, that Roosevelt would have pressed for a shorter and more fundamental list of rights and backed them up with the full weight of American political and military force. Had the United States done so, the record of human rights advancement and enforcement for the next seventy years might have looked very different indeed.

As it was, however, the Human Rights Commission believed they had achieved a compact for the ages. One can hear the faint echo of trumpets in Eleanor Roosevelt's address to the United Nations on December 10, 1948:

> We stand today at the threshold of a great event both in the life of the United Nations and in the life of mankind.... This Declaration may well become the international Magna Carta of all men everywhere. We hope its proclamation by the General Assembly will be an event comparable to the proclamation of the Declaration of the Rights of Man by the French people in 1789, the adoption of the Bill of Rights by the people of the United States, and the adoption of comparable declarations at different times in other countries.[17]

If these words read now like starry-eyed idealism, one must blame the times, not the author. There were glimmering, fleeting moments when it seemed as though it could almost have worked. A global community shattered by war and surrounded by the toppled idols of totalitarianism; dozens of new nations clamoring to be born; a transcendent desire for order and decency after a decade of chaos and barbarism; and, at the apex of it all, a vivified democratic nation with more raw power than any empire in history—never before and probably never again would the kaleidoscope of human events fall into such a perfect pattern for universal law.[18] A few months after the declaration was introduced, the State Department released a pamphlet reaffirming "the establishment of the methods and precedents of a world rule of law in which disputes among nations would be resolved just as most disputes among individuals are resolved today—through recourse to a proper and established court of justice."[19] The Universal Declaration of Human Rights must certainly be recognized as the founding charter for such a court. Notwithstanding its flaws, it was the first significant attempt to extend natural law principles beyond state parameters and make them truly universal. Article 1, quoted above (although "men" was fortunately changed to "human beings"), established the natural basis of law reaffirmed by scholars from Cicero to Kant. Article 3 echoed Grotius and Blackstone in its declaration that "everyone has the right to life, liberty and the security of person." Even the language of the preamble, cobbled together from such natural law texts as the Declaration of Independence, the Rights of Man, and FDR's Four Freedoms, was in its own way a reaffirmation of the legal foundation underlying them:

> Whereas recognition of the inherent dignity and of the equal and inalienable rights of all members of the human family is the foundation of freedom, justice and peace in the world,
>
> Whereas disregard and contempt for human rights have resulted in barbarous acts which have outraged the conscience of mankind, and the advent of a world in which human beings shall enjoy freedom of speech and belief and freedom from fear and want has been proclaimed as the highest aspiration of the common people,
>
> Whereas it is essential, if man is not to be compelled to have recourse, as a last resort, to rebellion against tyranny and oppression, that human rights should be protected by the rule of law.

❖ ❖ ❖

This language, steeped in Western liberalism, was inevitably going to produce a backlash. But the first sign of resistance came from an unexpected quarter closer to home. Isolationism in the United States held a long and distinguished pedigree, from George Washington's Farewell

Address in 1796 to the Red Scares of the early twentieth century. It reached its zenith in the months preceding the attack on Pearl Harbor, represented by such powerful organizations as America First and public figures like aviator Charles Lindbergh and endorsed by a significant portion of Congress. By the end of the decade, however, isolationism had become a tattered standard, frequently (and not unfairly) derided as xenophobic, obtuse, even fascist. Nevertheless, as universal law moved tantalizingly close to reality, the prospect of a "world court" reawakened old fears of foreign entanglements. Perversely but predictably, these domestic antagonists couched their critique in the language of their opponents: "The American people want to make certain that no treaty or executive agreement will be effective to deny or abridge their fundamental rights. Also, they do not want their basic human rights to be supervised or controlled by international agencies over which they have no control."[20]

The idea that international covenants designed to safeguard human rights could themselves be instruments of denying them was delusional on an Orwellian scale. Moreover, the isolationist horror of "international agencies" was oxymoronic: exercising its hegemony after the war, the United States had effectively fashioned a universal law in its own image. The same treaties and agencies that so terrified the isolationists were crafted, sponsored, staffed, and maintained by the Americans and their allies. Objective reality, however, has never been a serious hindrance to politics. In 1951, Ohio senator John W. Bricker introduced an amendment to Article 6 of the Constitution, certifying that no international treaty or covenant could alter domestic law unless specifically endorsed by congressional legislation. "My purpose in offering this resolution," Bricker said candidly, "is to bury the so-called covenant on human rights so deep that no-one holding high public office will ever dare to attempt its resurrection." Debate raged for nearly three years until the amendment was ultimately defeated by a razor-thin margin of two Senate votes.[21] This was hardly a victory for the universalists: in truth, the amendment died not because it was unpopular but because it was redundant. The American government did not need a constitutional amendment prohibiting it from doing something it had no intention of doing in the first place. "This whole damn thing is senseless," President Eisenhower complained.[22]

Senseless perhaps, but comprehensible. Beneath the convoluted logic of the Bricker amendment was a solid bedrock of fear. Its staunchest supporters were likewise enemies of unionization, social welfare, and—most particularly—desegregation. Far from curtailing basic rights, the real danger was that the Universal Declaration might ultimately compel the United States to recognize them. Someone, Bricker raved, had to "slow the State Department in its mad pursuit for a World Bill of Rights."[23] In actuality, the State Department had already begun applying the brakes. Secretary of State John Foster Dulles made a special trip to the Senate Judiciary Committee to assure them that the president would never seek ratification of any human rights covenants—not even the Genocide Convention of 1948. Sounding remarkably like a cultural relativist of the mid-1990s, Dulles opined that such agreements would force "one part of the world to impose its particular social and moral standards upon another."[24] So much for the Four Freedoms.

The intransigence of the Eisenhower Administration had a chilling effect on the United Nations itself. Since 1948 a draft committee within the UN had been doggedly attempting to transform the articles of the Universal Declaration into binding agreements. But even the friendlier Truman government had balked at adoption of "socialistic" protections for workers and families, and Republicans in Congress fumed at the "eager beavers" in the UN "grinding out treaties...which have an effect upon the rights of American citizens."[25] By 1952 it was abundantly clear that no single covenant would gain the support of both the United States and the Soviet Union, or their respective blocs. Accordingly, drafters codified reality by officially splitting the articles into two separate covenants: the International Covenant on Civil and Political Rights (ICCPR) and the International Covenant on Economic, Social and Cultural Rights (ICESCR). Then both drafts stalled, hors de combat within an escalating Cold War that made grand international agreements all but impossible. It would not be until 1966 that the two covenants even reached the General Assembly for a vote; another decade passed before ratification. The United States formally and finally ratified the ICCPR in 1992 (with numerous reservations); it has never ratified the ICESCR.

Even as the United States retrenched, other nations seemed eager to pick up the torch of natural law and liberalism. The postwar decolonization movement followed a pattern broadly similar to the French and Russian Revolutions, marked by constitutional restraint at the start but devolving rapidly into violence and extremism. The blame may be laid in part on the colonial powers themselves and more broadly on the bipolar geopolitics of the era. The Atlantic Charter of 1941, discussed in chapter 4, pledged the Allies to a policy of self-determination for all nations. The language was Roosevelt's; Winston Churchill signed on reluctantly, with fingers crossed behind his back. Less than a year later, when Churchill learned that FDR was secretly negotiating with Gandhi's Congress Party for postwar independence, he exploded with rage. "Anything like a serious difference between you and me would break my heart," he wrote to FDR, "and would surely deeply injure both our countries at the height of this terrible struggle."[26] Roosevelt took the hint and desisted.

But the matter was merely deferred. The Atlantic Charter had raised hopes around the world of a postwar dissolution of empire, and by 1945 emergent nations were ready to collect on the bond. In Vietnam, Ho Chi Minh began talks with American espionage agents for a pledge not to allow the resumption of French imperial rule. "He kept asking me if I could remember the language of our Declaration [of Independence]," one OSS operative recalled. "The more we discussed it, the more he actually seemed to know more than I did."[27] Not surprisingly, the Vietnamese Declaration of Independence of September 3, 1945, declared "All men are created equal, they are endowed by their Creator with certain unalienable rights; among theses are Life, Liberty and the pursuit of Happiness." Ho wrote the draft himself and added an observation of his own: "In a broader sense, this now means all the *peoples* have the right to live, to be happy and free." By this single phrase, dusty old natural law was wedded to the very new right of cultural self-determination.[28]

India quickly followed suit. The Indian Constitution of 1949 listed six "fundamental rights." The first three were distinctly Rooseveltian: freedom of speech and association, freedom of religion, and the right to due process of law. (One might also make the case that the fourth, freedom from want, was implied by the constitutional guarantee of a "right to employment and profession" regardless of caste.) The latter three were more culturally specific: prohibition of forced and child labor; the right to education; and the rights of minorities to their culture, language, and self-governance. After the partition, Pakistan's constitution contained nearly identical language, with the added provision that no law could contradict the teachings of Islam.[29]

Similar developments could be found on the African continent. Former British colonies including Ghana and Nigeria melded colonial law—which had often promised equal rights de jure while denying them de facto—with the new language of individualism. Thus natural law rights, as per Blackstone, were augmented with freedom of worship, speech, and protection of minorities. Cameroon, which achieved independence from France in 1960, invoked both the UN Charter and Universal Declaration in providing for the "inalienable rights" of its citizens.[30]

It should not be surprising to find such expressly Western language in these new constitutions. Like the American founding fathers, the architects of the postcolonial world were trained and immersed in the law of their colonizers. Gandhi studied law at University College London at roughly the same time that Mohammad Ali Jinnah was finishing his legal pupilage at Lincoln's Inn. Many African leaders attended universities in the United States on scholarships funded by American religious or political organizations, including Nnamdi Azikiwe of Nigeria and Kwame Nkrumah of Ghana, and thus returned to their countries well versed in Western liberalism.[31] Ho Chi Minh lived in France, England, and the United States and had even petitioned Georges Clemenceau and Woodrow Wilson to recognize Vietnamese independence at the conference of Versailles in 1919.

The response of the Western powers to their constitutional efforts, however, was anything but receptive. In the short term, Churchill's vision of status quo antebellum won out. Despite Ho Chi Minh's protests and those of other former colonies, the British quickly restored French Indochina and most of its possessions in West Africa to France, even as they attempted to salvage their own waning empire. The Congo, which had supplied uranium crucial for the making of the first atomic bomb, was likewise handed back to Belgium. Throughout it all the United States remained silent, as did the UN. This naked power grab, which occurred at precisely the same time drafters hammered out provisions for the Universal Declaration of Human Rights, must be understood in context. The Soviet Union had already engulfed the whole of Eastern Europe and was recommitting itself to the old Comintern idea of world socialism. American forces still occupied Japan and were busily drafting a *Showa* constitution intended to demilitarize the nation and place it forever within the Western liberal democratic sphere. By the end of 1945 the world was divided into spheres of influence, distinct but not wholly different from the empires of the previous century.

The American position, expressed by Presidents Truman and Eisenhower, was that it was preferable to maintain old colonial systems if they kept their colonies in the Western bloc—by force, if necessary. This betrayal was deeply disillusioning for those, like Ho Chi Minh, who had taken FDR's pledge to heart. As historian Samuel Moyn has written, after 1945 "Ho, who initially begged his American interlocutors to live up to the Atlantic Charter's promise of self-determination rather than allow the French to return, stopped asking and never again made even declaratory rights central."[32] Humayun Kabir's warning about the "fundamental flaw" in human rights had tragically come to pass.

The failure of Western liberalism provided an opening for its nemesis. Many anti-imperialists already identified themselves as Marxists, or at least sympathetic to communistic theories. Spurned by the west, Ho Chi Minh, Nkrumah, and others accepted aid and support from the Soviet Union. The second wave of independence movements from the mid-1950s through the 1960s thus emerged in a Manichaean geopolitical climate which effectively forced them to align with one side or the other. In contrast to individual human rights, the Soviet Union championed the collective "right of self-determination," which implicitly included wholesale rejection of the colonizer's legal, political, and cultural norms. The Declaration on the Granting of Independence to Colonial Countries and Peoples, proposed at the UN by Nikita Khrushchev in 1960, stated baldly that self-determination was not only an absolute human right, but a superseding one. Amilcar Cabral, a Guinean anti-imperialist (and covert agent of Czechoslovak state security) crowed, "The colonial system ... is now an international crime."[33]

What the Soviets had done, in fact, was dust off and update Xenophon's definition of law as the will of the state. If the primary right of all peoples was self-determination, this was tantamount to declaring that no law could exist that subordinated locality. In the guise of deferring to local custom (and in contrast to centuries of Western meddling under the banner of "civilization"), the Soviets were openly challenging the basis for all human rights—natural law. Its precepts, along with several centuries of Western liberalism, were collectively labeled imperialist oppression. Rejection of human rights was thus recast as an act of nationalism, even patriotism. Nuremberg might never have happened. From this admixture of anti-imperialism, positivism, and rejection of Western values came the germination of cultural relativism.

To the extent that the United States or any Western power could still claim to be invested in human rights, it was only in opposition to the perceived authoritarianism and brutality of their Soviet counterparts. Thus natural law was bound up in a kind of package deal along with democratic government, free speech, and free market economy, peddled to the postcolonial world with the same brio as Coca-Cola and Chryslers. The sales pitch was brilliantly on display at the 1964 World's Fair, where visitors passed through the General Foods Arch along United Nations Avenue to see Japan, Austria, and Seven-Up.

◆ ◆ ◆

Having returned, so to speak, to the fair, it is a fitting point to pause and consider in sum the two decades that preceded it. They began with enormous promise, embodied by the late President Roosevelt's efforts to secure universal law under a United Nations. In the early postwar years, the Truman administration and its State Department seemed genuinely committed to fulfilling Roosevelt's vision—none more than his wife. With her trademark tenacity, earnestness, and sense of duty, Eleanor devoted herself to the cause of human rights. But while she certainly shared her husband's passion, it is arguable that she lacked his political acumen. The same might be said of the Human Rights Commission itself, composed as it was primarily of scholars and jurists. Its achievements were titanic and world-altering, but so too were its mistakes.

In hindsight, there were three principal faults. First, instead of narrowing its focus to those rights universally agreed upon between cultures—rights that also, correspondingly, had centuries of precedent, application, and evolution in every nation's laws—the committee chose instead a broad list of "rights" that were in fact culturally specific norms:

democratic government, presumption of innocence, right to join trade unions, etc. In other words, rather than tackle the admittedly difficult question of what constitutes a universal right, they deferred to each ideological conception and incorporated the whole lot within the document. This is not to suggest such goals are not laudable, or that the world wouldn't be better if they were universally adopted. But the world of 1948 was not one where such a list could ever be realized; nor, for that matter, is ours today.

For the committee members that was immaterial. The declaration was meant to be aspirational, a foundation rather than a blood oath. But a foundation must be built upon solid ground, and the declaration was not. The lack of consensus within committee meetings should have been a warning for how the document would be received internationally. In fact, its trajectory mirrored the tribulations of its drafting, split into two covenants, one "democratic" and one "socialist," that withered on the vine for decades until their relevancy was moot. The inclusion of expressly political elements into the document guaranteed this outcome; it was, in effect, terming a host of rights "universal" that were not universal at all, nor likely to be. Mrs. Roosevelt compared the Universal Declaration of Human Rights to the Magna Carta, the Declaration of the Rights of Man, and the US Constitution. But a code, constitution, or charter does not allow its signatories to pick and choose which provisions they wish to follow. The declaration was drafted with the full knowledge that states would do exactly that. The fact that it was signed by nearly every nation in 1948 was not evidence of its acceptance but its impotence.

This leads us to the second fault, lack of enforcement. Mrs. Mehta was correct: declarations are words on paper, but laws are a combination of word and force. The simple truth was that there were far too many provisions in the declaration for any kind of enforcement mechanism. How could the international community or any of its members *force* a state to provide paid medical leave? The proposed remedy was to transform the unenforceable declaration into a series of treaties or covenants. But states could still choose whether to sign—choose, in effect, whether these "universal" rights applied to them. Clearly those states that signed the covenant were already in compliance with its provisions or expected soon to be. This meant that the covenants were not an impetus to further progress but yardsticks for how far each state had already come. Moreover, they listed no penalties for states that fall short—in other words, no enforcement.

Third, and most fatal, was the lack of differentiation between rights. A code of laws, as discussed above, requires equal compliance. This means that whether the law against murder is No. 1 or No. 2339, it is still enforced. Differentiation exists not within the code but in the penalties applied for breach—hence the difference in prison sentences, for example, between first-degree murder and involuntary manslaughter. But without enforcement, all we have left is the words. And here words were the problem. Nowhere in the Universal Declaration of Human Rights is it stated or implied that the right to life is more fundamental than the right to patents and royalties. This would not matter if the declaration were law, but it is not law. Stripped to its essence, it is a statement by the community of nations that there are certain things it must do and others it must not. The list was already too long, too controversial, and too divorced from geopolitical reality. Compounding these failings was a conspicuous moral vacuum. If states would ultimately choose which rights to uphold, what was to prevent a state from claiming the right to unemployment insurance trumped the right not to be tortured? Some logical division would be helpful, and William Blackstone's eighteenth-century distinction between "rights" and "liberties" is as sensible as any:

> For the principal aim of society is to protect individuals in the enjoyment of those absolute rights, which were vested in them by the immutable laws of nature, but which could not be preserved in peace without that mutual assistance and intercourse which is gained by the institution of friendly and social communities. Hence it follows, that the first and primary end of human laws is to maintain and regulate these absolute rights of individuals.... And, therefore, the principal view of human laws is, or ought always to be, to explain, protect, and enforce such rights as are absolute, which in themselves are few and simple: and then such rights as are relative, which, arising from a variety of connections, will be far more numerous and more complicated.... Thus much for the declaration of our rights and liberties.[34]

In sum, the abandonment of natural law principles for a catchall list with no enforcement mechanism left the Universal Declaration permanently crippled—broad and shallow rather than narrow and deep. The goodwill and fervor that led to its creation dissipated quickly in the wake of Cold War realities. Less than a decade after the destruction of Nazism, the world was consumed once again by a political, military, and ideological tug-of-war that subordinated all else. Even philosophic constructs of right, law, and duty were passed through its narrow prism. At the World's Fair, visitors tripped happily from the UNICEF Pavilion (sponsored by Pepsi) humming its irritating signature theme: *"It's a small world after all..."* Across from them rose the glittering striated hubcap of Progressland.

Yet what no one realized was that the Carousel of Progress had done a complete revolution and was back at the beginning once again.

— 8 —

THE LAST CRUSADE

In March 1975, a State Department official filed a brief regarding the rapidly developing situation in Cambodia. The pro-American yet corrupt and incompetent Lon Nol regime had fallen to the hands of rebels calling themselves the Khmer Rouge (KR). In a remarkably short time the rebels seized control of the country's limited resources, arms, and governmental apparatus. The last stronghold was the capital city, Phnom Penh. "The Communists," the official warned, "are waging a total war against Cambodia's civilian population with a degree of systematic terror unparalleled since the Nazi period—a clear precursor of the blood bath and Stalinist dictatorship they intend to impose on the Cambodian people."[1]

This time the warning was not too late. The capital had not fallen; American forces still could intervene and prevent what President Gerald Ford correctly predicted as a "massacre." US military commanders had extensive familiarity with the terrain, a legacy of the 1970 invasion during the Vietnam War. Nor could they claim to be unaware of the severity of Khmer Rouge tactics; in these final days, journalists and American envoys remained to witness the bloodshed themselves.

But the State Department memo disappeared into a void. After Vietnam, after Watergate, the American people had been lied to once too often. They had been cajoled into believing the Vietnam War was a humanitarian mission, not an exercise in cold realpolitik. The disillusionment of the early 1970s, coupled with the stunning downfall of President Nixon, ingrained a cynicism into the American mind that remains to this day. Even NGOs like Amnesty International refused to believe the worst. As Samantha Power writes: "To the extent that the apocalyptic warnings of US government officials were sincere, many Americans believed they stemmed from the Ford administration's anti-Communist paranoia or its desire to get congressional backing for an $82 million aid package for the Lon Nol regime."[2]

In early April, the Khmer Rouge began evacuating Phnom Penh. Ultimately the entire city, millions of inhabitants, were forced out of their homes and sent on death marches into the countryside. Embassies were abandoned. Prince Sirak Matak was offered a seat on an American evacuation plane but chose instead to remain with his people. He wrote to the US ambassador: "As for you and in particular your great country, I never believed for a moment that you would [abandon] a people which had chosen liberty.... If I shall die here on this spot in my country that I love...I have only committed the mistake of believing in you, the Americans."[3] Before the letter reached Washington, Matak was dead.

The pace of the genocide quickened past all comprehension in the weeks and months that followed. The Khmer Rouge ordered the execution of all military personnel down to the rank of lieutenant "and their wives and children." Clerics of every faith—Buddhists, Hindus, Christians, Muslims, Jews—were targeted as "class enemies." So too were those the KR considered intellectuals: writers, artists, journalists, academics, and indeed anyone with an education or even, incredibly, persons who wore glasses. Industrialists, aristocrats, farm owners, bureaucrats, schoolteachers...the list went on and on. Disloyalty was punishable by instant death and could take virtually any form; even the tiniest infraction of KR law—flirting, praying, reading, reminiscing— meant execution. "To keep you is no gain," the Khmer Rouge told its people, "to kill you is no loss."[4]

This genocide, the greatest since 1945, played out against a worldwide backdrop of disbelief and indifference. Nightly news programs devoted it scant attention, as did most American and European newspapers. By 1976, only fragmentary reports emerged of life and death within Cambodia; the KR had effectively shut down all contact with the outside world. In a move that has come to be axiomatic of impending atrocity, journalists and foreigners were expelled. But even the momentary glimpses that emerged were enough to horrify those who still bothered to pay attention. By early 1978, the administration of President Jimmy Carter had assembled enough evidence to spark an impassioned declaration, three years exactly since the fall of Phnom Penh: "America cannot avoid the responsibility to speak out in condemnation of the Cambodian government, the worst violator of human rights in the world today.... It is an obligation of every member of the international community to protest the policies of this or any nation which cruelly and systematically violates the right of its people to enjoy life and basic human dignities."[5]

This Grotian response, belated as it was, seemed to herald a new age. The Carter administration was in many ways better positioned to take up the banner of human rights than its predecessors: untarnished by the legacies of Vietnam or Watergate, it could (and did) reassert the image of the United States as a moral force. Carter's declaration drew prominent allies, some more expected than others. Democratic senator and former presidential candidate George McGovern came out boldly in favor of military intervention to stop what he described as a "genocide." McGovern, with his strong sense of duty, correctly understood Cambodia's predicament as a direct outgrowth of US presence and policy in Southeast Asia. The United States had a moral obligation to help. Moreover, he argued, such intervention would be swift and effective: the KR, despite their ferocity, were weak. Conservative commentator William F. Buckley agreed. Channeling the internationalist voice that still held some currency in the Republican Party, Buckley urged the president to assemble a coalition of neighbor states and intervene under US command.[6]

In the end, nothing came of these plans. It was Vietnam, not the United States, that finally invaded Cambodia, and its motives were anything but humanitarian. Just as McGovern predicted, the Khmer Rouge collapsed and fled. By that time, however, the Carter administration had done another about-face and condemned the Vietnamese for violating state sovereignty. The opportunity to reestablish the United States as preeminent defender of natural law principles and redress decades of stagnancy had come and gone before anyone was fully aware of the fact.

◆ ◆ ◆

Cambodia demonstrated that, in spite of the Nuremberg Principles and the repeated pledge "Never forget, and never again," a state could employ a policy of unlimited destruction against its own citizens as the international community stood idly by. On the one hand it was a colossal failure of diplomacy and international law, a refutation of the principle of progress that underlay the Nuremberg Tribunal. On the other, it was a wake-up call. The Carter administration was not singly responsible for American failure to intervene—causes extended all the way back to the Johnson and Nixon eras—but it was the first to receive a complete, devastating account of the atrocity. "The drama of human rights," wrote historian Samuel Moyn, "is that they emerged in the 1970s seemingly from nowhere."[7] Not from nowhere: from Cambodia.

The Cambodian genocide also coincided with a proliferation of NGOs. Amnesty International had been founded in the early 1960s but remained for over a decade a lone voice for human rights outside the usual government channels. For nearly thirty years, the dialog of rights had been consumed by the Cold War. Then, in 1978, a new organization was founded in New York City to ensure the Soviet Union obeyed the protocols of the Helsinki Accords. Helsinki Watch, as it was originally known, broadened its mandate and was retitled Human Rights Watch. It now has several thousand members and an annual budget of over $75 million.

These developments came in accordance with a renewed commitment from the Carter administration. Indeed, author and activist Stephen Hopgood describes Jimmy Carter's inauguration as "the turning point."[8] In 1978, Carter directed the State Department to begin publishing annual "country reports" detailing the human rights record of nations receiving US assistance. Congress later amended this list to include nearly all major states. The president also created the office of assistant secretary of state for human rights, ostensibly to oversee the creation and dissemination of these reports. The State Department complied reluctantly. Still staffed with holdovers from the Nixon and Ford administrations, it regarded such compilations as a distraction at best, or at worst imperiling valuable international relationships. This was particularly the case when President Carter openly criticized numerous Latin American dictators who had allied themselves with the United States, including Augusto Pinochet of Chile, Romeo Lucas Garcia of Guatemala, Anastasio Somoza in Nicaragua, and the right-wing death squads in Argentina. It must be admitted, however, that despite Carter's condemnation, US aid continued (for the most part) to flow to these countries. Nevertheless, the backlash among Republicans in Congress was fierce.[9]

In many ways, President Carter's position was untenable. As long as the United States remained locked in global combat with the Soviet Union it could not abandon its rightist allies; the best Carter could hope for was to use what diplomatic pressure he had to curb their worst excesses. It is interesting to speculate what the ultimate results might have been had the American electorate granted him a second term. As it was, however, the now-former president channeled his energies and global vision into an NGO of his own, the Carter Center. Founded just as he left office, it expounds "a fundamental commitment to human rights and the alleviation of human suffering...to prevent and resolve conflicts, enhance freedom and democracy, and improve health."[10] Thus it may certainly be said that Jimmy Carter has done more as an ex-president to promote human rights than the vast majority of his peers achieved while in office—including himself.

Ronald Reagan's election in 1980 was a victory for those within his party who regarded Carter's emphasis on human rights as naïve, wrongheaded, and antithetical to American interests. Acolytes of Henry Kissinger and Dean Acheson, their foreign policy could best be summed up as, "He may be a scumbag, but at least he's *our* scumbag." Jeane Kirkpatrick, chosen by President Reagan to represent the United States at the United Nations, was vociferous in her condemnation of Carter's foreign policy as responsible for the replacement of the corrupt Somoza and Shah of Iran with the infinitely worse Sandinistas and Ayatollah Khomeini. Under the "Kirkpatrick doctrine," the United States would willingly align itself with established dictatorships on the assumption that "traditional authoritarian governments are less repressive than revolutionary autocracies." Accordingly, President Reagan assumed office under a mandate to abandon human rights in favor of cold-eyed self-interest. The State Department's country reports became parodic, obviously weighted in favor of "friendly" nations and unnecessarily harsh toward leftist or revolutionary ones. The administration also turned a blind eye to atrocity whenever convenient, as in the case of a US-trained military force in El Salvador that brutally slaughtered over a thousand civilians in December 1981. Testifying before Congress, administration officials blithely denied the validity of the victims' accounts.[11]

But Reagan went further. In a speech before the British Parliament in June 1982, just as that nation emerged victorious from the Falklands War, he called for an international "crusade of democracy." The choice of words is revealing. A crusade, by definition and practice, is a holy war waged against an infidel enemy. The United States was thus pledging itself to spreading democracy around the world by any means necessary. As Human Rights Watch founder Aryeh Neier later recalled:

> Reagan equated advances in the direction of electoral democracy with human rights.... Whatever the initial inspiration for the speech, the way forward that it enunciated has had a profound impact. In the three decades since that speech, every American administration has committed itself in significant measure to the promotion of democracy on the international stage. Also, though the extent to which the promotion of democracy with the promotion of human rights has varied to some degree, in general the two are not distinguished by those who have spoken for the US government in the period since Reagan's address at Westminster. [*Note: Neier wrote these words in 2012, prior to the election of Donald Trump.*][12]

The conflation of human rights with Western democratic values did not originate with Ronald Reagan, but never had the ideological battle between democracy and communism been recast in such Manichaean terms. Reagan's natural law philosophy was very simple: for people to enjoy their natural rights to life and property, they must first be free; for them to be free, they must enjoy democratic government. Ironically, by predicating all other rights on the establishment of a particular form of government, his views matched exactly those of the communist delegation at the Human Rights Commission in 1948.

Like any good salesman, Reagan passionately believed his own pitch. In his inaugural address, the president invoked John Winthrop's depiction of America as a "shining city on a hill," a beacon and a model for peoples around the world. He returned to this image again in his farewell address eight years later: "I've spoken of the shining city all my political life, but I don't know if I ever quite communicated what I saw when I said it. But in my mind it was a tall, proud city built on rocks stronger than oceans, wind-swept, God-blessed, and teeming with people of all kinds living in harmony and peace; a city with free ports that hummed with commerce and creativity."[13] Or, as historian Nicolas Guilhot has written, Reaganite "human rights were primarily based on a set of values embedded in existing national political institutions and legal structures, of which the United States were at once the best historical example and the model."[14]

If the United States had at least been consistent in its objectives, this politicized definition of human rights might have produced dividends. During his second term, Reagan echoed the language of his Democratic predecessor by condemning human rights abuses in Haiti, Chile, and the Philippines. Moreover, his administration was quick to trumpet any incremental advances in US-allied nations toward democracy, however halting or illusory. Yet Reagan, while condemning human rights abuses in Grenada and using them as a justification for armed invasion, pointedly ignored them in South Africa—ultimately provoking Congress to pass sanctions against the apartheid regime over the president's veto. Thus the legacy of the Reagan era for natural law and human rights is twofold. First, his "crusade for democracy" was both the logical successor to Cold War containment theory and an evolution. It was not enough to protect democracy where it existed; the United States must henceforth place itself at the fore of a global democratic movement. This bound the United States to an internationalist foreign policy even as it recast objectives in starkly moralistic terms. Reagan's view of the United States' place in the world was a unique fusion of natural law, Western liberalism, and tub-thumping patriotism combined with even greater abstractions of Duty, Honor, and Right. Fittingly, it was best expressed at the unveiling of a restored Statue of Liberty on July 3, 1986:

> For love of liberty, our forebears—colonists, few in number and with little to defend themselves—fought a war for independence with what was then the world's most powerful empire. For love of liberty, those who came before us tamed a vast wilderness and braved hardships which, at times, were beyond the limits of human endurance. For love of liberty, a bloody and heart-wrenching civil war was fought. And for love of liberty, Americans championed and still champion, even in times of peril, the cause of human freedom in far-off lands.
>
> "The God who gave us life," Thomas Jefferson once proclaimed, "gave us liberty at the same time."... We are the keepers of the flame of liberty. We hold it high tonight for the world to see, a beacon of hope, a light unto the nations.[15]

Second, while Reagan's full-throated rejection of isolationism was laudable, in other respects his democratic view of human rights was deeply flawed. The ethical mandate of a "crusade" required consistency in application, but consistency was impossible. The United States could not champion democracy as the harbinger of human rights and at the same time turn a blind eye to abuses in democratic or protodemocratic nations. The charge levied by Ambassador Kirkpatrick against Jimmy Carter could apply equally to her boss: a foreign policy predicated on moral absolutes was bound to be undone by the essential amorality of statecraft. Moreover, the conflation of rights and democracy reinforced postcolonial suspicions that "human rights" were simply neoimperialism writ large—a charge often made by the Soviet Union which in the Reagan years had more than a kernel of truth.

❖ ❖ ❖

But suddenly everything changed. The Berlin Wall came down, and the Soviet Union collapsed under the weight of its own bloated bureaucracy. Geopolitical realities that had defined human rights discourse for decades evaporated. These events were viewed, not without merit, as a triumph of democracy generally—and specifically of the policies of

Presidents Reagan and George H. W. Bush. The "crusade for democracy" had, figuratively speaking, reached Jerusalem.

Contemporary observers, many of whom could not remember a world before the Cold War, were quick to assign messianic properties to the moment. Political scientist Francis Fukuyama famously termed it an "end of history," even as others—notably Henry Kissinger—cautioned that a unipolar world was an unsustainable model. But this was dismissed as so much carping. Victory in the West opened a clear path for the ultimate triumph of Western rights. As Peter Stearns describes it, "The collapse of communism and the advances of global capitalism without question reduced attention to social and economic rights. These rights had never secured an absolutely fixed place on the human rights agenda, but now they definitely trailed off."[16] For a brief moment it seemed as though the celestial clock had been turned back to 1945; once again the United States had triumphed over its ideological foes. But this time there was no other superpower sharing the stage; by 1990 it looked as though the United States would enjoy many decades of unchallenged hegemony. The opportunity to finally implement its vision of global justice had never seemed so close.

Yet, as is so often the case, the signal traces of a countervailing force were already there for those who could see them. In the same week in June 1989 when Poland held its first democratic elections in half a century, tanks rolled into Beijing's Tiananmen Square. Over a thousand democratic protestors were massacred. Even as the Soviet Union fell, China began its slow but steady rise as both market competitor and ideological foil to the West. This was not Maoist China, hidebound in its own political philosophies, but a nimble authoritarian regime that embraced the less controversial aspects of capitalism while still maintaining an iron grip on its people.

It was not long after that a warning came that would reverberate in the years to come. A conference of Asian states including China, Malaysia, Indonesia, and Singapore produced a startling critique of Western rights in an article entitled "Asia's Different Standard." "Many East and Southeast Asians" it began, "tend to look askance at the starkly individualistic ethos of the West in which authority tends to be seen as oppressive and rights are an individual's 'trump' over the state." It then went on to lay out its indictment with devastating candor:

> The hard core of rights that are truly universal is smaller than many in the West are wont to pretend.... It is not only pretentious but wrong to insist that everything has been settled once and forever. The Universal Declaration is not a tablet Moses brought down from the mountain. It was drafted by mortals. All international norms must evolve through continuing debate among different points of view if consensus is to be maintained.[17]

The plea for recognition of communitarian values echoed Dr. Chang and others at the drafting of the Universal Declaration. But there was also something new. In direct contrast to the Reagan model, which predicated all other rights on democratic government, the article argued the reverse: "Order and stability [are] preconditions for economic growth, and growth is the necessary foundation for any political order that advances human dignity." Freedom of the press, democratic elections, the right to political protest—these might be laudable, but they were not universal. This language was practically guaranteed to raise a storm of protest in the West, from human rights NGOs to neocon internationalists.

But it was not, ultimately, a rejection of *all* human rights. The proposition that the list of universal rights was "smaller" not only reaffirmed that such essential rights exist but was in fact correct. What, then, were "universal" rights in Asia? Life, liberty, and property, wrote Singaporean diplomat Bilahari Kausikan, speaking for the conference. Assaults on the essential life, freedom, or security of the person—as typified by genocide, slavery, or torture—were necessarily criminal regardless of the politics of the state undertaking them. "The West has a legitimate right and moral duty to promote those core human rights."[18]

Far from a relativist justification for tyranny, this was a reasoned and necessary corrective to decades of Western liberalism; better still, it was based entirely on the principles of natural law. Had it been heeded, the consensus that eluded the drafters in 1948 might actually have been reached and a genuinely universal law emerge as a result.

It was not heeded. The fall of communism was universally accepted as the triumph of Western democratic values, a neat syllogism that was not, in fact, true. Yet it had an attractive simplicity and a great deal of political mileage. Having "won" the Cold War, the United States saw its success as a moral mandate to continue the crusade until the whole world was democratized. "Flushed with victory," as Justice Jackson would have said, few realized the extraordinary opportunity available to them. For the first time in almost fifty years (or, arguably, almost eighty) there was no enemy, no competing ideology, no geopolitical necessity to peddle democracy around the world. In victory, the United States was liberated. It could finally engage with the community of nations in a real dialog about natural and universal law with no political blinkers on any side.

Inasmuch as it was perceived at all, it remained a dream of academics. There was virtually no support for a nuanced view of human rights in any governmental quarter. Neoconservatives saw the triumph of Reagan's crusade for democracy laying the political and diplomatic groundwork for events up to the Second Iraq War. Liberals saw a golden opportunity to translate American hegemony into global change—social, political, economic—a benign *Pax Americana* spreading democracy, human rights, and Coca-Cola throughout the world. The result was a masterpiece of perversity. The exact moment when the United States was most able to bring workable universal law into reality, it was least inclined to do so.

Nor, indeed, were other Western powers. The 1993 Vienna Declaration and Programme of Action, quoted earlier in this book, was a recommitment to the principles of the Universal Declaration, a kind of "amen" at the end of the 1948 prayer. "Invoking the spirit of our age," it began, "and the realities of our time which call upon the peoples of the world and all States Members of the United Nations to rededicate themselves to the global task of promoting and protecting all human rights and fundamental freedoms so as to secure full and universal enjoyment of these rights." The opportunity was there, but the next passages squandered it. "All human rights are universal, indivisible and interdependent and interrelated. The international community must treat human rights globally in a fair and equal manner, on the same footing, and with the same emphasis."[19] "All human rights" meant all provisions of the Universal Declaration.

Incredibly, the international community was stating that *every* right was equal and codependent—the right to life and the right to royalties, freedom from torture and freedom of cultural expression. It was as though they had learned nothing from the forty-five-year trajectory of the Universal Declaration; or, more likely, they regarded the fall of communism as an opportunity to undo several decades of stalemate. There is an almost mystical connection invoked between the 1948 and 1993 declarations, as though drafters of the latter were willfully trying to erase the intervening time.

But by ignoring past errors they were condemned to repeat them. The global community was no closer to adopting all thirty provisions of the Universal Declaration than it had been in 1948, and not even a unipolar US could compel it to do so (not to mention, of course, its own reservations about several articles). Article 8 of the Vienna Declaration compounded the folly:

> Democracy, development and respect for human rights and fundamental freedoms are interdependent and mutually reinforcing. Democracy is based on the freely expressed will of the people to determine their own political, economic, social and cultural systems and their full participation in all aspects of their lives. In the context of the above, the promotion and protection of human rights and fundamental freedoms at the national and international levels should be universal and conducted without conditions attached. The international community should support the strengthening and promoting of democracy, development and respect for human rights and fundamental freedoms in the entire world.[20]

Once again, overconfidence and a politicized vision of rights had won out. By the end of the decade, observers spoke of the so-called "global-ization era" as one of retrenchment rather than progress. As Michael Ignatieff described it, this neoimperialism was not "built on colonies, conquest and the white man's burden" but was instead "a global hegemony whose grace notes are free markets, human rights and democracy, en-forced by the most awesome military power the world has ever known."[21]

❖ ❖ ❖

Nevertheless, the "unipolar moment," lasting from 1991 to 2008, saw significant advances in one field of international law: accountability. The year of the Vienna Declaration also saw the establishment of the first international tribunal since Nuremberg: the International Criminal

Tribunal for Yugoslavia. Created to adjudicate crimes committed during the Yugoslav wars, it ultimately tried a total of 161 defendants from 1993 to 2017, ranging from head of state Slobodan Milosevic to ordinary soldiers and members of the security services. The UN was justly proud of its success, boasting that the tribunal "irreversibly changed the landscape of international humanitarian law, provided victims an opportunity to voice the horrors they witnessed and experienced, and proved that those suspected of bearing the greatest responsibility for atrocities committed during armed conflicts can be called to account."[22]

Success in adjudicating the crimes of Yugoslavia was coupled with colossal failure to stem genocide in Rwanda, occurring less than a year after the Vienna Declaration. The response of the international community, including the United States, Belgium, France, and the UN itself, has been the subject of widespread condemnation. The Canadian general leading the UN peacekeeping force, Romeo Dallaire, accused his employers of willful and cynical disregard of the unfolding crisis. In a speech delivered in Kigali four years after the massacre, President Bill Clinton admitted, "The international community, together with nations in Africa, must bear its share of responsibility for this tragedy, as well. We did not act quickly enough after the killing began." General Dallaire's response twenty years later is succinct: "Most of that is crap. A month before the genocide, [Clinton] produced a presidential directive that stated that the United States will not engage in any humanitarian operation, unless it's in its self-interest. He had instructed his staff…not to tell him what the hell was going on."[23]

It became a truism of the 1990s and early 2000s that nations that failed to prevent atrocities proved much more adept at adjudicating them. The International Criminal Tribunal for Rwanda was established only a few months after the genocide ended and remained in operation until December 31, 2015. In 1997, the Cambodian government formally requested UN assistance in creating a tribunal for the crimes of the Khmer Rouge; first convened in 2003, it exists to this day. The Special Court for Sierra Leone was established in 2002, in the aftermath of a bloody civil war resulting in thousands of civilian deaths. Nearly thirty defendants have been tried under its auspices, including former Liberian president Charles Taylor.

Most famous, and with arguably the most lasting impact, was the creation of an International Criminal Court in 2002. The court represented the fulfillment of a promise made during the Roosevelt administration, but the horrors of ethnic cleansing in the 1990s gave new urgency to the project. As M. Cherif Bassiouni has written: "If the lessons of the past are to instruct the course of the future, then the creation of a permanent system of international criminal justice with a continuous institutional memory is imperative."[24] The "institutional memory" to which Bassiouni referred is a combination of foundational law, in this case the Nuremberg Principles (given concrete form as the Rome Statute of 1999) and case law. Bassiouni correctly understood that individual tribunals convened for a specific set of offenses would never have the same weight in precedent as the decisions of a sitting judicial body.

President Clinton, himself a graduate of Yale Law School, agreed. Haunted perhaps by the memory of Rwanda, he pushed especially hard for a permanent international tribunal for war crimes and crimes against humanity. Yet, predictably, his internationalist zeal ran headlong into isolationist opposition. Old fears of surrendering American sovereignty, nearly identical in form and content to those of 1919 and 1945, rose once again. As a result, under the presidency of George W. Bush the United States declined to recognize the court it helped establish. To this date it remains something of an orphan on the international scene, with fifteen cases "under investigation" yet none resolved. Scholarly opinion on the tribunal—indeed, all tribunals—is mixed. Human Rights Watch founder Aryeh Neier has been optimistic: "Augusto Pinochet and Slobodan Milosevic are symbols of the cruelty and barbarity of the last third of the twentieth century, but they also inspired the most significant advances in international accountability for the authors of great crimes."[25] His fellow activist Stephen Hopgood disagreed. "International criminal tribunals," he wrote dismissively, "are grand ritualized spectacles that symbolize authority and power by dramatizing the archetypal myth of the hero defeating existential threats to the community."[26] That is a harsh judgment, surely. If civilization is once again the complaining party at the bar, it was not the prosecutors but the defendants who put it there.

Still and all, the list of former heads of state tried since 1990 of crimes against their citizens is growing. Milosevic and Taylor join the likes of

Jean Kambanda of Rwanda, Jorge Videla of Argentina, Alberto Fujimori of Peru, Khieu Samphan of Cambodia, and, of course, Saddam Hussein of Iraq. Add to this list of luminaries the hundreds of other lesser-rank individuals who worked for them, also successfully tried by the same tribunals. Indeed, if one wishes to find evidence of Dr. Peabody's "upward path" of social progress, the accountability for international crimes may be the best evidence available. Prosecutor David Crane opened his remarks at the 2004 Sierra Leone tribunal by invoking the "sober and steady climb upwards towards the towering summit of justice."[27]

◆ ◆ ◆

For all these successes, it remains indisputable that the great powers—Russia, China, and the United States—are effectively immune from international justice. This is troubling given the brutal treatment of minorities in the former two countries—homosexuals in Russia, numerous ethnic and religious sects in China—but the United States itself is likewise tainted. This was especially the case following the events of September 11, 2001. Al Qaeda was an enemy unique in the American experience: lacking any state authority or territory, recognizable military force, or—crucially—codes of conduct.[28] It was impervious to all the usual measures undertaken to chastise a state: shaming, sanctions, etc. The word most commonly (if controversially) used to describe Al Qaeda's nature and methods was "barbaric." Barbarism, by this understanding, meant not playing by the rules. In previous centuries a barbaric enemy was presumed not to comprehend "civilized" war; here, however, it was the terrorist organization's knowledge of the limitations of conventional warfare and diplomacy that made it so formidable a foe.

War with a barbaric enemy brought out the barbarism in ourselves. Less than a week after the attacks, Vice President Dick Cheney was typically unsparing in his assessment of this new form of conflict. "It is a mean, dangerous, dirty business out there, and we have to operate in that arena...sort of on the dark side, if you will."[29] What Cheney meant by "dirty business" was not yet clear, but it is certain the vast majority of Americans would have supported striking back at Al Qaeda by any means. The United States, which had not experienced a territorial invasion or attack since 1812, had grown complacent. From this complacency it critiqued other nations on the directed use of torture, suspension of civil liberties, and absence of due process—nations like Israel and the United Kingdom, which had been combating terrorist organizations for decades.

The US response to direct attack was no different; indeed, not having become accustomed to this kind of warfare, it was arguably worse. A 2006 report listed nearly one hundred deaths in US extralegal prison camps, of which at least thirty-four were probable homicides. Strangulation, asphyxia, and blunt-force injuries were cited as causes.[30] Prisoner abuse was graphically revealed in the circulation of the Abu Ghraib photographs, but it was much more common than anyone knew—in fact, more than we may ever know. Consumed by its War on Terror, and ultimately by Afghanistan and Iraq, the United States disengaged from the global dialog on human rights. Even before its own abuses were revealed, the Bush administration adopted the position that the promotion of rights was a luxury enjoyed in peacetime but a distraction during war. To the extent that it mentioned them at all, it did so in the familiar refrain of spreading democracy and liberty; fundamentalist regimes were a convenient stand-in for the "red menace" of the Comintern. This fierce retrenching filtered its way through American society, even academia. A 2006 study titled "Forging a World of Liberty under Law" by Princeton scholars G. John Ikenberry and Anne-Marie Slaughter reads as if it could have emerged intact from archaic debates over the Bricker Amendment: "The basic objective of US strategy must be to protect the American people and the American way of life. This overarching goal should comprise three more specific aims: 1) a secure homeland...2) a healthy global economy...and 3) a benign international environment grounded in security cooperation among nations and the spread of liberal democracy."[31] There was no mention of natural rights at all.

Marcus Tullius Cicero declared, "The security of the people is the highest law." He wrote these words as a former consul who, during the Catiline conspiracy, suspended Roman law and ruthlessly pursued the conspirators. Little has changed. As a Supreme Court justice wrote, challenges to our rights rarely occur in times of placidity. The American response to 9/11 illustrated (or reaffirmed) that no nation is immune from passions that may trump fundamental liberties in the name of collective security. This extends even to the presidency of Barack Obama and his decision to summarily execute Osama Bin Laden. It was the exact opposite of Nuremberg: instead of "staying the hand of vengeance," the United States allowed itself the pleasure of an assassination. Few would argue Bin Laden didn't deserve it; then again, few would have argued Goering or Kaltenbrunner didn't either. But the decision—made by a former University of Chicago law professor—transformed what might have been the most significant trial of the century (and an ennobling end to the War on Terror) into a squalid little scuffle in the dark. A trial, wrote human rights barrister Geoffrey Robertson, "would have been the best way of demystifying this man, debunking his cause and de-brainwashing his followers. In the dock he would have been reduced in stature...as a hateful and hate-filled old man, screaming from the dock or lying from the witness box."[32]

The legacy of 9/11 for American engagement in rights is profound. From Carter to Clinton, the United States spent over two decades reestablishing its position as global exemplar and authority; in eight years this legacy was undone. The American people themselves would come to feel a sense of shame for Abu Ghraib and other abuses, as well as outrage at the Bush administration for allowing them to continue. This reflects a curious duality: even as the government pursued its policies, donations poured into organizations like the ACLU at an unprecedented rate. A similar phenomenon occurred in the 1980s, leading to the establishment of several human rights watchdogs for the American government. Partly this can be accounted for by the partisanship of the electorate, but it also reminds us that not all understandings of rights emerge from governments. In present day America it is most often NGOs, corporations, or even individuals who have carried the torch after the Trump administration laid it down.

The last decade has witnessed the most abrupt about-face on human rights in American history, from pragmatic engagement and cautious optimism to near-complete rejection. As with most historical phenomena, its roots lie deep. In 2002, President Bush's UN ambassador (and Donald Trump's future national security adviser), John Bolton, formally withdrew the United States from the International Criminal Court, which he described as "my happiest moment at State."[33] Three years later, a global summit convened by the UN unanimously declared a "responsibility to protect" peoples in imminent danger from their governments for crimes against humanity. Hitherto the only convention to have a so-called "trigger mechanism" was the Genocide Convention of 1948, which pledged signatories to intervene once a genocide was formally recognized to have begun. The reluctance of states to do so is illustrated by the fact that neither Cambodia, Rwanda, Yugoslavia, nor any major atrocity until the Sudan was formally declared a genocide by the United Nations. Not surprisingly, this new responsibility to protect, or "R2P," came under withering fire from Asian, African, and Middle Eastern nations who regarded it as an open license for Western states to launch preemptive wars in the name of humanity—as, indeed, the United States was then doing in Iraq.[34]

The aftermath of the Iraq War accelerated a process that had been underway for some time: the concurrent rise of non-Western views of human rights (or lack thereof) and the decline of American hegemony. Syria, China, Brazil, Russia, Myanmar, and countless other states openly defied US warnings and pursued brutal and criminal policies against their own citizens. "American influence is weakening," Stephen Hopgood cautioned. "The distribution of power in the international system is shifting from unipolarity to multipolarity, and the institutions that are built on liberal hegemony are fatally at risk.... Our world will finally kill the European dream."[35] Hopgood wrote these words in 2013, at a time when—contrary to his pessimistic views—it appeared that the United States under President Obama was attempting to recapture some measure of moral authority it enjoyed during the Clinton years. But Hopgood must be credited as among the first scholars to sound the warning bell for the rise of neonationalism and fragmenting of traditional liberal institutions, which became all too apparent by decade's end.

Respect for natural rights had always been predicated on some overarching ideal of civilization, from Grotius and Blackstone to Wilson and FDR. Yet a condescending paternalism lay at the heart of the mission: if some states must "civilize" others, how was this any different from good old-fashioned nineteenth-century imperialism? President Clinton had been able to chart a narrow path, asserting America's engagement in human rights without overemphasizing its raw power post–Cold War. President Obama was forced to navigate a very different geopolitical reality: a resurgent Russia and China that frequently aligned themselves with criminal regimes and themselves engaged in criminal conduct against their citizens. "In other words," Hopgood declared, "the last great hope for humanist internationalism is an illusion. The United States, democratic, liberal, and successor to the great heritage of Western enlightenment, has avoided becoming embroiled in alliances and commitments that would restrain it.... R2P is a meaningless doctrine without US support, and the ICC is a European vanity project."[36]

This was not entirely fair. The European Union, Organization of American States (OAS), African Union, and Association of Southeast Asian Nations would certainly take umbrage at the United States as "the last great hope" for human rights and be right to do so. Even as America's voice on the international stage began to fade, others came forward. Globalization and the interlocking of nations' economic, social, and even political structures has introduced a new arsenal of weapons for enforcing human rights, and a new army to use them. Oil-rich nations, nations commanding critical trade routes, large corporations, and political blocs like the EU and OAS have been able to bring pressure to bear on recalcitrant states. While their record may be mixed, it is not without its victories—and indeed it is debatable whether the mobilization of world action and opinion might not have greater success than a hegemonic state power enforcing its will.

Yet it is undeniable that the old pas de deux between Western liberalism and cultural relativism continues. Even as new nations joined (and eventually eclipsed) the United States in their call for universal rights, other voices rose in protest. This was a classic example of the pillow effect: for example, as new claims for gender and sexual equality arose, they produced a push-back among religious, ethnic, and political bodies that zealously guarded their bias as a cultural heritage. International debates over burqas and marital enslavement at the beginning of the decade broadened to include state codes that penalize homosexuality (many of them legacies of colonialism) by the end. And in this new era of global movements and oversight, political action can cut both ways. One example is illustrative. In 2014, the Ugandan Parliament passed a law mandating the execution of persons convicted of homosexual acts. It was then duly signed by longtime Ugandan president Yoweri Museveni. International outcry was immediate. The European Union, along with the governments of Sweden, Germany, France, Norway, Denmark, the United Kingdom, and the United States all pledged to halt aid to Uganda. The World Bank withheld a $90 million loan. The so-called "Kill the Gays" bill was ultimately ruled unconstitutional on procedural grounds. In 2019, however, it returned. Faced with the same outrage and threats of cutting aid, the Ugandan government was intransigent. It later transpired that religious organizations within the United States, most notably the National Christian Foundation (NCF) had been actively financing the bill's reemergence and aided in its drafting. These organizations, in turn, were financed by conservative corporations, including the fast-food giant Chick-fil-A.[37] While the outcome of the Ugandan bill remains unclear, it demonstrates how global opinion and financing can promote human rights and hinder them.

One must also reckon with the failure of the Obama administration to respond effectively to the gravest humanitarian crisis during its tenure, the Syrian civil war. The war had dragged on for years, a grinding unequal struggle between rebel forces and the oppressive regime of Bashar al-Assad. In August 2012, a reporter asked President Obama what circumstances might lead him to authorize military force in Syria. "We have been very clear to the Assad regime," he answered, "that a red line for us is we start seeing a whole bunch of chemical weapons moving around or being utilized. That would change my calculus." In fact the regime had already begun stockpiling such weapons and distributing them to allies, including the terrorist organization Hezbollah. Just a week after President Obama issued his public warning, intelligence reports confirmed a sarin attack in Damascus had killed over one thousand people. Until that time, the balance of opinion within the Obama White House favored caution. According to one account, the chairman of the Joint Chiefs of Staff, Marty Dempsey, had argued that Syria was a "slippery slope, with little chance of success" and warned against being drawn into another Iraq situation. But after the Damascus attack, that thinking changed. "Now he said that something needed to be done even if we didn't know what would happen after we took action." The red line had been crossed.[38]

President Obama, careful and deliberative by nature, sought the advice of those around him. The consensus favored air strikes, but even this limited step was flagged as potentially bringing the United States into another war. Instead, the president began sounding out allies for an international coalition. This, after all, was the embodiment of the UN ideal: nations banded together to preserve and protect human rights norms. But the response was chilling. Chancellor Angela Merkel of Germany told the president, "I don't want you to get into a situation where you are left out on a limb," implying other European nations might not be quick to follow the US lead. Having pledged Britain's enthusiastic support, Prime Minister David Cameron was forced to apologize and withdraw after his own parliament vetoed the air strikes, 285-272.

Nor did the president fare any better with Congress. House speaker John Boehner was personally in favor of action but cautioned he could not move his caucus to support it. Senator Mitch McConnell was even more duplicitous, refusing to endorse the move and then criticizing the president afterward for not making it. "Real profiles in courage," Obama commented acerbically. Rank-and-file Republicans, many of whom had enthusiastically joined George W. Bush's call to arms in 2003, found various ways of ducking responsibility now. Even Democrats were gun-shy, the fear of another war overwhelming their humanitarian impulses. "People always say never again," President Obama lamented. "But they never want to do anything." In the end, the president chose to pursue a somewhat dubious diplomatic channel through Russia, and the prospect of military action receded. Ben Rhodes, a former deputy national security adviser, was fatalistic. "Thousands of tons of chemical weapons would be removed from Syria and destroyed," he wrote, "far more than could have been destroyed through military action."[39] That might be true, but it was also true that the president had promised retribution if his "red line" was crossed, and none came. The precedent was set.

Despite its faults, the Obama administration must be credited with reestablishing international bonds that had frayed under George W. Bush and providing a steady and reassuring presence on the world stage. In 2016, as the outgoing administration prepared to hand over the reins, they could congratulate themselves that the next president would be well positioned to continue American stewardship of human rights.

That person was all but certain to be Hillary Clinton, who had served as President Obama's secretary of state and could be relied upon to protect his legacy and continue his policies abroad. The possibility of a Trump presidency was terrifying but remote: his reactionary, incendiary, and boneheaded comments seemed to make the outcome foreordained. "Yes, I think the Republican nominee is unfit to serve as president," Obama said during a joint press conference with Singapore's prime minister, Lee Hsien Loong, in August 2016. "I said so last week, and he keeps on proving it. The notion that he would attack a Gold Star family [the name for a family whose relative has died in service] that had made such extraordinary sacrifices on behalf of our country, the fact that he doesn't appear to have basic knowledge around critical issues in Europe, in the Middle East, in Asia means that he's woefully unprepared to do this job." He went on:

> I think I was right and Mitt Romney and John McCain were wrong on certain policy issues but I never thought that they couldn't do the job. And had they won, I would have been disappointed but I would have said to all Americans: this is our president and I know they're going to abide by certain norms and rules and common sense, will observe basic decency, will have enough knowledge about economic policy and foreign policy and our constitutional traditions and rule of law that our government will work and then we'll compete four years from now to try and win an election.
>
> But that's not the situation here. And that's not just my opinion. That is the opinion of many prominent Republicans. There has to come a point at which you say enough. The alternative is that the entire party, the Republican Party, effectively endorses and validates the positions that are being articulated by Mr. Trump.

These words now ring with prophecy.

— 9 —

AMERICAN CARNAGE

There is a scene in Robert Graves's epic novel *I, Claudius* that recent events have often brought to mind. Poor, stammering Claudius is summoned before the emperor Caligula, who confides that he, the emperor, has been transformed into a god. Not just any god, but Jove himself. Claudius is seemingly awestruck. "I don't know how I could have been so blind," he exclaims. "Your face shines in this dim light like a lamp!" But when he leaves the divine presence, Claudius exults to himself: "*This has happened for the best. Everyone will soon see he's mad, and lock him up.... The Republic will be restored.*" Yet on the morrow, when the emperor makes his divinity known to the Senate, they rush to prostrate themselves before him.[1]

So it was with Donald Trump. From his first candidacy speech to his final ignominious exit—an absurdist coup d'etat—the same narrative played again and again. The president mouthed inanities, which were instantly accepted, adopted, and defended by his apparatchiks, supporters, and fellow party members. No lie was too brazen; even the risible could be labeled "alternative facts." For over four years Trump and his team waged the greatest and most successful war on truth in human history. Falsehoods dropped endlessly like stones into a pond, sending out ripples beyond just the president and his staff. Again and again, wearily but inevitably, senators and congresspeople found some way to rationalize the nonsensical: how could you prove the emperor was *not* a god? Sympathetic news anchors and talk show hosts carried his message through the airwaves, broadcasting it to the remotest corners of the nation and the world. Even respectable journalists didn't know quite what to make of it all. "That's just the way Trump is, and we have to cover him no matter what he says," went the refrain. Yet as one wrote later, the price of covering Trump was becoming a pollinator for his torrent of misinformation and slander. "We journalists should have been tougher on Mr. Trump," the reporter concluded, "questioning his every lie and insult. We should not have let him get away with his racism and xenophobia. We should never again allow someone to create an alternative reality in order to seize the presidency."[2]

One would assume, given the stupendous scale of misinformation emerging from the White House, that fashioning a cohesive narrative of human rights in the Trump era would be daunting. Beyond obfuscation and chaos there is also the problem of detachment. History requires a measure of distance before establishing objectivity, and the significance of events may not become fully known until sometime after the fact. When Neville Chamberlain returned from Munich in 1938 declaring "peace in our time," the crowds cheered; neither he nor they could have imagined that the moment would come to represent a nadir in the twentieth century. But fortunately this is not the case with Donald Trump. Paradoxically, despite—or, indeed, *because of*—its obfuscations, the Trump administration in retrospect has a crystalline transparency. From the moment Trump descended the infamous escalator, the shocking nature of his words and deeds generated correspondingly intense journalistic analysis. If we cannot say that every lie was reported (all 30,000 of them, by one count), we may say that almost every *new* lie was.

Perusing the list of his misdeeds, falsehoods, scandals, insults, blunders, and crimes, one apprehends two truths. First, neither the media nor the public ever became indifferent or desensitized to Trump's actions. Each provoked a fresh storm of outrage, which reverberated within the echo chamber of the public sphere. What happened instead was that the list simply grew too long for any mortal imagination to comprehend. Not desensitization but deluge.

Second, the real-time analysis of the Trump presidency—and of the man himself—was both accurate and prescient. This is especially true on the subject of human rights. In July 2016, then candidate Trump was asked if he would address President Recep Erdogan's numerous violations of the rule of law. Years before he declared himself a "big fan" of the Turkish autocrat, Trump's answer was illuminating: "[W]hen it comes to civil liberties, our country has a lot of problems, and I think it's very hard for us to get involved in other countries when we don't know what we are doing and we can't see straight in our own country." He referred to "policemen being shot in the streets, when you have riots, when you have [the protests in] Ferguson." On the one hand, Trump was previewing the race-baiting rhetoric that would become a staple of his presidency. On the other, he was laying down groundwork for an abandonment of human rights, at home and abroad. As the *New York Times* was quick to point out, "This argument—that the United States could not be a model because of its domestic problems—was made during the early years of the Cold War, when racial segregation and violence against civil rights demonstrators generated international criticism. But this case was made by Soviet propagandists, not American presidential candidates." Its conclusion was even more foreboding, as it came four months before the 2016 election:

> Mr. Trump's war on American values, and his effort to hollow out the nation's image in the world, was, of course, already apparent in his rhetoric about Mexican immigrants and Muslims. As the world looks at the United States' election this year, it is ultimately the American electorate that will have a final say about whether we, as a nation, are ready to embrace the idea that American democracy has nothing to offer the world.[3]

So it came to pass. Within months of taking office, Donald Trump withdrew the United States from both the Paris climate accord and the Iran nuclear treaty. To this list he would later add the Trans-Pacific Partnership negotiations; the Treaty on Open Skies; the UN Educational, Scientific and Cultural Organization; the Intermediate-Range Nuclear Forces Treaty; and, just over a year before a global pandemic killed hundreds of thousands of Americans, the World Health Organization.

President Trump mused about revoking the lease on the UN building and sent Nikki Haley, a politician with no foreign policy experience, to represent the United States in the General Assembly. Her inaugural speech set the tone for an isolationist, xenophobic, and transactional foreign policy—exactly what Mr. Trump wanted. Ms. Haley insisted the United States get "value for its money" from the UN and suggested that all human rights issues should be settled exclusively by NATO. Speaking to a crowd of career diplomats and foreign policy experts, she went on to claim—without evidence—that the UN Human Rights Council "is so corrupt," and left them with this chilling line: "The fact is, a wave is building throughout the world. It's a wave of populism that is challenging institutions like the United Nations, and shaking them to their foundations." Similar arguments had been made about the League of Nations in the face of Nazism, but they had been warnings, not aspirations. To this thuggish threat she added another: "[F]or those who don't have our back, we're taking names." Even as she declared the UN moribund, the ambassador went on to state—with no apparent irony—that America was "the moral conscience" of the world.[4]

After this clarion call, the disintegration of American human rights policy occurred in stages, marked by incidents large and small. In March 2017, the United States refused for the first time in decades to appear before the Inter-American Human Rights Commission—despite the fact that the event took place in Washington, DC. The American president was in a pique that certain Latin American nations had criticized his attempted Muslim travel ban. "The refusal to appear placed Washington in dubious company of Nicaragua, Venezuela and Cuba on accountability for human rights compliance," one journalist noted laconically.[5] Not long after, the State Department quietly proffered a plan to alter its mission statement. The old statement read: "The department's mission is to shape and sustain a peaceful, prosperous, just and democratic world and foster conditions for stability and progress for the benefit of the American people and people everywhere." Secretary of State Rex Tillerson proposed dropping the words "just and democratic." As one commentator wrote, "such a change might reflect a growing feeling that most of the programs to support democracy abroad and the importance of democratic ideals are wasteful, inefficient, unappreciated or even damaging."[6]

Meanwhile, the full dimensions of President Trump's transactional foreign policy began to take shape. Two months after his nonappearance at the Inter-American Human Rights Commission, Trump visited Saudi Arabia and dismissed any questions about that nation's checkered human rights record. "We are not here to lecture," he announced. "We are not here to tell other people how to live, what to do, who to be or how to worship. Instead, we are here to offer partnership—based on shared interests and values—to pursue a better future for us all." A few days later, Secretary Tillerson offered the pious hope that Iran "restores the rights of Iranians to freedom of speech, to freedom of organization," but ignored questions about Saudi abuses on both grounds. He went on to rationalize this hypocrisy:

> If we condition too heavily that others must adopt this value that we've come to over a long history of our own, it really creates obstacles to our ability to advance our national security interests, our economic interests.... It doesn't mean that we don't advocate for and aspire to freedom, human dignity and the treatment of people the world over. We do. But that doesn't mean that's the case in every situation.

The message was clear: America was out for itself and willing to do business with anyone on their terms. Woodrow Wilson's "moral diplomacy" was officially dead. "To the president and his advisors," wrote the *New York Times,* "human rights concerns can be an impediment to the flow of commerce between countries and a barrier to beneficial partnerships for the United States."[7] To be sure, Trump and his cabinet were not the first to choose commerce over rights; American presidents had been straddling that line for decades. Trump was, however, unique in dispensing with the choice altogether. His personal diplomacy underscored this new amorality. He showed disdain for staunch allies like Angela Merkel of Germany and Emmanuel Macron of France while basking in the mutual approval of strongmen: President Xi Jinping of China was "a very special man," Egypt's military dictator Adbel Fattah el-Sisi was "doing a fantastic job," and Rodrigo Duterte of the Philippines was "a great guy" with whom the president had a "fantastic relationship."

Worse was to come, as the consequences of American withdrawal began to manifest themselves. Authoritarian regimes started borrowing from Trump's playbook, especially his dismissal of all factual evidence as "fake news." During the Rohingya genocide in Myanmar, a security official told reporters blithely, "There is no such thing as Rohingya. It is fake news." The Russian Foreign Ministry began affixing a red stamp reading "FAKE" to website news content it did not like. President Nicolas Maduro of Venezuela blamed criticism of his government's appalling human rights record on "lots of lies.... This is what we call 'fake news' today." Finally, upon receipt of an Amnesty International report on prison deaths in Syria, President Bashar al-Assad was unmoved: "We are living in a fake-news era."[8] Trump had provided human rights abusers with a new weapon for their rhetorical arsenal.

Moreover, they knew they would face no threat of censure from the American president. After Syrian governmental forces began bombarding Aleppo and Eastern Ghouta in February 2018, killing nine hundred civilians including many women and children, the governments of France and Britain convened an emergency meeting of the UN Security Council. Over 400,000 Syrians remained trapped within their own cities, in what the French ambassador described as "a siege worthy of the Middle Ages." A coalition of nations demanded enforcement of a ceasefire; American ambassador Nikki Haley declined to attend the session. The United States ultimately did not join in the demand. A year later, in a sop to Turkish strongman Recep Erdogan, Trump abruptly withdrew support for the Kurdish militia, allowing Turkish-backed Syrian armed groups to perpetrate a massacre. Women were dragged from their cars and beaten to death; Turkish-allied forces used napalm and white phosphorus on civilians. President Trump said the Kurds were "no angels" and compared the slaughter to children fighting in a vacant lot. "This is an obscene and ignorant statement," his own former special envoy, Brett McGurk, wrote. Senator Mitt Romney agreed: "What we have done to the Kurds will stand as a bloodstain in the annals of American history."[9]

It was one stain among many. Not long after meeting with President Trump, Viktor Orban of Hungary flatly rejected a pledge to "the rule of law and respect for human rights" under the European Union, declaring instead: "We do not want to be diverse and do not want to be mixed; we do not want our own color, traditions and national culture to be mixed with those of others."[10] There was no response from Washington.

But when Canadian Prime Minister Justin Trudeau gently criticized American demands to lower tariffs on milk, cheese, and yogurt from the United States, President Trump accused him of "betrayal," backstabbing, and deserving of "a special place in hell."[11]

When the administration did choose to highlight human rights abuses—which was rare—it did so for nakedly political ends. Again, it is not uncommon for presidents to use human rights as a weapon for shaming, or indeed to be politically motivated in whom they target. Donald Trump, however, took this to a new and profoundly cynical level. As one commentator wrote, "Mr. Trump rarely condemns repression overseas, except when Christians are being persecuted by Muslim extremists, or when human rights are abused by longtime foes of the United States— particularly Iran, Syria, Cuba, Venezuela and North Korea.... Instead of viewing human rights as a universal ideal, Mr. Trump invokes them only strategically, when they are useful as a geopolitical cudgel."[12] Trump, lacking empathy, regarded victims as nothing more than convenient props. This was vividly on display when the president invited a number of former child sex slaves from various nations and paraded them before the cameras in the White House. "My administration is putting unprecedented pressure on traffickers at home and abroad," he announced. "We've had a tremendous track record—the best track record in a long time." This was not true. The number of prosecutions and crackdowns actually declined significantly under Trump, and available resources were not funneled to recognized NGOs but to dubious organizations with names like "Hookers for Jesus." The *New York Times* was scathing: "Few people on earth are so exploited as children trafficked into the sex trade. And now they are being exploited again, by President Trump."[13]

The president's callousness seemed to strike an unlovely chord with many others. "Trump's America does not care," historian Robert Kagan summarized. "It is unencumbered by historical memory. It recognizes no moral, political or strategic commitments. It feels free to pursue objectives without regard to the effect on allies or, for that matter, the world. It has no sense of responsibility to anything beyond itself."[14] The world was taking notice. President Duterte of the Philippines began jailing journalists; the ruling party of Cambodia purged all parliamentary opposition; Viktor Orban instituted a systematic rollback of LGBTQ rights in

Hungary and a purge of the independent judiciary; the Modi government of India implemented a docket of anti-Muslim legislation; the Chinese government chipped away at democracy in Hong Kong. These were in addition to ongoing human rights crises in Eastern Europe, Africa, Latin America, and Asia. As one commentator noted, "Authoritarian forces everywhere perceive that there is no longer any price to pay for ruling as nastily as they want."[15] Zeid Ra'ad al-Hussein, the United Nations high commissioner for human rights, was horrified:

> Today oppression is fashionable again; the security state is back, and fundamental freedoms are in retreat in every region of the world. Shame is also in retreat. Xenophobes and racists in Europe are casting off any sense of embarrassment.... Have we all gone completely mad?[16]

To the long list of international human rights violations ticking up around the world, the Trump administration in 2018 added its own: migrant children forcibly separated from their parents at the Mexican border and incarcerated. The base cruelty of the practice appalled even many traditional Republicans. Former first lady Laura Bush condemned the practice and demanded the children be restored to their families. But time and again, Trump and his circle proved themselves impervious to shame. Before a hearing of the ninth circuit, an attorney for the administration claimed that soap, toothbrushes, and bedding were unnecessary for the children to enjoy "safe and sanitary" captivity. One of the judges asked incredulously: "Are you arguing seriously that you do not read the agreement as requiring you do something other than what I described: Cold all night long. Lights on all night long. Sleep on the concrete floor and you get an aluminum blanket?" The Trump team was unconcerned and unrepentant. Fox News host Laura Ingraham compared the prisons to "summer camps" and speculated the children were better off than they had been at home. Journalists from the Associated Press found instead a bleak and hellish reminiscence of the very darkest moments in American history:

> A 2-year-old boy locked in detention wants to be held all the time. A few girls, ages 10 to 15, say they've been doing their best to feed and soothe the clingy toddler who was handed to them by a guard days ago.

> Three girls told attorneys they were trying to take care of the 2-year-old boy, who had wet his pants and had no diaper and was wearing a mucus-smeared shirt when the legal team encountered him....
>
> A 14-year-old girl from Guatemala said she had been holding two little girls in her lap. 'I need comfort, too. I am bigger than they are, but I am a child, too,' she said.[17]

On June 18, 2018, with furor mounting around the world, the UN Human Rights Council entered the fray. Cannily, it referred to a statement by the president of the American Association of Pediatrics that called the separation and detainment policy a form of "government-sanctioned child abuse." Such actions violated numerous articles of the Universal Declaration of Human Rights, including Article 9, prohibiting arbitrary arrest and detention, and Article 16, which stated, "The family is the natural and fundamental group unit of society and is entitled to protection by society and the State." The UN high commissioner for human rights said baldly, "The thought that any state would seek to deter parents by inflicting such abuse on children is unconscionable."[18]

One day later, the United States formally withdrew from the Human Rights Council. No nation had ever voluntarily resigned, and among all the nations of the world only North Korea, Iran, and Eritrea were not members. Consistent with its habit of deflecting blame, the Trump administration insisted its withdrawal was due not to any criticism over child separation but rather in protest over the council's unfair treatment of Israel. "If the Human Rights Council is going to attack countries that uphold human rights and shield countries that abuse human rights, then America should not provide it with any credibility," Haley announced. Secretary of State Mike Pompeo concurred, calling the Human Rights Council "an obstacle to the progress of human rights and a threat to the United States." This was an Orwellian inversion the Trump team used often: slavery was liberty, peace was war, and human rights organizations curtailed human rights. But there was a glimmer of honesty in Pompeo's concluding remark: "When organizations undermine our national interests and our allies, we will not be complicit.... When they seek to infringe on our national sovereignty, we will not be silent."[19]

The concept that fundamental rights supersede national sovereignty is the bedrock upon which all human rights rest. Yet the Trump administration regarded even polite criticism as an attack on its sovereignty, in effect articulating a legal vision synonymous with Xenophon's: law was the will of the state, nothing more. Worse yet, the withdrawal formalized what had already been an accepted fact. The United States no longer had any voice on human rights. Rob Berschinski, senior vice president of Human Rights First, warned: "Countries like China, Russia and Venezuela will applaud this decision because we are freely giving up leverage over them that we previously had."

The most pernicious attack on human rights was yet to come. Beyond abrogating its responsibilities, the Trump administration in its waning days embarked on a quixotic crusade to undermine the very definition of "right" under law. In May 2019 Pompeo ordered the establishment of a "Commission on Unalienable Rights." The commission's goals seemed, at first glance, laudable: "To provide the Secretary of State advice and recommendations concerning international human rights matters [and] fresh thinking about human rights discourse where such discourse has departed from our nation's founding principles of natural law and natural rights."[20] In abstract, the mandate appeared not unlike that proposed by this book: reconsidering and determining the difference between essential rights and privileges—or, as Pompeo put it, "ad hoc rights created by politicians and bureaucrats." That was the first clue something was not quite right. Certainly politicians and bureaucrats had been manufacturing rights, even relabeling privileges as rights, but most of these—labor, welfare, education, etc.—were centuries old. What "ad hoc rights" was the secretary referring to?

Writing in the *Wall Street Journal,* Pompeo defended the commission by saying the administration "takes seriously the founders' ideas of liberty and constitutional government." The purpose of the commission, he insisted, was to "address basic questions: What are our fundamental freedoms? Why do we have them? Who or what grants these rights?... What does it mean to say or claim that something is, in fact, a human right? How can there be human rights, rights we possess not as privileges we are granted or even earn, but simply by virtue of our humanity?"[21] These were old questions, and good ones.

But then Pompeo went on: "Rights claims are often aimed more at rewarding interest groups and dividing humanity into subgroups. Oppressive regimes like Iran and Cuba have taken advantage of this cacophonous call for 'rights,' even pretending to be avatars of freedom." This was dangerous language. The secretary of state appeared to be casting doubt not merely on the subject of rights but the entire mechanism for identifying and protecting them—in other words, the UN itself. The purposes of the commission were becoming clearer.

A group of Democratic senators wrote in June to "express our deep concern with the process and intent behind the Department of State's recently announced Commission on Unalienable Rights.... With deep reservations about the Commission, we request that you not take any further action regarding its membership or proposed operations without first consulting with congressional oversight and appropriations committees."[22] A few days later the House voted to defund the Commission on Unalienable Rights. Representatives of GLAAD, Amnesty International, and the Cato Institute also criticized the commission's mandate, which they feared might have a deleterious effect on women's and LGBTQ rights.

Neither Trump nor his advisers have ever been accused of subtlety, and the consensus was that the commission was a blatant attempt by the president to redefine rights out of existence and thus give the United States a plausible excuse for disengagement on the world stage. Writing for the *New York Times,* columnist Roger Cohen warned: "Trump, having shown willful neglect toward human rights, now wants to redefine them. The exercise can only reflect his contempt for the rule of law, a free press, an independent judiciary, gays, minorities, women's reproductive rights, the safety of migrant children, truth and decency—as well as his boundless affection for human rights violators. It is, in other words, a disaster in the making."[23] This was fair criticism. Unto itself, the commission seemed harmless enough. But placed in the broader context of the assault on human rights outlined earlier, a different image appears. The Trump administration began by ignoring human rights, then progressed to formally abandoning them, and was now attempting to delegitimize the very concept.

But why bother? Trump had already walked off the stage; why tear it down too? Michael H. Fuchs of the *Guardian* provided a possible answer:

"The Trump administration wants to gaslight Americans into believing that this new commission is necessary because the fight to expand rights protections somehow gives cover to other countries to abuse the language of human rights to defend their repression." In other words, Trump and Pompeo sought a new relativist standard, so reductive as to be virtually worthless, that gave an automatic pass to both the United States and all other nations that didn't wish to be niggled by pesky accusations of atrocity. It was the same old Orwellian inversion. "Don't be surprised," Fuchs warned, "if one of the conclusions of this new commission is 'human rights is repression.'" The irony of a nihilist administration founding a commission on human rights would be laughable if it wasn't also terrifying:

> They want everyone to believe that what they are doing is in support of laudable goals—freedom, democracy, security, choose your own lofty noun. They make racist and antisemitic comments against others while claiming that they are somehow fighting antisemitism and defending Israel. They tear children from their parents and place them in cages and claim that it is all a deterrent to protect those same migrants from the dangers of the journey to the United States."[24]

Perhaps the most disturbing aspect of the commission was its deliberate mutilation of natural law. When Secretary Pompeo mused on how America and other nations had drifted away from the principles of "natural law and natural rights," what exactly did he mean? The rights to life, liberty, property, and security are enshrined by the Constitution and upheld by every court in the land. So are they in almost all of America's traditional allies. Which "natural law" rights were being abused, and which "ad hoc" rights had usurped them?

The composition of the commission offered a clue to Pompeo's thinking. It featured, among a collection of relative nonentities (many of whom had no prior experience or knowledge of legal issues), Islamicist scholar Hamza Yusuf Hanson; Rabbi Meir Soloveichik of the Straus Center for Torah and Western Thought; and Mary Ann Glendon, a devout Catholic, avowed antiabortionist, and former US ambassador to the Holy See. Dr. Glendon once remarked that giving the Pulitzer Prize to the *Boston Globe* journalists who uncovered decades of child sexual abuse by Catholic clergy "would be like giving the Nobel Peace Prize to Osama bin Laden." She was also Pompeo's former mentor. "For Pompeo, 'unalienable rights' comes from God," wrote Jayne Huckerby, a law professor at Duke University. "It's shorthand for erasing subsequent rights guarantees for LGBTI persons and rights guarantees for sexual and reproductive health."[25]

The Catholic Church often refers to God's law as "natural law," borrowing the term from medieval understandings of law emerging from the mind of God. A handful of fundamentalist legal scholars, among them Princeton professor Robert P. George, have also espoused this view. But it has not been the accepted meaning among states for centuries; natural law is not divine law. As Grotius wrote, *Etiamsi daremus non esse Deum,* "Such things as these would still be true even without God." Nevertheless, Secretary Pompeo appeared to be favoring abandonment of traditional human rights—which themselves rested upon a foundation of natural law—for a new "ad hoc" understanding based on religious principles. As one correspondent wrote of the commission, "One concern is the reference to 'natural law,' which is held to be more powerful than the laws people write, and can suggest a narrower, religious sensibility. When the term natural law has been thrown about, it's often been by people concerned with what they think is unnatural—homosexuality, transgender rights, reproductive choice and sexual equality." Yale law professor Harold Hongju Koh was equally dismissive: "Modern rights are based on the dignity inherent in all human beings, not on God-given rights."[26]

Any lingering doubt about Pompeo's motives was put to rest in a speech given at the National Constitution Center in July 2020 announcing the completion of the commission's report. The event began, appropriately, with an invocation by Cardinal Timothy M. Dolan. Then Pompeo took the stage. "America is fundamentally good, and has much to offer the world, because our founders recognized the existence of God-given unalienable rights and designed a durable system to protect them," he declared. The commission's report, Pompeo went on, would enshrine religious liberty as the paramount human right "for decades to come": "It's important for every American, and for every American diplomat, to recognize how our founders understood unalienable rights. Foremost among these rights are property rights and religious liberty." How the secretary arrived at this remarkable (and false) conclusion he did not say. Instead he went on to name, for the first time, those "ad hoc" rights that in his view usurped the church's supremacy in law. "Today, the very core of what it means to be an American, indeed the American way of life itself, is under attack," he said. "Instead of seeking to improve America, too many leading voices promulgate hatred of our founding principles." He was referring to the 1619 Project, a scholarly reexamination of the legacy of slavery in contemporary American culture, which Pompeo called "a dark vision of America's birth" and a "disturbed reading of our history."[27] By dismissing the corrosive effects of slavery on the lives and legal status of African Americans in favor of illusory threats against Christianity, the Trump administration finally had its own Magna Carta: rights to life, liberty, equality before the law, and security were out, property and religion (at least some religions) were in. Even more incredibly, this was alleged to be a reaffirmation of both the founders' intent and natural law.

The response among legal scholars and within the global community was derisive. "Human rights are not a choose-your-own-adventure," said Tarah Demant of Amnesty International. "The U.S. State Department's effort to cherry-pick rights in order to deny some their human rights is a dangerous political stunt that could spark a race to the bottom by human rights-abusing governments around the world."[28] Later that year, the State Department reached out to the European Union, Britain, and other nations to drum up support for the commission's report. It was a signal failure. Changing tack, the department then tried to convince the UN to issue a statement reaffirming its commitment to rights as defined by the 1948 Universal Declaration of Human Rights. This seemingly innocent request was seen through at once; what Pompeo and Trump actually wanted was to rhetorically erase decades of evolution in human rights. Or, as the director of Human Rights Watch described pithily, "It's moving backward. It's returning us back to some kind of 'Leave It to Beaver' world where the international protections against racial discrimination, against discrimination against women, people with disabilities and LGBT people don't exist." Scholars and experts noted that the commission and its proponents might encourage other nations to attempt to "redefine" human rights, fueling debates over cultural relativism—debates in which, until recently, the United States always stood as a bulwark for universalism. No fewer than 230 human rights organizations, religious groups, and former US government officials wrote a public letter to Pompeo condemning the commission and its report. Its vision, they declared, "will undermine American commitments to human rights and provide cover for those who wish to narrow certain categories of rights protections, resulting in a weakening of the international human rights system and its protections in the process."[29] Other organizations went so far as to file an injunction in federal court to prevent the State Department from adopting the report's recommendations, on the grounds it violated constitutional protections.

In the end, the Commission on Unalienable Rights was a Pyrrhic victory for Trump and Pompeo. Scorned by the US allies and the UN, condemned by experts, and ultimately dismissed by the incoming Biden administration, it disappeared within State Department archives: one failed draft among many. Yet it was also a tragically wasted opportunity. The fundamental question put before the commission—the distinction between right and liberty—urgently needs to be addressed. As this book has argued, the list of "rights" has grown exponentially over the last century into an unworkable compendium in which basic rights to life, liberty, and security under natural law are lost within a deluge of other claimants. A serious scholarly endeavor might have yielded useful results. Instead, Pompeo convened a kind of twenty-first-century theological *disputatio,* as King James I of Aragon once summoned Dominicans and Jews to settle questions between the faiths. The result of the 1263 Dispute of Barcelona, in fact, gave judgment to the Jews, but the Dominicans claimed victory anyway and had all the proceedings burned—a historical precedent Donald Trump certainly would favor.

Of the last few fevered months of the Trump administration, little need be said. When in August of 2020 the International Criminal Court began investigations into possible war crimes committed by American troops in Afghanistan, Secretary Pompeo decried it as an attack on American sovereignty. He described the ICC as a "thoroughly broken and corrupted institution" and took the extraordinary step of imposing sanctions on its chief prosecutor, Fatou Bensouda. Ms. Bensouda abruptly learned that her bank account had been frozen, as well as those of several family members—even though none was connected to the ICC. The top diplomat of the European Union called Pompeo's actions "unacceptable and unprecedented," while the German foreign minister warned they were "a serious mistake." Weeks later, the State Department revoked Ms. Bensouda's visa, as well as those of several of her colleagues.[30]

Considering the provocation, Ms. Bensouda was surprisingly unruffled. "It definitely is quite unprecedented," she admitted in an interview. "These are the kind of sanctions that we normally reserve to be used as a mechanism to target narcotic traffickers, notorious terrorists and the like. But not professional lawyers, not prosecutors, not investigators, not judges or others who are working tirelessly to prevent atrocity crimes." Still, she refused to be fazed by acts of petty spite, even when they took the form of American foreign policy. "This will not deter us. This will not stop us. We will continue to do our work."[31]

A measured but devastating coda came from the president of the ICC, Chile Eboe-Osuji. "These acts of coercion and their premises are wrong," he wrote bluntly. "The ICC is not intent on 'hauling' Americans up to trial before it. The real issue is whether investigations—and any resulting prosecution—may be conducted to examine allegations of violations committed mostly in Afghanistan by the Taliban, Afghan security personnel and, yes, United States security personnel while stationed in Afghanistan." Having laid down the parameters of the dispute, Judge Eboe-Osuji offered an indictment of his own. Referencing the Nuremberg Tribunals and chief prosecutor Robert Jackson (who had famously warned of the "poisoned chalice" passing to American lips one day), the judge concluded:

> It is not impressive that the American leadership insists that these questions of justice dare not be asked, if they might implicate Americans in allegations of wrongdoing abroad. It is enough that senior American officials, well attuned to the old-fashioned American sense of justice, readily accept that not even American soldiers are immune from accountability when they are suspected of committing crimes in foreign countries.[32]

At last, on November 8, 2020, the fever broke. Even as Trump and his advisers spun fantastical claims of election fraud and suborned party regulars to indulge these dangerous absurdities, President-elect Joe Biden began quietly assembling a team of foreign policy advisers to begin righting the ship on day one. Several months before the election, Biden laid out an ambitious foreign policy agenda in *Foreign Affairs* magazine. It began as an indictment. "For 70 years," wrote Mr. Biden, "the United States, under Democratic and Republican presidents, played a leading role in writing the rules, forging the agreements, and animating the institutions that guide relations among nations and advance collective security and prosperity—until Trump. If we continue his abdication of that responsibility, then one of two things will happen: either someone else will take the United States' place, but not in a way that advances our interests and values, or no one will, and chaos will ensue." The only error in Mr. Biden's analysis was his use of the future tense; in fact, the worst had already happened. But it was not too late to reverse course. For the incoming president, said Biden, the first and most important goal must be to "place the United States back at the head of the table," reestablishing connections with allies and reengaging with the United Nations and its ancillaries. Beyond rebuilding bridges, he pledged in his first year of office to host a Summit for Democracy to "bring together the world's democracies to strengthen our democratic institutions, honestly confront nations that are backsliding, and forge a common agenda." More specifically, the summit was intended to foster commitment to fighting corruption, defending against authoritarianism, and advancing human rights. On the one hand, this vision of America and its role was a clear break from the isolationism and amorality of his predecessor; on the other, it was couched in terms familiar to anyone who remembered Ronald Reagan's "city on a hill." Like Reagan, Mr. Biden is fond of homilies, and expressed himself in similar language: "The triumph of democracy and liberalism over fascism and autocracy created the free world. But this contest does not just define our past. It will define our future, as well.... As a nation, we have to prove to the world that the United States is prepared to lead again—not just with the example of our power but also with the power of our example."[33]

It was not entirely clear, however, whether the rest of the world was ready to allow the United States to regain its moral authority. The lacerations of the previous four years did not fade so easily, especially with the possibility of a second Trump administration in 2024. Questions were being asked that had been unthinkable a decade before: could the United States be trusted to remain a steady hand, or would it backslide into xenophobia and isolation? Moreover, during its absence, other nations had stepped up. In July 2020, Britain announced it had blacklisted a long roster of suspected human rights abusers from Myanmar, Russia, and Saudi Arabia, charged with acts ranging from executions to beatings to the persecution of minorities.[34] Even as they welcomed the end of the Trump era, the international community was not about to fall obligingly back into its Cold War–era role of approving chorus for American policy. As one op-ed summed up pithily: "Biden Wants America to Lead the World. It Shouldn't." This was not a defense of isolationism, the author explained, but a caution against presuming the old order of things could be reestablished. Indeed, it mustn't be: the vision of human rights interwoven with liberal democratic values was precisely what had hampered US policy for years and allowed nations like China and Russia to dismiss such rights as imperialist propaganda. A renewed commitment to internationalism meant that the United States shouldn't try to sit at the head of the table but among its peers: "The point isn't that American participation in common global efforts is unnecessary. To the contrary—it's vital. But most of the time, America best serves these efforts less by dictating the rules than by agreeing to them. Choosing partnership over leadership may strike some as un-American. But it's what most Americans want."[35]

Nevertheless, it was a mark of how dearly American engagement was missed that the global community—and the United Nations in particular—reacted to Joe Biden's electoral victory with modified rapture. "I have never known nor can I ever imagine the secretary general doing cartwheels in his office or anywhere else," his spokesperson said repressively. "What I can tell you is that the secretary general has always worked very closely with every US permanent representative that has been sent by Washington and will do so in the future." Behind her careful words was the discreet sound of champagne being popped. "Under Joe Biden, the international human rights community and beyond will breathe a sigh of relief," said Agnès Callamard, the UN Human Rights Council's special investigator on extrajudicial killings. She particularly hoped that President Biden would rejoin the Human Rights Council, as he was almost certain to do. "The absence of the US there in some of the council's difficult debates and issues has led to a weakening of those espousing positions supportive of human rights protection," she admitted. Most discussions were now "largely taken by countries whose primary interest is to weaken international scrutiny over their human rights records." Similar expressions of relief and reengagement came from almost every quarter. Richard Gowan, UN liaison for the International Crisis Group, dismissed the argument that America had somehow forfeited a place at the table. Yes, he said, "Biden faces a very difficult world, but a very easy pathway to gaining some political good will at the United Nations." He concluded bluntly: "Biden and his UN ambassador just need to be human, and they will be treated as conquering heroes."[36]

Such expressions of relief and optimism were perhaps inevitable, but they must not be taken too far. It is a human trait to want to turn the page, put uncomfortable memories behind us. Thus it is tempting to dismiss Donald Trump as an aberration, a brief, chaotic interregnum between the ordered administrations of Barack Obama and his former vice president, Joe Biden. Perhaps eventually it will come to be regarded as such. But if so, it will not be because of the passage of time but rather because of the proactive efforts of Trump's successors to completely and thoroughly destroy every vestige of Trumpism at home and abroad, and sow the fields with salt. That has not yet been done.

Consequently, it is necessary to regard the narrative of events described above not as mere history, but as a warning. To quote Faulkner: "The past isn't dead. It isn't even past." We are still reckoning with the damage wrought by four years of mismanagement, ignorance, avarice, indifference, and cruelty. The word most commonly used to describe Trump and his actions is "unprecedented." Now there are precedents. It was unimaginable that the United States, which crafted both the UN and much of the postwar geopolitical landscape, should abandon its own creation. It was unimaginable the American president would willfully disparage democratic allies and coddle dictators instead. But it did, and he did, and they may do so again.

Trump's presidency might be unprecedented, but there are still discernible patterns worth considering. The withdrawal from all rights organizations and duties was part policy, part pique. When the Inter-American Human Rights Commission dared criticize Trump's Muslim ban, he withdrew from the commission. When the UN Human Rights Council criticized his incarcerating children, he withdrew from the Human Rights Council. When the ICC began investigating possible war crimes by American soldiers, he did not withdraw from the ICC (he couldn't, as the United States is not a member) but instead imposed sanctions on the chief prosecutor. In every instance—as with other inter-actions in his presidency—he turned charges against himself back at the accuser and had his underlings do the same: thus Nikki Haley accused the council of being "so corrupt," as Pompeo did the ICC. American foreign and domestic policy became reduced to a series of Orwellian in-versions. In the end, to reach the bedrock truth of the Trump presidency, one need only revert all the accusations it made against others back upon itself: weak, broken, treacherous, untruthful, vacillating, ungrateful, and so, so corrupt.

— 10 —

PROGRESSLAND

Finally, a cautionary tale. It is late November, and the world is gripped by the greatest economic crisis in generations. Despair, fueled by xenophobia and outright racism, brings a surge of populist strongmen on every continent, each claiming the national emergency requires unprecedented, coordinated, and concentrated power. Democratic institutions suddenly seem fragile. While the United States is consumed by the aftershocks of a raucous election, across the Atlantic a quiet revolution is underway. A democratically elected European head of state suddenly begins disenfranchising minorities, blaming them for the "moral rot" of the nation. He attacks his own nation's judiciary, compromising their independence and "coordinating" them—a favorite phrase of the majority party that means complete and total subjugation. All political dissent disappears seemingly overnight. The parliament, still housed in grand offices from the last century, becomes nothing more than a rubber stamp. Once he is sure of his ground, the dictator persuades this complacent body to suspend term limits, allowing him to govern indefinitely. He cites the worldwide crisis as justification for a broad range of emergency powers which, once given, will never be relinquished.

There is a mechanism in place to deal with this problem: an international coalition of democratic states created to prevent another world war. But they are divided amongst themselves and ultimately more interested in recouping debts than curbing authoritarianism. The United States, too, remains silent. Emboldened, the dictator continues to press his claims at home and abroad. Other nations stand idly by; a few, led by "strongmen" themselves, watch with interest.

This story has played out twice in the last century. We know how the first ended: in the conflagration of the Second World War. The second, however, is still being written. In November 2020, the governments of Hungary and Poland threatened to dismantle a multitrillion-euro stimulus package for European Union members because the language of the agreement enjoined them to abide by the "rule of law." This threat of veto sent other nations scrambling, and there was reason to anticipate the offending language would be removed from the final draft. Many states, in fact, didn't want it there in the first place.

Hungary, formerly a democratic republic and model for its Eastern European neighbors, had backslid into autocracy under President Viktor Orban. Civil rights for minority groups, particularly the LGBTQ community, were curtailed. An independent judiciary no longer existed. Mr. Orban exploited the pandemic to justify emergency measures intended to allow him unlimited and indefinite rule, much as his ideological predecessor seized upon the Great Depression and Reichstag fire in 1933.

Once again, as in 1933, the international community turned a blind eye. At the height of the Depression, desperate to collect their long-standing debts, Europe and America willfully ignored Nazi Germany's abandonment of the rule of law in favor of its promise to pay. Germany, whose chancellor served as acting president of the EU, appeared ready to do the same for Hungary and Poland. At this point, as Winston Churchill would have it, "the New World in all its power and might" should have stepped forth to liberate the Old. The United States alone had the ability to prevent this second red tide of appeasement. Wounded as it may be, it was still the largest, wealthiest, and most powerful democracy in the world. The United States also had a long history of defending democratic values and human rights around the globe under presidents of both political parties.

In another world, the EU stalemate could have been a perfect test case for American reengagement on human rights. Here was a crime against humanity unfolding in real time: withdrawal from the rule of law in Hungary was not yet at terminal stage. There was a window of opportunity for the United States to safeguard the rights of the Hungarian people and strike a chord for American democratic values revivified. Mr. Orban had placed the EU in the invidious position of denying its own founding principles in order to reestablish financial solvency. The question was not whether they would take his devil's bargain but if the United States should allow them to.

Of course, the United States did nothing. President Trump counted Mr. Orban among his closest allies, one of a collection of strongmen the president found appealing. It is more than likely American silence enabled Orban to consolidate his position in the first place, much like Erdogan of Turkey and many others. In the twilight of his presidency—though loath to admit it—Mr. Trump would no more offer democratic assistance to the EU than concede gracefully on his electoral loss. Both actions were entirely out of character.

That problem, like so many others, would ultimately fall into the lap of the president-elect. Singly, it counted for relatively little. But it was part of a much larger and more disturbing pattern: an authoritarian surge unchecked—indeed encouraged—by an ersatz authoritarian American president. It is impossible to overstate the impact four years of silence had upon the world stage. As we have seen, Trump and his allies attempted to deconstruct the entire postwar system of alliances, rejecting nearly every human rights norm and concept of accountability, giving comfort to dictators and the back of their hand to everyone else. The shocking, unprecedented character of Trumpian foreign policy (if it can be dignified with that title) will doubtless be felt for decades to come.

Nevertheless, there is cause for hope. President Joe Biden's earnestness and decency stand in stark contrast to his predecessor, and thus his interactions with men like Putin and Orban have the catalytic quality of salt on slugs. No less significant is his resolute faith in the "upward path" of history, as espoused by men like Wilson and FDR. The strength of his convictions, in fact, recalls the motto of Dr. Martin Luther King Jr. invoked in the introduction to this work: "The arc of the moral universe is long, but it bends towards justice." Until 2016, one might have read these words as a promise at least partially fulfilled; in 2011, for example, the MLK Memorial was unveiled with the same quote etched in stone. Yet Dr. King's aphorism also contains a warning: just as certain as the arc's direction is the uncertainty of its length. King understood that humanity's inclination toward justice does not necessitate a smooth or rapid progression.

Likewise, the defense of natural rights does not consist of demonstrating, vide Émile Coué, that every day and in every way we are getting better and better. *Jus naturale* may be immutable and perfect, but those tasked with determining and upholding it are not. The central irony to the concept of a justice transcending individuals is that it relies on those individuals for its relevance. Without human interpretation there would still be law, but it would stand like a marble monument in a vast wilderness. It was for this reason that Cicero, Aquinas, Grotius, and countless others emphasized the importance of wise and good legislators to divine the law; a foolish or cruel one may seemingly negate its progress. As we have recently seen.

The trajectory of natural law encompasses such reverses. Even as it acknowledges the role of individual sovereigns, it places them on a temporal curve where their actions, good or ill, are absorbed by the collective. "For all their activity," F. W. Maitland wrote of English kings, jurists, and reformers, "they changed, and could change, but little in the great body of law which they inherited from their predecessors."[1] Not only is the law greater than individuals, it is greater than events. As Franklin Roosevelt's mentor Dr. Peabody phrased it, when "all will seem to reverse itself and start downward...the great fact to remember is that the trend of civilization itself is forever upward." The arc of the moral universe is long; it is also bumpy.

This doesn't make the journey any easier to bear. It is not my intention to mitigate the catastrophe of the Trump presidency, nor to ignore the real suffering inflicted upon countless persons as a result of his actions and inactions. Likewise, in a broader context, the enormous strides undertaken both nationally and globally in the field of human rights have come at nearly equal cost. Every country that embraces a "universal" right is counterbalanced by another that expressly denies it. What, then, of universality? And, as we saw in previous chapters, rights themselves have become political lightning rods. How do we distinguish between privilege and freedom, cultural practice and crime? Is it proper for one state to "blackmail" another into compliance with universal norms? If it declines to do so, is that a failure as well?

The domestic landscape in our own nation is no less baffling. With the advancement of civil liberties and recognition of new minority groups comes a plethora of claimants for protected rights and status. How do we weigh their respective claims, and what happens if they conflict? This *embarras de richesses* raises a vexing question unimagined by the framers of the Constitution, or even their twentieth-century successors: is it possible to have *too many* rights? In our Age of Rights, as one author termed it,[2] the stark outline of natural law seems ever more obscured.

There is, however, no doubt that the *idea* of natural law has had a profound impact on the development of states. We have seen the law's evolution from justice to right, extending its protection from the few to the many to the whole and ultimately transcending national boundaries to encompass the world entire. Likewise, because of natural law, heads of state are no longer immune from justice, even if that justice is difficult, politicized, and all too rare. It is hard not to interpret these transformations as a form of progress. Yet as the global community continues to engage with a natural law understanding of human rights, "progress" today is erratic, indefinable, incremental, and maddening. Measuring ourselves against the unachieved standard of utopia means that we are perpetually consigned to fall short. Until the twentieth century, a genocidal sovereign could die unlamented but unpunished and nothing would be felt but relief. Now, since Nuremberg, every Pinochet or Pol Pot becomes a collective moral failure.[3] Little wonder that even idealists become frustrated, or cynical.

It is rather like a game we played in elementary school. Each student would take one step forward, then divide it in half and step again, half again, and so on. Our destination was the other side of the room. Did one regard this progression with despair, knowing they would never reach their goal? Or with hope, since each step brought them closer? That is the conundrum of natural law. It is defined by belief in a transcendent universal order; therefore its trajectory is progressive, as humanity gradually comes to know more of that order and incorporates it within itself. The inverse posits a Hobbesian universe where all is chaos and law is the mechanism by which we are forcibly restrained from destroying ourselves. Success is not progress but stasis, which is a much lower bar.

Natural law is infinitely harder. "We shall not attain a Utopia," Franklin Roosevelt cautioned in 1944, even as many in the world community—including his own administration—sought precisely that. "Indeed, in our own land, the work to be done is never finished." This harsh lesson has been passed down from antiquity. By positing that natural law resided "in the mind of Jupiter," Cicero recognized it as perfect, complete, and impenetrably isolated from total human understanding. Through logic we could discover its elements but never the whole. If we knew the totality of Jupiter's mind, Cicero implied, we would be gods ourselves. Thomas Aquinas made a similar point. "The rational creature," he wrote, "is subject to divine providence in the most excellent way, in so far as it partakes a share of providence.... It is therefore evident that the natural law is nothing else than the rational creature's participation in the eternal law."[4] We may always partake of that share of natural law that can be known by us, a share that increases as we evolve. Thus Renaissance humanists likened the contemplation of natural law to astronomy, a reference Winston Churchill might have had in mind when he called the Atlantic Charter "a star." It was beautiful and remote, essentially unknowable yet ever within sight.

To seek a perfection that can never be realized is a paradox as ancient as human thought. In the nineteenth century, some synthesis was achieved by recasting progress as an end in itself. Utopia might remain forever distant, but that hardly mattered as long as one could measure humanity's march toward it. In a time of profound and rapid change—political, social, technological—there was comfort to be found in the immutable character of natural law and its evolving influence on the polity. In contrast to a physical landscape whose transformation seemed both hurried and haphazard, the works of historians William Stubbs, Thomas Macaulay, and F. W. Maitland offered a vision of orderly, measured progress. While their historical perspective might be Olympian, it had the virtue of relegating the ephemera of the moment to a broader context. "Law is a body, a living body," Maitland wrote in his *Constitutional History of England.*[5] Like any body, it grew and matured; like any life, a single moment—however critical—would inevitably be absorbed within its long arc of existence:

> When we speak of a body of law, we use a metaphor so apt that it is hardly a metaphor. We picture to ourselves a being that lives and grows, that preserves its identity while every atom of which it is composed is subject to a ceaseless process of change, decay and renewal. At any given moment of time—for example, in the present year—it may, indeed, seem as though our legislators have, and freely exercise, an almost boundless power of doing what they will with the laws under which we live; and yet we know that, do what they may, their world will become an organic part of an already existing system.[6]

How comforting to think of a foolish legislator as an atom! The Whig narrative has much to criticize, but there is a stark beauty as well. For Maitland and his colleagues, humanity's struggle to better itself through the law was the best and most enduring proof of humanity's essential goodness. The lesson, long obscured under a heavy imperialist encrustation, has relevance today: so long as we continue to strive, our collective efforts outweigh any individual failings or frailties. Ennobling that struggle allows us to suffer reverses and even catastrophes without losing faith in the ultimate trajectory of the law and human society.

As the nineteenth century gave the crusade for natural law its nobility, the twentieth proved its necessity. This was the abiding lesson of Nuremberg: if the Nazis' actions were not a crime, no rational conception of criminality could exist. "At length," Robert Jackson declared at the trial, "bestiality and bad faith reached such excess that they aroused the sleeping strength of imperiled Civilization."[7] The issue at Nuremberg was greater than the guilt of the accused, greater even than their crimes. Civilization itself was on trial—a civilization defined by law. This was a truism that men like Henry Stimson and Robert Jackson understood, yet Churchill and Stalin (and even, for a time, Roosevelt) did not. Stalin's solution—line the Nazi leaders up and shoot them—had the virtue of expediency but no lasting precedent. Victor's justice would do nothing to prevent another Holocaust. The choice of justice over vengeance was explicitly one of natural over positivist law, as Jackson made clear in his opening statement.

It could be no other way. While a catalog of broken treaties might enable the Allies to build a case for war crimes, nothing in the legal philosophy of Xenophon or Ulpian could reach the deeds committed by the Nazis against their own citizens and those of captive nations. Consequently the tribunal established a set of principles that survive to this day: negating both sovereign immunity and deference to superior orders, while enumerating a list of crimes so heinous that they transcended state law as offenses against the law of nations. The Nuremberg Principles, reinforced and restated numerous times (including in the foundational charter of the International Criminal Court), are natural law codified. On the one hand it may seem incredible it took until 1948 for such principles to achieve international recognition; on the other, one might equally make the case that it took the supreme horror of the Holocaust to make them so.

Having established the doctrine of individual responsibility and a catalog of international crimes, we then spent the next seventy-five years lamenting their failure to be universally prosecuted. It is right that we should feel thus. As with the ongoing debate over human rights, frustration and anger are healthy emotions. To continue Professor Maitland's metaphor of the "body of law," one might compare such feelings with the pain of a limb that has suddenly regained sensation. Pain is preferable to numbness, as it means the body is functioning as it should. In the slow progression toward utopia it is anger as much as hope that drives us: outrage at an atrocity helps us redouble our efforts to do justice and prevent similar abuses in the future.

Anger and frustration are congruous with natural law; despair is not. I am often amazed at the cynicism many of my students share at the prospect of universal human rights. Not that I blame them. They are inundated with a daily catalog of horrors on their television sets, Facebook pages, Twitter feeds, and so on. This intimacy with atrocity can lead to resignation: clearly, if the world is such a mess, the law must be failing. At such times Dr. King's words seem like cold comfort. Yet it is also worth considering how Professor Maitland would regard these developments. In the vast expanse of legal history, human rights and international criminal law are in their barest stages of infancy. To declare them a failure at this juncture is to commit the same shortsighted error as those smug nineteenth-century imperialists who congratulated themselves prematurely on their success. As the Victorians themselves would have said, it is the progression, not the destination, that matters. And the arc of the moral universe is long indeed.

With that in mind, let us consider the work ahead. The question is not whether the United States will reengage with the global community on human rights, but how. One thing is certain: old playbooks are out. A Western, liberal democratic vision of human rights is an anachronism of the past century. Not only does it compound the charge of neoimperialism, it remains hopelessly out of step with present geopolitical circumstances. The United States is not a hegemon. It now competes with Russia and China for markets, political influence, and ultimately hearts and minds. This is not the Manichaean struggle of democracy versus communism: today it is between engagement and indifference. These states are not questioning a Western conception of rights but the validity of rights themselves. We must have an answer, and it cannot be predicated on any political philosophy.

A return to the austere simplicity of natural rights has numerous advantages. First, it ends stale cyclical debate on neoimperialism. Natural rights are not Western or democratic; they predate modern democracy and may be found, as we have seen, in every society. Life, liberty, security, and property are the cornerstones of every nation's laws. That is why abuses are easy to identify: they transcend individual cultures, faiths, and circumstances. But as I have said, these are categories, not definitions. When we speak a new language of rights, we need to know exactly what life or liberty means. Hence it will be the job of the State Department or like agencies to offer narrow, well-reasoned definitions for each right.

Second, and even more importantly, a return to natural rights is not only expedient but logical. History has provided two watershed moments where universal law came tantalizingly close. The first was at the end of the eighteenth century, when the political philosophy of the Enlightenment transformed into revolution. That momentum ended in the Industrial Era as new philosophies introduced new understandings of rights based not on universality but individual circumstance. The tattered standard of natural law was shredded further by European imperialism, which attempted to export (by force) Western principles of law in a package with political institutions, cultural norms, religion, technology, capitalism, and guns.

The next moment was during the Second World War. "This generation of Americans has a rendezvous with destiny," Franklin Roosevelt declared in 1936. He was more right than he knew. By 1941, Roosevelt correctly perceived that the complete destruction of Nazism—along with much of the developed world—necessitated social, political, and legal reconstruction postwar. Roosevelt did not wholly reject a democratized vision of rights, but his Four Freedoms and other writings suggested a strong natural law foundation, perhaps emerging from the wellspring of his own deep faith. It was Roosevelt who, with his unshakable belief in human progress, redefined "civilization" for the twentieth century not as an imperialist construct but as a shared set of values under universal law. Even in death, his legacy remains in the United Nations and the numerous international criminal tribunals of the last seventy-five years.

The third moment is now. In the next decade the United States will have no choice but to reengage with human rights, lest it abandon the field to authoritarian regimes altogether. The task will be to work with those nations, and the global community as a whole, to agree upon universal legal standards independent of politics, economics, or faith. In 1850, Senator William Henry Seward spoke of a "higher law" greater than constitutions, untouched by the political tumult of the day. We must invoke that same spirit. The United States must prove through words and action that it will defend natural rights around the globe. Only in this way can we compel a recalcitrant nation to deal justly with its own people. We don't need to rediscover natural law; we just need to stop ignoring it.

This raises a final point on the character of that law. Just as it is presumed to reside within the individual conscience, it is likewise only as viable as individual resolve. Many persons erroneously conflate natural law with divine law, but there is a crucial difference. Religious faith allows us to surrender to God's will, mercy, and judgment. Natural law offers no such consolation. It demands the best within us by declaring we are greater than we appear now to be. There is no original sin, no comforting acknowledgment of perpetual frailty. We stand in judgment of our own selves against a future perfection that may never be reached.

Yet it drives us to excel and evolve. If blind faith says to us, "It's not your fault," natural law admonishes, "You are better than this." The interrelationship of natural law and statecraft is thus a common search for utopia led by those who truly wish to reach it.

Our generation has its own rendezvous with destiny. The most tantalizing and terrifying aspect of utopia is that its vision is always within sight, but just beyond grasp. There is no biological law preventing humans from coexisting peacefully; indeed, our natural impulses propel us toward sociability. Likewise there is no reason why the community of nations, and each person within, may not choose to live under agreed standards of decency, respect, and justice. This should not be seen as an impossible goal, but a necessary and even inevitable one. As FDR once said, this is no vision of a distant millennium. It is a definite basis for a kind of world attainable in our own time. Yet our disenchanted age has conditioned us to look askance at lofty ambitions, much less utopian ones. That defeatist spirit saw its champion and avatar in Donald Trump, a living embodiment of lethargy, cynicism, indifference, selfishness, and vice. But if we reach beyond his sorry example, there are others who speak to us still. John F. Kennedy: *"No problem of human destiny is beyond human beings"*; Ronald Reagan: *"America is too great for small dreams"*; and, once again, the last words of Franklin Delano Roosevelt: *"The only limitation to our realization of tomorrow will be our doubts of today."*

Let us, as a nation, heed their words. Let us move forward, with strong and active faith.

— Acknowledgments —

I am profoundly grateful to my editor, Kevin Stevens, who shepherded this project from start to finish and provided insightful comment that has helped it immeasurably. I must also thank my good friend and agent, Kimberley Cameron, for her faith in me and in this work. The greatest debt must go to my husband, Tonmoy Hassan, who has shown unflagging patience and offered encouragement through every stage of the process.

Last, I wish to acknowledge my mother, Shannon, for her constant support, and my father, Doug Sr., whose capacious view of the law and its majesty shaped my own. It is to him this book is respectfully dedicated.

— Notes —

Introduction [*Pages 1–17*]

1. It is the privilege of every incoming president to redesign their office to suit their tastes. Donald Trump replaced the Obama rug with a rather frowsy laurel-wreath design dating from the Reagan administration.

2. Ezra Klein, "Why Ta-Nehisi Coates Is Hopeful," *Vox*, June 5, 2020.

3. P. Schofield, ed., *Rights, Representation and Reform: "Nonsense upon Stilts" and Other Writings of the French Revolution* (Oxford: Oxford University Press, 2002), 317.

4. See Chester James Antieau, "Natural Rights and the Founding Fathers—The Virginians," *Washington and Lee Law Review* 17(1) (1960), 43–81.

5. See Lynn Hunt, *Inventing Human Rights* (New York: Norton, 2008).

6. William Blackstone intriguingly wrote that a fetus *en ventre á sa mere* could indeed own property, but this was done more to ensure clean passage of title than for whatever enjoyment and use an unborn infant could derive from a freehold estate in Leeds.

7. William Blackstone, *Commentaries on the Laws of England* (Oxford: Oxford University Press reprint, 2008), 133.

8. "Will John Bolton Bring On Armageddon, or Stave It Off?" *Atlantic*, March 9, 2019.

9. See Samantha Power, *A Problem from Hell: America and the Age of Genocide* (New York: Basic Books, 2002).

10. Vienna Declaration and Programme of Action, June 14, 1993.

11. Peter N. Stearns, *Human Rights in World History* (New York: Routledge, 2012), 15.

The Mind of Jupiter [*Pages 18–37*]

1. "World Leaders See Washington Turmoil as Warning for Democracies Everywhere," *New York Times*, January 7, 2021. (hereafter *NYT)*

2. Tweet by the president of Zimbabwe, @edmangagwa, January 7, 2021.

3. Lee Moran, "Fox News' Pete Hegseth Defends Capitol Rioters: They Just Love Freedom," *Huffington Post*, January 7, 2021.

4. Jonathan Martin and Alexander Burns, "Republicans Splinter over Whether to Make a Full Break from Trump," *NYT*, January 7, 2021.

5. See Herbert J. Muller, *Freedom in the Ancient World* (New York: Bantam, 1961).

6. *The Overland Monthly*, v. LV (January-June 1910), 524.

7. See Michel Foucault, *Discipline and Punish: The Birth of the Prison* (New York: Vintage Books, 1993).

8. Paul Rahe, *Republics Ancient and Modern: The Ancien Regime in Classical Greece* (Chapel Hill: University of North Carolina Press, 1994), 100.

9. Gary Herbert, *A Philosophical History of Rights* (London: Transaction Publishers, 2002), 24–5.

10. Mencius, VII, B, 14, ed. D. C. Lau (New York: Penguin Books, 1970).

11. Ibid., I, A, 4.

12. Ibid., VI, A, 1.

13. The Mahabharata, *Karna Parva,* Chapter 69, verse (6) 58.

14. Chakradhar Jha, *History and Sources of Law in Ancient India* (New Delhi: Ashish Publishing, 1987), 7.

15. S. V. Puntambekar, "Human Rights" in Jacques Maritain, ed., *Human Rights: Comments and Interpretations* (New York: Columbia University Press, 1949), 197.

16. A. Ezzati, *Islam and Natural Law* (London: ICAS Press, 2002), 85.

17. Muhammed Shahrastani; Alfred Guillaume, ed., *Kitabo Nihayat al-Iqdam fi 'Ilm al-Kalam* (Oxford: Oxford University Press, 1934), 90–1.

18. Quran, 49:13.

19. Ezzati, *Islam,* 68.

20. Micheline Ishay, *The History of Human Rights: From Ancient Times to the Globalization Era* (Berkeley: University of California Press, 2004), 23.

21. Marcus Tullius Cicero, *De Legibus,* Book II (4).

22. Ibid., Book III (3).

23. See Anthony Everitt, *Cicero: A Turbulent Life* (New York: John Murray, 2001).

24. Marcus Tullius Cicero, *De Republica,* Book III (22).

25. Cicero, *De Legibus,* Book II (4).

26. Ibid., Book II (10).

27. Ibid., Book I (10).

28. Ibid., Book II (5).

29. Hadley Arkes, "That Nature Herself Has Placed in Our Ears the Power of Judging: Some Reflections on Cicero's Naturalism," in Robert P. George, ed., *Natural Law Theory: Contemporary Essays* (Oxford: Oxford University Press, 1992), 255.

30. Quoted in A. P. d'Entreves, *Natural Law: An Historical Survey* (New York: Harper, 1965), 25.

31. Ibid., 25.

32. Ibid., 25.

33. Jacob Giltaij and Kaius Tori, "Human Rights in Antiquity? Revisiting Anachronism and Roman Law," in Pamela Slotte and Miia Halme-Tuomisaari, eds., *Revisiting the Origins of Human Rights* (Cambridge: Cambridge University Press, 2015), 62.

34. D'Entreves, *Natural Law,* 38.

35. For complete analysis see Anthony Lisska, *Aquinas's Theory of Natural Law: An Analytic Reconstruction* (Oxford: Clarendon Press, 1996).

36. Thomas Aquinas, *Summa Theologica,* I (91), art. 1 and 2.

37. Ibid., I (91), art. 1 and 2.

38. Ibid., 2ae (104).

39. Quoted in Stearns, *Human Rights*, 46.

40. R. H. Helmholz, *Natural Law in Court: A History of Legal Theory and Practice* (Cambridge: Harvard University Press, 2015), 17.

41. See Samuel Moyn, *The Last Utopia: Human Rights in History* (Cambridge: Harvard University Press, 2010).

42. Virpi Makinen, "Medieval Natural Rights Discourse" in *Revisiting the Origins of Human Rights*, 68.

43. Annabel Brett, *Changes of State: Nature and the Limits of the City in Early Modern Natural Law* (Princeton: Princeton University Press, 2011), 43.

44. Ibid., 12–14.

45. Bartolome de las Casas, *In Defense of the Indians* (De Kalb: Northern Illinois University Press, 1970), 42–43.

46. Quoted in Brett, *Changes,* 31.

47. Quoted in Ibid., 32.

THE TREE OF LIBERTY *[Pages 38–60]*

1. Michael P. Zuckert, *The Natural Rights Republic* (Notre Dame: University of Notre Dame Press, 1996), 148–193.

2. Brett, *Changes of State*, 63.

3. Philip Melanchthon, *Philosophae moralis epitome,* 2–3.

4. Brett, *Changes,* 83.

5. See Edmund S. Morgan, ed., *Puritan Political Ideas* (Indianapolis: Hackett Publishing, 1965).

6. Cicero, *De Legibus*, I, 4.

7. Zuckert, *Republic,* 118.

8. See Max Weber, *The Protestant Ethic and the Spirit of Capitalism* (reprint New York: Courier Corp., 2003).

9. See C. B. MacPherson, *The Political Theory of Possessive Individualism: From Hobbes to Locke* (Oxford: Oxford University Press, 1962).

10. Brett, *Changes,* 69.

11. See M. van Ittersum, *Profit and Principle: Hugo Grotius, Natural Rights Theories and the Rise of Dutch Power in the East Indies, 1595–1615* (Leiden: Brill, 2006).

12. Hugo Grotius, *De Iure Belli et Pacis,* I, i, x.

13. Ibid., Prolegomena, 11.

14. Ibid., Prolegomena, 39.

15. Luis de Molina, *De iustitia et iure,* I, 2, 33, n.3.

16. Quoted in Brett, *Changes,* 103.

17. Grotius, *De iure praedae,* 1, Prolegomena, v. II, cap. 2.

18. See Weber, *The Protestant Ethic.*

19. Quoted in Ishay, *The History of Human Rights*, 92.

20. Ronald Bosco, "Lectures on the Pillory: The Early American Execution Sermon," *American Quarterly,* v. 30, 2 (Summer 1978), 156–176.

21. Hunt, *Inventing Human Rights,* 30.

22. Ibid., 81.

23. Blackstone, *Commentaries,* v. IV, 3.

24. See Annabel Brett, "Natural Right and Civil Community: The Civil Philosophy of Hugo Grotius," *Historical Journal* 45 (2002), 31–51.

25. See Katherine Gerbner, *Christian Slavery: Conversion and Race in the Protestant Atlantic World* (Philadelphia: University of Pennsylvania Press, 2018).

26. *In re Antelope,* 23 U.S. 66 (1825).

27. Cicero, *De Legibus,* I, 2.

28. Ibid., II, 4.

29. Execution Speech of Charles I (1649).

30. Thomas Hobbes, *De Corpore,* 14, 3.

31. Ibid., 1, 7.

32. Ibid., 1, 7. See also Peter Zagorin, *Hobbes and the Law of Nature* (Princeton: Princeton University Press, 2009), 26–28.

33. Hobbes, *Leviathan,* II, XVII, 2.

34. *English Bill of Rights* (1689).

35. John Locke, *Two Treatises on Government,* II, ii, 7.

36. Quoted in Zagorin, *Hobbes,* 27.

37. Ibid., 26.

38. Locke, *Treatises,* II, ii, 8.

39. Ibid., II, ii, 15.

40. Hunt, *Inventing,* 118.

41. Levy and Young, "Preface," in Morgan, ed., *Puritan,* v–vi.

42. Governor Clarke to the Rhode Island Assembly, British National Archives, Colonial Series, 5, f. 1259.

43. John Carter Brown Library, *Stevens Collection,* v. VIII, n. 510.

44. Blackstone, *Commentaries,* I, 129.

45. Quoted in Hunt, *Inventing,* 120.

46. Quoted in Zuckert, *Republic,* 149.

47. Hunt, *Inventing,* 122.

48. Quoted in Michael Zuckert, "Natural Rights and Imperial Constitutionalism: The American Revolution and the Development of the American Amalgam," in Ellen Frankel Paul et al., eds., *Natural Rights Liberalism from Locke to Nozick* (Cambridge: Cambridge University Press, 2005), 43.

49. Board of Trade to Governor Clarke, December 29, 1697, *Calendar of State Papers, Colonial Series 1696–1697,* n. 132.

50. William Popple to William Blathwayt, August 11, 1699. *Blathwayt Papers* Add. Ms. 9747, f. 19.

51. Addington's remarks, January 5, 1700, *CSP 1700,* n. 14, viii.

52. Quoted in Zuckert, "Natural Rights," 40.

53. See T. J. Hochstrasser, *Natural Law Theories in the Early Enlightenment* (Cambridge: Cambridge University Press, 2000).

54. Declaration of Independence (1776).

55. Hunt, *Inventing,* 17.

56. Ibid., 24–25.

57. Declaration of the Rights of Man and of the Citizen (1789).

THE CIVILIZATION GAME *[Pages 61–82]*

1. "Mark Twain Home, an Anti-Imperialist," *New York Herald,* October 16, 1900.

2. Mark Twain, "To the Person Sitting in Darkness" (New York: Anti-Imperialist League, 1901).

3. Stearns, *Human Rights,* 89.

4. *General Law Code for the Prussian States, proclaimed on February 5, 1794, effective June 7, 1794* (1794).

5. *The French Civil Code Translated* (London: William Benning, 1827), 3.

6. "Chartist Petition Agreed to at the Crown and Anchor Tavern Meeting in London, February 28, 1837" (1837).

7. Karl Marx and Friedrich Engels, *The German Ideology, Including the Theses of Feurbach [Feuerbach?]and the Introduction to the Critique of Political Economy* (New York: Progress Publisher, 1968), 35.

8. Friedrich Engels, "Herr Eugen Duhring's Revolution in Science" in Friedrich Engels and Karl Marx, *Basic Writings on Politics and Philosophy* (Garden City: Doubleday, 1959), 270.

9. Friedrich Engels and Karl Marx, *The Marx-Engels Reader* (New York: W. W. Norton, 1972), 726.

10. Geoffrey Marcus, *The Maiden Voyage* (New York: Viking Press, 1969), 94.

11. Pierre-Joseph Proudhon, *What Is Property? Or an Inquiry into the Principle of Right and Government* (London: New Temple Press, 1902), 179.

12. See Douglas Hay, et al. *Albion's Fatal Tree: Crime and Society in 18th Century England* (New York: Pantheon, 1976).

13. Susan B. Anthony and Elizabeth Cady Stanton, "The Declaration of Sentiments" (Seneca Falls, 1848) in Ishay, *Human Rights,* 164.

14. See Jenny S. Martinez, *The Slave Trade and the Origins of International Human Rights Law* (Oxford: Oxford University Press, 2012).

15. David Brion Davis, *The Problem of Slavery in the Age of Revolution, 1770–1823* (Ithaca: Cornell University Press, 1999), 485.

16. *Somerset v. Stewart* (1772), 98 Eng. Rep. 499 (K.B.).

17. Martinez, *Slave Trade,* 23–29.

18. Thomas Jefferson, Sixth Annual Presidential Message to Congress, December 2, 1806, in Julius W. Muller, ed. *Presidential Messages and State Papers* v. 2 (New York: Review of Reviews, 1917), 390.

19. *In re Antelope,* 23 U.S. 66 (1825).

20. Gerald S. Graham, *A Concise History of the British Empire* (New York: Viking, 1978), 132.

21. G. M. Trevelyan, *A History of England* (London: Longman, 1946), 342.

22. Graham, *Empire,* 140.

23. Ibid., 128–129.

24. See Jill Lepore, *The Name of War: King Philip's War and the Origins of American Identity* (New York: Penguin, 1999).

25. Quoted in Graham, *Empire,* 142.

26. John Stuart Mill, *Three Essays* (New York: Oxford University Press, 1975), 401.

27. Ibid., 408.

28. Quoted in Ishay, *Human Rights,* 153.

29. George Bernard Shaw, *Fabianism and the Empire* (London: Fabian Society, 1900), 22–39.

30. *Records of the Delhi Residency and Agency* (Lahore: 1911), 2.

31. Lawrence James, *Raj: The Making and Unmaking of British India* (New York: Little, Brown, 1998), 201.

32. Ibid., 151.

33. Archibald Primrose, Lord Rosebery, "Speech before the Colonial Institute," March 1, 1893.

34. Lord Rosebery, "Glasgow Rectorial Address," November 23, 1900.

35. Thomas R. Metcalf, *An Imperial Vision: Indian Architecture and Britain's Raj* (London: Faber and Faber, 2002), 225.

36. *British Parliamentary Papers: Colonies and East Indies 1804–1874* (Shannon: 1970), v. 15, 205.

37. See Douglas Burgess, *Engines of Empire: Steamships and the Victorian Imagination* (Stanford: Stanford University Press, 2016).

38. Abdul Hamid, *A Chronicle of British Indian Legal History* (Jaipur: RBSA Publishers, 1991), 129.

39. M. P. Jain, *Outlines of Indian Legal History* (Delhi: Wadhwa International, 1999), 230.

40. Quoted in Hamid, *Chronicle,* 150.

41. Quoted in Ibid., 151.

42. G. S. Chhabra, *Advance Study in the History of Modern India, Volume 2* (Delhi: Lotus Press, 2005), 265.

43. Neier, *Rights,* 48.

44. Quoted in James, *Raj,* 158.

45. Quoted in Graham, *Empire*, 208.

46. James, *Raj*, 178.

THE GREAT ADVENTURE *[Pages 83–104]*

1. John Malcolm Brinnin, *The Sway of the Grand Saloon* (New York: Delacorte Press, 1971), 333–334.

2. See Adam Hochschild, *King Leopold's Ghost: A Story of Greed, Terror and Heroism in Colonial Africa* (New York: Houghton Mifflin, 1998).

3. Ibid., 243.

4. Edmund Morris, *Theodore Rex* (New York: HarperCollins, 2001), 243.

5. Power, *A Problem from Hell*, 5.

6. Ibid., 7.

7. See Taner Akcam, *The Young Turks' Crime against Humanity: The Armenian Genocide and Ethnic Cleansing* (Princeton: Princeton University Press, 2012).

8. Power, *Problem from Hell*, 11.

9. Albert Fried, ed., *A Day of Dedication: The Essential Writings & Speeches of Woodrow Wilson* (New York: Macmillan, 1965), 301.

10. Margaret MacMillan, *Paris 1919: Six Months That Changed the World* (New York: Random House, 2001), 18.

11. Ibid., 91.

12. Ibid., 5.

13. Patricia O'Toole, *The Moralist: Woodrow Wilson and the World He Made* (New York: Simon & Schuster, 2018), 141.

14. E. David Cronon, ed., *The Political Thought of Woodrow Wilson* (Indianapolis: Bobbs-Merrill, 1965), 269.

15. Ibid., 275.

16. Ibid., 269.

17. Ibid., 275.

18. Arthur S. Link, *Wilson: The Struggle for Neutrality, 1914–1915* (Princeton: Princeton University Press, 1960), 512–514.

19. Cronon, *Thought*, 294–295.

20. O'Toole, *The Moralist*, 112–113.

21. Ibid., 113.

22. Ibid., 205.

23. Ibid., 241.

24. Fried, *Day of Dedication*, 305.

25. Cronon, *Thought*, 269.

26. Edwin Rozwenc and Thomas Lyons, eds., *Realism and Idealism in Wilson's Peace Program* (Boston: D. C. Heath, 1965), 33.

27. Cronon, *Thought,* 433.

28. Fried, *Day of Dedication,* 322.

29. Rozwenc and Lyons, *Realism and Idealism,* 13.

30. Fried, *Day of Dedication,* 360.

31. O'Toole, *The Moralist,* 343.

32. Rozwenc and Lyons, *Realism and Idealism,* 44.

33. Macmillan, *Paris 1919,* 92–93.

34. Ibid., 317–318.

35. Ibid., 318.

36. Ibid., 7.

37. O'Toole, *The Moralist,* 358.

38. Ibid., 360.

39. Ibid., 395.

40. Ibid., 409.

41. Fried, *Day of Dedication,* 400.

42. Ibid., 408.

43. Ibid., 417.

44. Ibid., 453.

45. Ibid., 459.

46. Ibid., 472.

THE PRESIDENT'S GHOST [Pages 105–141]

1. Doris Kearns Goodwin, *No Ordinary Time: Franklin and Eleanor Roosevelt—the Home Front in World War II* (New York: Simon & Schuster), 1994, 39.

2. Michael Dobbs, *Six Months in 1945: FDR, Stalin, Churchill and Truman—From World War to Cold War* (New York: Vintage, 2013), 78.

3. Goodwin, *No Ordinary Time,* 573.

4. Walter White, *A Man Called White* (New York: Viking Press, 1948), 179.

5. Goodwin, *No Ordinary Time,* 193.

6. See Mary Ann Glendon, *A World Made New: Eleanor Roosevelt and the Universal Declaration of Human Rights* (New York: Random House, 2001).

7. Glen M. Johnson, "The Contributions of Eleanor and Franklin Roosevelt to the Development of International Protection for Human Rights," *Human Rights Quarterly* 9 (February 1987), 19–48.

8. See Allida Black, *Casting Her Own Shadow: Eleanor Roosevelt and the Shaping of Postwar Liberalism* (New York: Columbia University Press, 1996).

9. Brian Bix, "Natural Law Theory," in Dennis Patterson, ed., *A Companion to Philosophy of Law and Legal Theory* (Oxford: Blackwell Publishers, 1996), 223–40.

10. See Elmer Bendiner, *A Time for Angels: The Tragicomic History of the League of Nations* (New York: Knopf, 1975).

11. See Antony Alcock, *A History of the International Labor Organization* (New York: Octagon Books, 1971).

12. "Traité général de rénonciation à la guerre…" *League of Nations Treaty Series* 94 (no. 2137), 57.

13. Speech before the League of Free Nations Association, March 1, 1919, found in the *Franklin Delano Roosevelt Papers,* Speech File, Box 1, Franklin D. Roosevelt Library. Summary of remarks given in *NYT,* March 2, 1919. (Hereafter *Roosevelt MSS*)

14. Speech at the League to Enforce Peace, July 18, 1919, reported in *Poughkeepsie Evening Star and Enterprise,* July 19, 1919.

15. Roosevelt explicitly references the league as the basis of a "new international law" in a speech given in Milwaukee, Wisconsin, August 20, 1920, *Roosevelt MSS.*

16. Speech accepting the Democratic nomination for vice president, August 9, 1920, *Roosevelt MSS.*

17. Draft of Jefferson Day Dinner Speech, April 13, 1945, *Roosevelt MSS.*

18. Robert Sherwood, *Roosevelt and Hopkins: An Intimate History* (New York: Harper, 1948), 9.

19. See Clifford Putney, *Muscular Christianity: Manhood and Sports in Protestant America, 1880–1920* (Cambridge: Harvard University Press, 2001).

20. Eleanor Roosevelt, *This I Remember* (New York: Harper, 1949), 69.

21. Quoted in Rowland Brucken, *A Most Uncertain Crusade: The United States, the United Nations, and Human Rights 1941–1953* (De Kalb: NIU Press, 2014), 42.

22. Susan Dimock, "The Natural Law Theory of St. Thomas Aquinas" in Joel Feinberg and Jules Coleman, *Philosophy of Law* (Belmont: Wadsworth/Thompson Learning, 2000), 19–32. See also Rev. John Jenkins, "Aquinas, Natural Law and the Challenges of Diversity" in Edward B. McLean, *Common Truths: New Perspectives on Natural Law* (Wilmington: ISI Books, 2000), 57–72.

23. Fourth Inaugural Address, January 25, 1945, *Roosevelt MSS.*

24. Speech in Mitchell, South Dakota, August 14, 1920, *Roosevelt MSS.*

25. Speech before the Old Town Merchants and Manufacturers' Association, reported in *Baltimore American,* March 7, 1919.

26. Speech given at Worcester Polytechnic Institute, June 25, 1919, *Roosevelt MSS.*

27. John Gunther, *Roosevelt in Retrospect* (New York: Harper, 1950), 216.

28. Josephus Daniels, *The Wilson Era: 1917–1923* (Chapel Hill: University of North Carolina Press, 1946), 273.

29. Emil Ludwig, *Roosevelt: A Study in Fortune and Power* (New York: Viking Press, 1938), 71.

30. The full draft of Roosevelt's "A Plan to Preserve World Peace" may be found in the appendices of Eleanor Roosevelt, *This I Remember,* 353–366.

31. Ibid., 34.

32. Statement prepared for Esther Lape of the American Peace Award Committee, July 1923, *Roosevelt MSS.*

33. Roosevelt to Edward Bok, August 12, 1923, *Roosevelt MSS.*

34. See Robert Dallek, *Franklin D. Roosevelt and American Foreign Policy, 1932–1945* (New York: Oxford University Press, 1979).

35. For a comprehensive history of international response to the Congo atrocities, see Hochschild, *King Leopold's Ghost.*

36. Speech given in Chicago on October 5, 1937, *Roosevelt MSS.*

37. Frederick Pollack, "The King's Peace in the Middle Ages" in *Select Essays of Anglo-American Legal History* v. 2 (Boston: Little Brown & Co., 1907), 334; see also F. W. Maitland, *The Constitutional History of England* (Cambridge: Cambridge University Press, 1919).

38. Originally published in *Reichsgesetzblatt* I, 1935, 1146.

39. See Richard Lawrence Miller, *Nazi Justiz: Law of the Holocaust* (Westport: Praeger, 1995).

40. For multiple accounts see Erik Larson, *In the Garden of Beasts: Love, Terror and an American Family in Hitler's Berlin* (New York: Broadway Paperbacks, 2011).

41. Brendan F. Brown, "Natural Law and the Law-Making Function in American Jurisprudence," *Notre Dame Law Review* 9 (1939), 9–25.

42. Clarence Streit, *Union Now: A Proposal for a Federal Union of the Democracies of the North Atlantic* (New York: Harper, 1939).

43. Eleanor Roosevelt, "My Day," January 1, 1941.

44. Samuel I. Rosenman, *Working with Roosevelt* (New York: Harper, 1952), 263.

45. State of the Union Address, January 6, 1941, *Roosevelt MSS.*

46. For analysis of the text and its impact, see Frank Donovan, *Mr. Roosevelt's Four Freedoms: The Story behind the United Nations Charter* (New York: Dodd Mead, 1966).

47. Brucken, *Crusade,* 11–16. See also Elizabeth Borgwardt, *A New Deal for the World: America's Vision for Human Rights* (Cambridge: Harvard University Press, 2005).

48. Sumner Welles, *The World of the Four Freedoms* (New York: Columbia University Press, 1943), 30.

49. Jane H. Pease, "The Road to the Higher Law," *New York History* 40, 2 (April 1959), 117–136.

50. See Jo Renee Formicola, *The Catholic Church and Human Rights* (New York: Garland Publishing, 1988).

51. Brucken, 27.

52. Richard H. Immerman, *John Foster Dulles: Piety, Pragmatism, and Power in U.S. Foreign Policy* (Wilmington: Scholarly Resources, 1999); see also Ronald Pruessen, *John Foster Dulles: The Road to Power* (New York: Free Press, 1982).

53. "'Six Pillars Peace Program' of Federal Council of Churches," *NYT,* June 6, 1943.

54. See Douglas Brinkley and David R. Facey-Crowther, eds., *The Atlantic Charter* (New York: St. Martin's, 1994).

55. Townsend Hoopes and Douglas Brinkley, *FDR and the Creation of the U.N.* (New Haven: Yale University Press, 1997), 36–40; see also Theodore Wilson, *The First Summit: Roosevelt and Churchill at Placentia Bay, 1941* (Lawrence: University Press of Kansas, 1991).

56. Quoted in Quincy Wright, "Human Rights and the World Order," *International Conciliation* (April, 1943), 238.

57. Hoopes and Brinkley, *Creation of the U.N.*, 45–47.

58. See Tony Evans, *U.S. Hegemony and the Project of Universal Human Rights* (New York: St. Martin's, 1996).

59. Catherine Grollman, "Cordell Hull and His Concept of a World Organization," PhD dissertation, University of North Carolina, 1965.

60. Cordell Hull, "The War and Human Freedom," radio address delivered July 23, 1942 (New York: Literary Licensing LLC, 2013).

61. Third Inaugural Address, January 20, 1941, *Roosevelt MSS.*

62. For Berle's account of the committee proceedings, see Beatrice B. Berle and Francis Jacobs, eds., *Navigating the Rapids, 1918–1971: From the Papers of Adolf A. Berle* (New York: Harcourt Brace Jovanovich, 1973).

63. Quoted in Brucken, *Crusade,* 27.

64. Percy Bordwell to Franklin Roosevelt, January 18, 1943, *Roosevelt MSS.*

65. Brucken, *Crusade,* 49.

66. Harley Notter, *Postwar Foreign Policy Preparation, 1939–1945* (Washington, DC: US Government Printing Office, 1950), 526–32.

67. Quincy Wright, "Human Rights and the World Order," *International Conciliation* 389 (April 1943), 238–62.

68. Daniel Gorman, "International Law and the International Thought of Quincy Wright, 1918–1945," *Diplomatic History* 41, 2 (April 2017), 336–361.

69. Sherwood, *Roosevelt and Hopkins,* 363.

70. Goodwin, *No Ordinary Time,* 211.

71. Clark Eichelberger, *Organizing for Peace: A Personal History of the Founding of the United Nations* (New York: Harper & Row, 1977), 193.

72. Quoted in Brucken, *Crusade,* 37.

73. William D. Hassett, *Off the Record with F.D.R.* (New Brunswick: Rutgers University Press, 1958), 166–7.

74. Ruth B. Russell, *A History of the United Nations Charter: The Role of the United States, 1940–1945* (Washington, DC: Brookings Institution, 1958), 219–20.

75. Brucken, *Crusade,* 55.

76. See, generally, Hoopes and Brinkley, *Creation.*

77. Brucken, *Crusade,* 11.

78. Jim Bishop, *FDR's Last Year* (New York: William Morrow, 1974), 419.

79. Robert A. Divine, *Second Chance: The Triumph of Internationalism in America during World War II* (New York: Atheneum, 1967), 132–3. For a complete account of Vandenberg's political transformation, see David C. Tompkins, *Senator Arthur H. Vandenberg: The Evolution of a Modern Republican, 1884–1945* (Lansing: Michigan State University Press, 1970).

80. Ibid., 150–153.

81. Quoted in Bishop, *Last Year*, 56–7.

82. Robert C. Hilderbrand, *Dumbarton Oaks: The Origins of the United Nations and the Search for Postwar Security* (Chapel Hill: University of North Carolina Press, 1990), 105.

83. Hoopes and Brinkley, *Creation*, 143.

84. Diary of Edward Stettinius, September 21, 1944, Thomas Campbell and George Herring, eds., *The Diaries of George Stettinius, Jr.* (New York: New Viewpoints, 1975).

85. Speech given in Chicago, October 28, 1944, *Roosevelt MSS*.

86. Robert Summers, ed. *Dumbarton Oaks* (New York: H. W. Wilson, 1945), 138–9; see also "Davis Sees Dark Future if Present Efforts Fail," *Changing World* 17 (January 1945), 5.

87. Quincy Wright, review, "*The World of the Four Freedoms*, Sumner Welles," *Journal of Political Economy* 52, 1 (March 1944), 95.

88. Department of State, *Report on the Delegation of the United States of America to the Inter-American Conference on Problems of War and Peace* (Washington, DC: US Government Printing Office, 1946); see also "Resolution 30 of the Inter-American Conference on Problems of War and Peace," *US Department of State Bulletin* 12 (March 18, 1945), 449; US Department of State, *The United Nations Conference on International Organization: Selected Documents* (Washington, DC: US Government Printing Office, 1946), 92.

89. State of the Union, January 6, 1945, *Roosevelt MSS*.

90. Address to Congress, March 1, 1945, *Roosevelt MSS*.

91. David B. Woolner, *The Last 100 Days: FDR at War and Peace* (New York: Basic Books, 2017), 224.

92. US Department of State, *The United Nations Conference on International Organization, San Francisco, April 25 to June 26, 1945. Selected Documents* (Washington, DC: US Government Printing Office, 1946).

93. Johnson, "Contributions," 19–32.

94. Diary of Margaret Suckley, March 31, 1945, *Roosevelt MSS*.

95. Bishop, *Last Year*, 551.

96. Diary of Margaret Suckley, April 6, 1945, *Roosevelt MSS*.

97. Hassett, *Off the Record*, 335.

98. *New Republic*, April 23, 1945.

99. Address to the United Nations Conference, San Francisco, April 25, 1945, *Public Papers Harry S. Truman, 1945–1953*, Harry S. Truman Presidential Library.

100. Robert Schlesinger, *White House Ghosts: Presidents and Their Speechwriters* (New York: Simon & Schuster, 2008), 31.

101. Leland M. Goodrich and Edvard Hambro, *Charter of the United Nations: Commentary and Documents* (Boston: World Peace Federation, 1949).

102. Divine, *Second Chance*, 296.

103. See Dorothy B. Robins, *Experiment in Democracy: The Story of U.S. Citizen Organizations in Forging the Charter of the United Nations* (New York: Parkside Press, 1971).

104. See Stuart Murray and James McCabe, eds., *Norman Rockwell's Four Freedoms: Images that Inspire a Nation* (Stockbridge: Berkshire House, 1993).

105. Rosenman, *Working with Roosevelt*, 167.

106. Justice Robert Jackson's Address for the Prosecution at Nuremberg, November 21, 1945, *Speeches-Nuremberg Prosecutor, Robert H. Jackson Center*.

107. Speech before the Foreign Policy Association, October 21, 1944, *Roosevelt MSS*.

THE ADVANTAGE OF THE STRONGER *[Pages 142–172]*

1. Quoted in Telford Taylor, *Anatomy of the Nuremberg Trials* (New York: Alfred Knopf, 1992), 44–45.

2. See Varkhan Dadrian, *The History of the Armenian Genocide* (New York: Bergahn Books, 2003).

3. See Douglas Kelley, *22 Cells at Nuremberg* (New York: McFadden, 1961).

4. Eden war criminals memorandum, June 22, 1942, in British National Archives Cabinet Papers 66/25.

5. Hannah Arendt to Karl Jaspers, August 17, 1946, in *Correspondence, 1926–1949* (New York: Harcourt Brace, 1992), 54.

6. In retrospect we now recognize that the tribunal proceedings that began in November 1945 were the first of numerous such tribunals both in Germany and Japan. That was not, however, universally envisioned at the time of planning.

7. *Report of Robert H. Jackson, United States Representative to the International Conference on Military Trials: London, 1945* (Washington, DC: US Department of State, 1947), 48–50.

8. Robert Jackson, "Nuremberg in Retrospect: Legal Answer to International Lawlessness," XXXC *American Bar Association Journal* (October 1949), 813–887.

9. *Trial of the Major War Criminals before the International Military Tribunal* (Washington, DC: US Government Printing Office, 1947), v. 2, 101.

10. Harold Nicholson, *Spectator*, May 10, 1946.

11. Airey Neave, *On Trial at Nuremberg* (Boston: Little Brown, 1978), 230–231.

12. Plato, *Republic* (New York: Basic Books, 1968), 16.

13. Michael Stolleis, *The Law under the Swastika* (Chicago: University of Chicago Press, 1998), 15.

14. Hermann Rauschning, *The Voice of Destruction* (New York: Putnam's, 1940), 223.

15. Arthur Wellesley, Duke of Wellington, *Supplementary Despatches and Memoranda of Field Marshal Arthur, Duke of Wellington, K.G.* (London: John Murray, 1863), v. 10, 631.

16. Ibid., v. 11, 95.

17. Quoted in Gary Jonathan Bass, *Stay the Hand of Vengeance: The Politics of War Crimes Tribunals* (Princeton: Princeton University Press, 2000), 50.

18. Imperial War Cabinet minutes, British National Archive Cabinet Papers, 23/43.

19. *Public Papers of Woodrow Wilson: War and Peace, Presidential Messages, Addresses and Public Papers 1917–1924* (New York: Harper, 1925), v. 5, 11.

20. Quoted in James F. Willis, *Prologue to Nuremberg: The Politics and Diplomacy of Punishing War Criminals of the First World War* (Westport: Greenwood, 1982), 25.

21. Committee on the Responsibility of the Authors of the War and on Enforcement of Penalties, British National Archives Foreign Office Papers, 1201/3.

22. This is not to say that Napoleon was an ideal candidate either. In fact the history of his political rise was long and convoluted, and it is not at all clear whether it could be termed "usurpation" by even the most liberal understanding of the term. What is clear is that, had it been so, the legitimacies of a great many of Europe's monarchies—including Britain herself—would fall into question. So perhaps it was best they sent him to St. Helena.

23. Quoted in Egon Schwelb, "Crimes against Humanity," 23 *British Year Book of International Law* (1946), 178–226.

24. *Punishment for War Crimes: The Inter-Allied Declaration Signed at St. James' Palace, London,* January 13, 1942 (London: Inter-Allied Information Committee, 1942), 3–4.

25. See Leonard Baker, *Brahmin in Revolt: A Biography of Herbert C. Pell* (Garden City, NY: Doubleday, 1972).

26. Taylor, *Anatomy,* 28.

27. *International Conference on Military Trials* (Washington, DC: US Government Printing Office, 1949), 9.

28. Ibid., 9.

29. Taylor, *Anatomy,* 29.

30. *History of the United States War Crime Commission and the Development of the Laws of War* (London: United States War Crimes Commission, 1948), 107–108.

31. Taylor, *Anatomy,* 29.

32. Bass, *Hand of Vengeance,* 147.

33. Eden memorandum, June 22, 1942, British National Archives Cabinet Papers 66/25.

34. Drexel A. Sprecher, *Inside the Nuremberg Tribunal: A Prosecutor's Comprehensive Account* (New York: University Press of America, 1999), 27.

35. See Power, *A Problem from Hell.*

36. Michael B. Oren, *Power, Faith and Fantasy: Americans in the Middle East, 1776 to the Present* (New York: W. W. Norton, 2007), 334.

37. John Morton Blum, *Roosevelt and Morgenthau* (Boston: Houghton Mifflin, 1970), xvi.

38. Goodwin, *No Ordinary Time,* 299.

39. Henry Morgenthau, *Diaries of Henry Morgenthau Jr.,* September 22, 1944, FDR Library.

40. "Post Surrender Germany Program," September 4, 1944, in Ibid.

41. Ibid., September 4, 1944.

42. Ibid., September 4, 1944.

43. Ibid., September 4, 1944.

44. Henry L. Stimson, August 25, 1944, *The Politics of Integrity: The Diaries of Henry L. Stimson* (New York: McGraw-Hill, 1976); see also "Diary of Henry L. Stimson, 1923–1945, Yale University Archives.

45. Goodwin, *No Ordinary Time,* 543–544.

46. Ibid., 234.

47. Stimson, *Diary,* September 27, 1940.

48. Ibid., September 16, 1944.

49. Ibid., October 25, 1944.

50. Gary Jonathan Bass writes, "Stimson's approach is the kind of legal reasoning that would not have considered it a murder when Cain slew Abel, because such a crime had not been committed before." Bass, *Stay,* 175.

51. Stimson to FDR, *Diary,* September 9, 1944.

52. Bass, *Stay,* 155–156.

53. Stimson to FDR, *Diary,* September 9, 1944.

54. *Journal of the United Nations,* No. 58. Supp. A-A/P.V./55, 185.

55. Taylor, *Anatomy,* 4.

56. Conot, *Justice,* 11.

57. Bradley F. Smith, *Reaching Judgment at Nuremberg* (New York: Basic Books, 1977), 27.

58. Quoted in Taylor, *Anatomy,* 38.

59. Rosenman, *Working with Roosevelt,* 472.

60. *International Conference on Military Trials* (Washington, DC: US Government Printing Office, 1949), 3–17.

61. Robert C. Jackson, "The Challenge of International Lawlessness," 374 *International Conciliation* (1940–1941), 683–691.

62. Speech by Robert Jackson, 35 *American Journal of International Law* (1941), 355–356.

63. Telford Taylor, "The Nuremberg Trials," *International Reconciliation* 450 (1949), 241–372.

64. *Trial of the Major War Criminals before the International Military Tribunal* (Washington, DC: US Government Printing Office, 1947), v. 2, 103.

65. Sprecher, *Inside,* 65.

66. *Trial,* v. 2, 109.

67. Ibid., 113.

68. Ibid., 115.

69. Ibid., 123.

70. Ibid., 103.

71. Quincy Wright, "The Law of the Nuremberg Tribunal," 41 *American Journal of International Law* (1947), 38–72.

72. Thomas J. Dodd, "The Nuremberg Trials," 37 *Journal of Criminal Law and Criminology* (January 1947), 357–367.

73. *Trial,* v. 17, 553.

74. Ibid., 514.

75. Ibid., v. 2, 125.

THE CAROUSEL OF PROGRESS *[Pages 173–190]*

1. See Lawrence Samuel, *The End of the Innocence: The 1964–1965 New York World's Fair* (Syracuse: Syracuse University Press, 2007).

2. Preamble to the Charter of the United Nations, June 26, 1945.

3. Glendon, *A World Made New,* 21.

4. Eleanor Roosevelt, "The Promise of Human Rights," *Foreign Affairs* (April 1948), 473.

5. Glendon, *World,* 72.

6. Martain, *Human Rights: Comments and Interpretations,* 186.

7. Mohandas Gandhi, "Letter Addressed to the Director-General of UNESCO" in Ibid., 18.

8. Humayun Kabir, "Human Rights: The Islamic Tradition and the Problems of the World Today" in Ibid., 191.

9. Human Rights Commission, First Session, Summary Records, quoted in Glendon, *World,* 37.

10. Ibid., 37.

11. Ibid., 146.

12. Eleanor Roosevelt, "Making Human Rights Come Alive," in Allida Black, ed., *What I Hope to Leave Behind: The Essential Essays of Eleanor Roosevelt* (New York: Carlson Press, 1995), 559.

13. Eleanor Roosevelt, *On My Own* (New York: Harper Publishing, 1958), 77.

14. Glendon, *World,* 37–8.

15. Ibid., 166.

16. See, for example, Henry Steiner and Philip Alston, *International Human Rights in Context* (Oxford: Clarendon Press, 1996). For an alternative view, see Elizabeth Borgwardt, *A New Deal for the World: America's Vision for Human Rights* (Cambridge: Harvard University Press, 2006).

17. "Statement by Mrs. Franklin D. Roosevelt," *Department of State Bulletin,* December 19, 1948, 751–2.

18. See, generally, Borgwardt, *New Deal.*

19. US Department of State, *The United Nations: Four Years of Achievement,* Department of State Publication 3624 (September 1949), 1–2.

20. Elizabeth Borgwardt, "Constitutionalizing Human Rights: The Rise and Rise of the Nuremberg Principles" in Akira Iriye, et al., eds., *The Human Rights Revolution: An International History* (Oxford: Oxford University Press, 2012), 78.

21. See Mark Bradley, "The Ambiguities of Sovereignty: The United States and the Global Rights Cases of the 1940's" in Douglas Howland and Luise White, eds., *Art of the State: Sovereignty Past and Present* (Bloomington: Indiana University Press, 2008).

22. Richard Davies, *Defender of the Old Guard: John Bricker and American Politics* (Columbus: Ohio State University Press, 1993), 155.

23. Duane Tananbaum, *The Bricker Amendment Controversy: A Test of Eisenhower's Political Leadership* (Ithaca: Cornell University Press, 1988), 35.

24. Department of State, *Bulletin,* 28, no. 721 (April 20, 1953), 591.

25. Borgwardt, "Constitutionalizing," 79.

26. Goodwin, *No Ordinary Time,* 343.

27. Dixie Bartholomew-Frees, *The OSS and Ho Chi Minh: Unexpected Allies in the War against Japan* (Lawrence: University of Kansas Press, 2006), 243. See also Samuel Moyn, "Imperialism, Self-Determination and the Rise of Human Rights" in Iriye, *Human Rights,* 159–160.

28. Moyn, "Imperialism," 160.

29. Stearns, *Human Rights,* 129.

30. Ibid., 130–1.

31. See Bonny Ibhawoh, *Imperialism and Human Rights: Colonial Discourses of [on?] Rights and Liberties in African History* (Albany: State University of New York Press, 2007).

32. Moyn, "Imperialism," 163.

33. Amilcar Cabral, "Anonymous Soldiers for the United Nations" in Richard Handyside, ed., *Revolution in Guinea: Selected Texts* (New York: Monthly Review Press, 1969), 50–1.

34. Blackstone, *Commentaries,* I, 129.

THE LAST CRUSADE [Pages 191–212]

1. Jamie Metzl, *Western Responses to Human Rights Abuses in Cambodia, 1975–1980* (New York: St. Martin's, 1996), 11.

2. Power, *A Problem from Hell,* 103.

3. Ibid., 89–90.

4. Joan Criddle and Teeda Butt Mam, *To Destroy You Is No Loss: The Odyssey of a Cambodian Family* (New York: Atlantic Monthly Press, 1987), 105.

5. "Human Rights Violations in Cambodia," April 21, 1978, *Public Papers of the Presidents of the United States: Jimmy Carter, 1978,* v. 2 (Washington, DC: GPO, 1979), 767–768.

6. Power, *Problem,* 133–134.

7. Moyn, *The Last Utopia,* 3.

8. Stephen Hopgood, *The Endtimes of Human Rights* (Ithaca: Cornell University Press, 2013), 98.

9. Aryeh Neier, *The International Human Rights Movement: A History* (Princeton: Princeton University Press, 2012), 169.

10. Mission statement available on www.cartercenter.org.

11. Neier, *International,* 171–175.

12. Ibid., 174.

13. Ronald Reagan, "Farewell Address to the Nation," January 11, 1989.

14. Nicolas Guilhot, *The Democracy Makers: Human Rights and International Order* (New York: Columbia University Press, 2005), 75.

15. Ronald Reagan, "Speech Commemorating the Statue of Liberty Restoration," July 3, 1986.

16. Stearns, *Human Rights,* 147.

17. Bilahari Kausikan, "Asia's Different Standard," *Foreign Policy* (Fall 1993), 24–41.

18. Ibid., 41.

19. Vienna Declaration and Programme of Action, June 25, 1993.

20. Ibid.

21. Quoted in Ishay, *Human Rights,* 289.

22. www.icty.org.

23. "'My soul is still in Rwanda': 25 years after the genocide, Roméo Dallaire still grapples with guilt," *CBC Radio,* April 7, 2019.

24. M. Cherif Bassiouni, "From Versailles to Rwanda in Seventy-Five Years: The Need to Establish a Permanent International Criminal Court," *Harvard Human Rights Journal* 10 (1997), 12–13.

25. Aryeh Neier, *Taking Liberties: Four Decades of the Struggle for Rights* (New York: Public Affairs, 2003), 363.

26. Hopgood, *Endtimes,* 126.

27. Tim Kelsall, *Culture under Cross Examination: International Justice and the Special Court for Sierra Leone* (Cambridge: Cambridge University Press, 2009), 36.

28. See my own study, Douglas Burgess, *World for Ransom: Piracy Is Terrorism, Terrorism Is Piracy* (New York: Prometheus Books, 2010).

29. Vice President Dick Cheney on *Meet the Press,* September 16, 2001.

30. Jameel Jaffer and Amrit Singh, *Administration of Torture* (New York: Columbia University Press, 2008), 29–30.

31. G. John Ikenberry and Anne-Marie Slaughter, "Forging a World of Liberty under Law: US National Security in the 21st Century," Princeton Project on National Security, September 2006.

32. Geoffrey Robertson, "Why It's Absurd to Claim that Justice Has Been Done," *Independent,* May 3, 2011.

33. Hopgood, *Endtimes,* 164.

34. Neier, *International,* 311.

35. Hopgood, *Endtimes,* 142.

36. Ibid., 163.

37. "Chic-fil-A's Ties to a Controversial Christian Charity Are Going Viral," *Business Insider*, October 17, 2019.

38. Ben Rhodes, "Inside the White House during the Syrian 'Red Line' Crisis," *Atlantic*, June 3, 2018.

39. Ibid.

AMERICAN CARNAGE *[Pages 213–232]*

1. Robert Graves, *I, Claudius* (New York: Harrison Smith, 1934), 395.

2. Jorge Ramos, "What I Learned from My Brush with Trump," *NYT*, December 4, 2020.

3. Mary Druziak, "Donald Trump and America's Moral Authority," *NYT*, July 22, 2016.

4. Somini Sengupta, "Nikki Haley Calls United Nations Human Rights Council 'So Corrupt,'" *NYT*, March 29, 2017.

5. Jorge D. Castaneda, "The Cost of Trump's Retreat from Rights," *NYT*, April 26, 2017.

6. Pippa Norris, "Trump's Global Democracy Retreat," *NYT*, September 17, 2017.

7. "To Trump, Human Rights Concerns Are Often a Barrier to Trade," *NYT*, May 20, 2017.

8. "'Fake News,' Trump's Obsession, Is Now a Cudgel for Strongmen," *NYT*, December 12, 2017.

9. "Trump Takes Incoherence and Inhumanity and Calls It Foreign Policy," *NYT*, October 19, 2019.

10. "Trump's World and the Retreat of Shame," *NYT*, March 9, 2018.

11. "Trump to Dictators: Have a Nice Day," *NYT*, June 19, 2018.

12. Gary J. Bass, "Trump's Cynical Use of Human Rights," *NYT*, February 12, 2018.

13. "Trump Uses Kids Sold into Sex Slavery to Score Political Points," *NYT*, February 26, 2020.

14. Ibid.

15. "The Trump Musical: Anything Goes," *NYT*, March 5, 2019.

16. "Trump's World," op. cit.

17. "Trump's 'Concentration Camps.'" *NYT*, June 23, 2019.

18. "U.N. Rights Chief Tells U.S. to Stop Taking Children from Parents," *NYT*, June 18, 2018.

19. "Trump Withdraws U.S. from U.N. Human Rights Council," *NYT*, June 19, 2018.

20. "Commission on Unalienable Rights," *Federal Register*, May 30, 2019.

21. Michael Pompeo, "Unalienable Rights and U.S. Foreign Policy," *Wall Street Journal*, July 7, 2019.

22. *US Senate Committee on Foreign Relations*, June 12, 2019.

23. Roger Cohen, "Trump's Ominous Attempt to Redefine Human Rights," *New York Times*, July 12, 2019.

24. Michael Fuchs, "Donald Trump Is on an Orwellian Mission to Redefine Human Rights," *The Guardian,* July 18, 2019.

25. Pranshu Verma, "Pompeo's Quest to Redefine Human Rights Draws Concern at UN," *NYT,* September 20, 2020.

26. "A New Trump Battleground: Defining Human Rights," *NYT,* June 17, 2019.

27. "Pompeo Says Human Rights Policy Must Prioritize Property Rights and Religious Liberty," *NYT,* July 16, 2020.

28. Ibid.

29. "Pompeo's Quest," op. cit.

30. "At the State Dept., Calling for Alliances and Acting as a Coalition of One," *NYT,* November 2, 2020.

31. "Trump's Sanctions May Do Little Beyond Alienating Allies," *NYT,* October 18, 2020.

32. Chile Eboe-Osuji, "All We Want Is Justice for Victims, Says the I.C.C.," *NYT,* June 18, 2020.

33. Joe Biden, "Why America Must Lead Again," *Foreign Affairs,* March/April, 2020.

34. "Britain, Charting Its Own Course on Human Rights, Imposes New Sanctions," *NYT,* July, 6, 2020.

35. "Biden Wants America to Lead the World. It Shouldn't." *NYT,* December 2, 2020.

36. "Feeling Spurned by Trump, UN Sees Redemption in Biden and His Team," *NYT,* December 3, 2020.

PROGRESSLAND *[Pages 233–243]*

1. F. W. Maitland and Francis C. Montague, *A Sketch of English Legal History* (New York: G. P. Putnam, 1915), 2.

2. Henkin, *The Age of Rights.*

3. See Power, *A Problem from Hell.*

4. Quoted in Susan Dimock, "The Natural Law Theory of St. Thomas Aquinas" in Joel Feinberg and Jules Coleman, *Philosophy of Law* (New York: Wadsworth, 1999), 19–33.

5. Maitland, *Constitutional History of England,* 539.

6. Maitland and Montague, *A Sketch of English Legal History,* 1.

7. Robert Jackson, "Opening Statement for the Prosecution at the International Military Tribunal," November 21, 1945.

— Bibliography —

Primary Sources Cited

Thomas Aquinas, *Summa Theologica* (1485).

"Chartist Petition Agreed to at the Crown and Anchor Tavern Meeting in London, February 28, 1837" (1837).

Marcus Tullius Cicero, *De Legibus, De Republica.*

Declaration of Independence (1776).

Declaration of the Rights of Man and of the Citizen (1789).

English Bill of Rights (1689).

Execution Speech of Charles I (1649).

The French Civil Code Translated (London: William Benning, 1827).

General Law Code for the Prussian States, Proclaimed on February 5, 1794; Effective June 7, 1794 (1794).

Hugo Grotius, *De Iure Belli et Pacis* (1625).

Thomas Hobbes, *De Corpore* (1655).

In re Antelope, 23 U.S. 66 (1825).

Robert Jackson's Address for the Prosecution at Nuremberg, November 21, 1945, *Speeches-Nuremberg Prosecutor, Robert H. Jackson Center.*

John Locke, *Two Treatises on Government* (1689).

The Mahabharata, *Karna Parva.*

Philip Melanchthon, *Philosophae moralis epitome* (1539).

Luis de Molina, *De iustitia et iure* (1733).

Archibald Primrose, Lord Rosebery, "Speech before the Colonial Institute," March 1, 1893.

Records of the Delhi Residency and Agency (Lahore: 1911).

Lord Rosebery, "Glasgow Rectorial Address," November 23, 1900.

Somerset v. Stewart (1772), 98 Eng. Rep. 499 (K.B.).

"Traité général de rénonciation à la guerre..." *League of Nations Treaty Series* 94 (no. 2137), 57.

Vienna Declaration and Programme of Action, June 14, 1993.

PERIODICALS AND ARCHIVAL COLLECTIONS CITED

Atlantic Monthly

Baltimore American

Boston Globe

British National Archives

Business Insider

Changing World

Federal Register

Foreign Affairs

*Franklin Delano Roosevelt
Presidential Library*

The Guardian

Harry S. Truman Presidential Library

Huffington Post

Independent

John Carter Brown Library

New York Herald

New York Times

Overland Monthly

*Poughkeepsie Evening Star
and Enterprise*

Spectator

Vox

Wall Street Journal

Washington Post

JOURNAL ARTICLES CITED

Antieau, Chester James, "Natural Rights and the Founding Fathers—The Virginians," *Washington and Lee Law Review* 17(1) (1960), 43–81.

Bassiouni, M. Cherif, "From Versailles to Rwanda in Seventy-Five Years: The Need to Establish a Permanent International Criminal Court," *Harvard Human Rights Journal* 10 (1997), 12–13.

Bosco, Ronald, "Lectures on the Pillory: The Early American Execution Sermon," *American Quarterly*, v. 30, 2 (Summer 1978), 156–176.

Brett, Annabel, "Natural Right and Civil Community: The Civil Philosophy of Hugo Grotius," *Historical Journal* 45 (2002), 31–51.

Brown, Brendan F., "Natural Law and the Law-Making Function in American Jurisprudence," *Notre Dame Law Review* 9 (1939), 9–25.

Dodd, Thomas J., "The Nuremberg Trials," 37 *Journal of Criminal Law and Criminology* (January 1947), 357–367.

Gorman, Daniel, "International Law and the International Thought of Quincy Wright, 1918–1945," *Diplomatic History* 41, 2 (April 2017), 336–361.

Ikenberry, G. John, and Anne-Marie Slaughter, "Forging a World of Liberty under Law: US National Security in the 21st Century," *Princeton Project on National Security*, September 2006.

Jackson, Robert, "The Challenge of International Lawlessness," 374 *International Conciliation* (1940–1941), 683–691.

Jackson, Robert, "Nuremberg in Retrospect: Legal Answer to International Lawlessness," XXXC *American Bar Association Journal* (October 1949), 813–887.

Jackson, Robert, "Speech," 35 *American Journal of International Law* (1941), 355–356.

Johnson, Glen M., "The Contributions of Eleanor and Franklin Roosevelt to the Development of International Protection for Human Rights," *Human Rights Quarterly* 9 (February 1987), 19–48.

Kausikan, Bilahari, "Asia's Different Standard," *Foreign Policy* (Fall 1993), 24–41.

Pease, Jane H., "The Road to the Higher Law," *New York History* 40, 2 (April 1959), 117–136.

Roosevelt, Eleanor, "The Promise of Human Rights," *Foreign Affairs* (April 1948), 473.

Schwelb, Egon, "Crimes against Humanity," 23 *British Year Book of International Law* (1946), 178–226.

Taylor, Telford, "The Nuremberg Trials," *International Reconciliation* 450 (1949), 241–372.

Twain, Mark, "To the Person Sitting in Darkness" (New York: Anti-Imperialist League, 1901).

Wright, Quincy, "Human Rights and the World Order," *International Conciliation* (April 1943), 238.

Wright, Quincy, "The Law of the Nuremberg Tribunal," 41 *American Journal of International Law* (1947), 38–72.

Wright, Quincy, review, "*The World of the Four Freedoms,* Sumner Welles," *Journal of Political Economy* 52, 1 (March 1944), 95.

SECONDARY SOURCES CITED

Akcam, Taner, *The Young Turks' Crime against Humanity: The Armenian Genocide and Ethnic Cleansing* (Princeton: Princeton University Press, 2012).

Alcock, Antony, *A History of the International Labor Organization* (New York: Octagon Books, 1971).

Arendt, Hannah, *Correspondence, 1926–1949* (New York: Harcourt Brace, 1992).

Baker, Leonard, *Brahmin in Revolt: A Biography of Herbert C. Pell* (Garden City, NY: Doubleday, 1972).

Bartholomew-Frees, Dixie, *The OSS and Ho Chi Minh: Unexpected Allies in the War against Japan* (Lawrence: University of Kansas Press, 2006).

Bass, Gary Jonathan, *Stay the Hand of Vengeance: The Politics of War Crimes Tribunals* (Princeton: Princeton University Press, 2000).

Bendiner, Elmer, *A Time for Angels: The Tragicomic History of the League of Nations* (New York: Knopf, 1975).

Berle, Beatrice B., and Francis Jacobs, eds., *Navigating the Rapids, 1918–1971: From the Papers of Adolf A. Berle* (New York: Harcourt Brace Jovanovich, 1973).

Bishop, Jim, *FDR's Last Year* (New York: William Morrow, 1974).

Black, Allida, *Casting Her Own Shadow: Eleanor Roosevelt and the Shaping of Postwar Liberalism* (New York: Columbia University Press, 1996).

Black, Allida, ed., *What I Hope to Leave Behind: The Essential Essays of Eleanor Roosevelt* (New York: Carlson Press, 1995).

Blackstone, William, *Commentaries on the Laws of England* (Oxford: Oxford University Press reprint, 2008).

Blum, John Morton, *Roosevelt and Morgenthau* (Boston: Houghton Mifflin, 1970).

Borgwardt, Elizabeth, *A New Deal for the World: America's Vision for Human Rights* (Cambridge: Harvard University Press, 2005).

Brett, Annabel, *Changes of State: Nature and the Limits of the City in Early Modern Natural Law* (Princeton: Princeton University Press, 2011).

Brinkley, Douglas, and David R. Facey-Crowther, eds., *The Atlantic Charter* (New York: St. Martin's, 1994).

Brinnin, John Malcolm, *The Sway of the Grand Saloon* (New York: Delacorte Press, 1971).

British Parliamentary Papers: Colonies and East Indies 1804–1874 (Shannon: 1970).

Brucken, Rowland, *A Most Uncertain Crusade: The United States, the United Nations, and Human Rights 1941–1953* (De Kalb: NIU Press, 2014).

Burgess, Douglas, *Engines of Empire: Steamships and the Victorian Imagination* (Stanford: Stanford University Press, 2016).

Campbell, Thomas, and George Herring, eds., *The Diaries of George Stettinius Jr.* (New York: New Viewpoints, 1975).

Chhabra, G. S., *Advance Study in the History of Modern India, Volume 2* (Delhi: Lotus Press, 2005).

Criddle, Joan, and Teeda Butt Mam, *To Destroy You Is No Loss; The Odyssey of a Cambodian Family* (New York: Atlantic Monthly Press, 1987).

Cronon, E. David, ed., *The Political Thought of Woodrow Wilson* (Indianapolis: Bobbs-Merrill, 1965).

Dadrian, Varkhan, *The History of the Armenian Genocide* (New York: Bergahn Books, 2003).

Dallek, Robert, *Franklin D. Roosevelt and American Foreign Policy, 1932–1945* (New York: Oxford University Press, 1979).

Daniels, Josephus, *The Wilson Era: 1917–1923* (Chapel Hill: University of North Carolina Press, 1946).

Davies, Richard, *Defender of the Old Guard: John Bricker and American Politics* (Columbus: Ohio State University Press, 1993).

Davis, David Brion, *The Problem of Slavery in the Age of Revolution, 1770–1823* (Ithaca: Cornell University Press, 1999).

De las Casas, Bartolome, *In Defense of the Indians* (De Kalb: Northern Illinois University Press, 1970).

D'Entreves, A. P., *Natural Law: An Historical Survey* (New York: Harper, 1965).

Department of State, *Report on the Delegation of the United States of America to the Inter-American Conference on Problems of War and Peace* (Washington, DC: US Government Printing Office, 1946).

Dimock, Susan, "The Natural Law Theory of St. Thomas Aquinas" in Joel Feinberg and Jules Coleman, *Philosophy of Law* (New York: Wadsworth, 1999).

Divine, Robert A., *Second Chance: The Triumph of Internationalism in America during World War II* (New York: Atheneum, 1967).

Dobbs, Michael, *Six Months in 1945: FDR, Stalin, Churchill and Truman—From World War to Cold War* (New York: Vintage, 2013).

Donovan, Frank, *Mr. Roosevelt's Four Freedoms: The Story behind the United Nations Charter* (New York: Dodd Mead, 1966).

Eichelberger, Clark, *Organizing for Peace: A Personal History of the Founding of the United Nations* (New York: Harper & Row, 1977).

Engels, Friedrich, and Karl Marx, *The Marx-Engels Reader* (New York: W. W. Norton, 1972).

Evans, Tony, *U.S. Hegemony and the Project of Universal Human Rights* (New York: St. Martin's, 1996).

Everitt, Anthony, *Cicero: A Turbulent Life* (New York: John Murray, 2001).

Ezzati, A. *Islam and Natural Law* (London: ICAS Press, 2002).

Feinberg, Joel, and Jules Coleman, *Philosophy of Law* (Belmont: Wadsworth/Thompson Learning, 2000).

Formicola, Jo Renee, *The Catholic Church and Human Rights* (New York: Garland Publishing, 1988).

Foucault, Michel, *Discipline and Punish: The Birth of the Prison* (New York: Vintage Books, 1993).

Fried, Albert, ed., *A Day of Dedication: The Essential Writings & Speeches of Woodrow Wilson* (New York: Macmillan, 1965).

George, Robert P., *Natural Law Theory: Contemporary Essays* (Oxford: Oxford University Press, 1992).

Gerbner, Katharine, *Christian Slavery: Conversion and Race in the Protestant Atlantic World* (Philadelphia: University of Pennsylvania Press, 2018).

Glendon, Mary Ann, *A World Made New: Eleanor Roosevelt and the Universal Declaration of Human Rights* (New York: Random House, 2001).

Goodrich, Leland M., and Edvard Hambro, *Charter of the United Nations: Commentary and Documents* (Boston: World Peace Federation, 1949).

Goodwin, Doris Kearns, *No Ordinary Time: Franklin and Eleanor Roosevelt—The Home Front in World War II* (New York: Simon & Schuster, 1994).

Graham, Gerald S., *A Concise History of the British Empire* (New York: Viking, 1978).

Graves, Robert, *I, Claudius* (New York: Harrison Smith, 1934).

Grollman, Catherine, "Cordell Hull and His Concept of a World Organization," PhD dissertation, University of North Carolina, 1965.

Guilhot, Nicholas, *The Democracy Makers: Human Rights and International Order* (New York: Columbia University Press, 2005).

Gunther, John, *Roosevelt in Retrospect* (New York: Harper, 1950).

Hamid, Abdul, *A Chronicle of British Indian Legal History* (Jaipur, RBSA Publishers, 1991).

Handyside, Richard, ed., *Revolution in Guinea: Selected Texts* (New York: Monthly Review Press, 1969).

Hassett, William D., *Off the Record with FDR* (New Brunswick: Rutgers University Press, 1958).

Hay, Douglas, *Albion's Fatal Tree: Crime and Society in 18th Century England* (New York: Pantheon, 1976).

Helmholz, R. H., *Natural Law in Court: A History of Legal Theory and Practice* (Cambridge: Harvard University Press, 2015).

Herbert, Gary, *A Philosophical History of Rights* (London: Transaction Publishers, 2002).

Hilderbrand, Robert C., *Dumbarton Oaks: The Origins of the United Nations and the Search for Postwar Security* (Chapel Hill: University of North Carolina Press, 1990).

History of the United States War Crime Commission and the Development of the Laws of War (London: United States War Crimes Commission, 1948).

Hochschild, Adam, *King Leopold's Ghost: A Story of Greed, Terror and Heroism in Colonial Africa* (New York: Houghton Mifflin, 1998).

Hochstrasser, T. J. *Natural Law Theories in the Early Enlightenment* (Cambridge: Cambridge University Press, 2000).

Hoopes, Townshend, and Douglas Brinkley, *FDR and the Creation of the UN* (New Haven: Yale University Press, 1997).

Hopgood, Stephen, *The Endtimes of Human Rights* (Ithaca: Cornell University Press, 2013).

Howland, Douglas, and Luise White, eds., *Art of the State: Sovereignty Past and Present* (Bloomington: Indiana University Press, 2008).

Hunt, Lynne, *Inventing Human Rights* (New York: Norton, 2008).

Ibhawoh, Bonny, *Imperialism and Human Rights: Colonial Discourses of Rights and Liberties in African History* (Albany: State University of New York Press, 2007).

Immerman, Richard H., *John Foster Dulles: Piety, Pragmatism, and Power in U.S. Foreign Policy* (Wilmington: Scholarly Resources, 1999).

International Conference on Military Trials (Washington, DC: US Government Printing Office, 1949).

Iriye, Akira, ed., *The Human Rights Revolution: An International History* (Oxford: Oxford University Press, 2012).

Ishay, Micheline, *The History of Human Rights: From Ancient Times to the Globalization Era* (Berkeley: University of California Press, 2004).

Jaffer, Jameel, and Amrit Singh, *Administration of Torture* (New York: Columbia University Press, 2008).

Jain, M. P., *Outlines of Indian Legal History* (Delhi: Wadhwa International, 1999).

James, Lawrence, *Raj: The Making and Unmaking of British India* (New York: Little, Brown, 1998).

Jha, Chakradhar, *History and Sources of Law in Ancient India* (New Delhi: Ashish Publishing, 1987).

Kelley, Douglas, *22 Cells at Nuremberg* (New York: McFadden, 1961).

Kelsall, Tim, *Culture under Cross Examination: International Justice and the Special Court for Sierra Leone* (Cambridge: Cambridge University Press, 2009).

Larson, Erik, *In the Garden of Beasts: Love, Terror and an American Family in Hitler's Berlin* (New York: Broadway Paperbacks, 2011).

Lepore, Jill, *The Name of War: King Philip's War and the Origins of American Identity* (New York: Penguin, 1999).

Link, Arthur S., *Wilson: The Struggle for Neutrality, 1914–1915* (Princeton: Princeton University Press, 1960).

Lisska, Anthony, *Aquinas's Theory of Natural Law: An Analytic Reconstruction* (Oxford: Clarendon Press, 1996).

Ludwig, Emil, *Roosevelt: A Study in Fortune and Power* (New York: Viking Press, 1938).

MacMillan, Margaret, *Paris 1919: Six Months That Changed the World* (New York: Random House, 2001).

MacPherson, C. B., *The Political Theory of Possessive Individualism: From Hobbes to Locke* (Oxford: Oxford University Press, 1962).

Maitland, F. W., *The Constitutional History of England* (Cambridge: Cambridge University Press, 1919).

Maitland, F. W., and Francis C. Montague, *A Sketch of English Legal History* (New York: G. P. Putnam, 1915).

Marcus, Geoffrey, *The Maiden Voyage* (New York: Viking Press, 1969).

Maritain, Jacques, ed., *Human Rights: Comments and Interpretations* (New York: Columbia University Press, 1949).

Martinez, Jenny S., *The Slave Trade and the Origins of International Human Rights Law* (Oxford: Oxford University Press, 2012).

Marx, Karl, *Basic Writings on Politics and Philosophy* (Garden City: Doubleday, 1959).

Marx, Karl, and Friedrich Engels, *The German Ideology, Including the Theses of Feuerbach and the Introduction to the Critique of Political Economy* (New York: Progress Publisher, 1968).

Mencius, ed. D. C. Lau, *Mencius* (New York: Penguin Books, 1970).

Metcalf, Thomas R., *An Imperial Vision: Indian Architecture and Britain's Raj* (London: Faber and Faber, 2002).

Metzl, Jamie, *Western Responses to Human Rights Abuses in Cambodia, 1975–1980* (New York: St. Martin's, 1996).

Mill, John Stuart, *Three Essays* (New York: Oxford University Press, 1975).

Miller, Richard Lawrence, *Nazi Justiz: Law of the Holocaust* (Westport: Praeger, 1995).

Morgan, Edmund S., ed., *Puritan Political Ideas* (Indianapolis: Hackett Publishing, 1965).

Morris, Edmund, *Theodore Rex* (New York: HarperCollins, 2001).

Moyn, Samuel, *The Last Utopia: Human Rights in History* (Cambridge: Harvard University Press, 2010).

Muller, Herbert J., *Freedom in the Ancient World* (New York: Bantam, 1961).

Muller, Julius W., ed. *Presidential Messages and State Papers* v. 2 (New York: Review of Reviews, 1917).

Murray, Stuart, and James McCabe, eds., *Norman Rockwell's Four Freedoms: Images That Inspire a Nation* (Stockbridge: Berkshire House, 1993).

Neave, Airey, *On Trial at Nuremberg* (Boston: Little Brown, 1978).

Neier, Aryeh, *The International Human Rights Movement: A History* (Princeton: Princeton University Press, 2012).

Neier, Aryeh, *Taking Liberties: Four Decades of the Struggle for Rights* (New York: Public Affairs, 2003).

Notter, Harley, *Postwar Foreign Policy Preparation, 1939–1945* (Washington, DC: US Government Printing Office, 1950).

Oren, Michael B., *Power, Faith and Fantasy: Americans in the Middle East, 1776 to the Present* (New York: W. W. Norton, 2007).

O'Toole, Patricia, *The Moralist: Woodrow Wilson and the World He Made* (New York: Simon & Schuster, 2018).

Patterson, Dennis, ed., *A Companion to Philosophy of Law and Legal Theory* (Oxford: Blackwell Publishers, 1996).

Paul, Ellen Frankel, ed., *Natural Rights Liberalism from Locke to Nozick* (Cambridge: Cambridge University Press, 2005).

Plato, *Republic* (New York: Basic Books, 1968).

Power, Samantha, *A Problem from Hell: America and the Age of Genocide* (New York: Basic Books, 2002).

Proudhon, Pierre-Joseph, *What Is Property? Or an Inquiry into the Principle of Right and Government* (London: New Temple Press, 1902).

Public Papers of the Presidents of the United States: Jimmy Carter, 1978, v. 2 (Washington, DC: GPO, 1979).

Public Papers of Woodrow Wilson: War and Peace, Presidential Messages, Addresses and Public Papers 1917–1924 (New York: Harper, 1925).

Punishment for War Crimes: The Inter-Allied Declaration Signed at St. James' Palace, London, January 13, 1942 (London: Inter-Allied Information Committee, 1942).

Putney, Clifford, *Muscular Christianity: Manhood and Sports in Protestant America, 1880–1920* (Cambridge: Harvard University Press, 2001).

Rahe, Paul, *Republics Ancient and Modern: The Ancien Regime in Classical Greece* (Chapel Hill: University of North Carolina Press, 1994).

Rauschning, Hermann, *The Voice of Destruction* (New York: Putnam's, 1940).

Report of Robert H. Jackson, United States Representative to the International Conference on Military Trials: London, 1945 (Washington, DC: US Department of State, 1947).

Robins, Dorothy B., *Experiment in Democracy: The Story of U.S. Citizen Organizations in Forging the Charter of the United Nations* (New York: Parkside Press, 1971).

Roosevelt, Eleanor, *On My Own* (New York: Harper Publishing, 1958).

Roosevelt, Eleanor, *This I Remember* (New York: Harper, 1949).

Rosenman, Samuel I., *Working with Roosevelt* (New York: Harper, 1952).

Rozwenc, Edwin, and Thomas Lyons, eds., *Realism and Idealism in Wilson's Peace Program* (Boston: D. C. Heath, 1965).

Russell, Ruth B., *A History of the United Nations Charter: The Role of the United States, 1940–1945* (Washington, DC: Brookings Institution, 1958).

Samuel, Lawrence, *The End of the Innocence: The 1964–1965 New York World's Fair* (Syracuse: Syracuse University Press, 2007).

Schlesinger, Robert, *White House Ghosts: Presidents and Their Speechwriters* (New York: Simon & Schuster, 2008).

Schofield, Paul, ed., *Rights, Representation and Reform: "Nonsense upon Stilts" and Other Writings of the French Revolution* (Oxford: Oxford University Press, 2002).

Shahrastani, Muhammed; Alfred Guillaume, ed. *Kitabo Nihayat al-Iqdam fi 'Ilm al-Kalam* (Oxford: Oxford University Press, 1934).

Shaw, George Bernard, *Fabianism and the Empire* (London: Fabian Society, 1900).

Sherwood, Robert, *Roosevelt and Hopkins: An Intimate History* (New York: Harper, 1948).

Slotte, Pamela, and Miia Halme-Tuomisaari, eds., *Revisiting the Origins of Human Rights* (Cambridge: Cambridge University Press, 2015).

Smith, Bradley F., *Reaching Judgment at Nuremberg* (New York: Basic Books, 1977).

Sprecher, Drexel A., *Inside the Nuremberg Tribunal: A Prosecutor's Comprehensive Account* (New York: University Press of America, 1999).

Stearns, Peter N., *Human Rights in World History* (New York: Routledge, 2012).

Stimson, Henry L., *The Politics of Integrity: The Diaries of Henry L. Stimson* (New York: McGraw-Hill, 1976).

Stolleis, Michael, *The Law under the Swastika* (Chicago: University of Chicago Press, 1998).

Streit, Clarence, *Union Now: A Proposal for a Federal Union of the Democracies of the North Atlantic* (New York: Harper, 1939).

Summers, Robert, ed. *Dumbarton Oaks* (New York: H. W. Wilson, 1945).

Tananbaum, Duane, *The Bricker Amendment Controversy: A Test of Eisenhower's Political Leadership* (Ithaca: Cornell University Press, 1988).

Taylor, Telford, *Anatomy of the Nuremberg Trials* (New York: Alfred Knopf, 1992).

Trevelyan, G. M., *A History of England* (London: Longman, 1946).

Trial of the Major War Criminals before the International Military Tribunal (Washington, DC: US Government Printing Office, 1947).

US Department of State, *The United Nations Conference on International Organization, San Francisco, April 25 to June 26, 1945. Selected Documents* (Washington, DC: Government Printing Office, 1946).

US Department of State, *The United Nations: Four Years of Achievement*, Department of State Publication 3624 (September 1949).

Van Ittersum, M., *Profit and Principle: Hugo Grotius, Natural Rights Theories and the Rise of Dutch Power in the East Indies, 1595–1615* (Leiden: Brill, 2006).

Weber, Max, *The Protestant Ethic and the Spirit of Capitalism* (reprint New York: Courier Corp, 2003).

Welles, Sumner, *The World of the Four Freedoms* (New York: Columbia University Press, 1943).

Wellesley, Arthur, Duke of Wellington, *Supplementary Despatches and Memoranda of Field Marshal Arthur, Duke of Wellington, K.G.* (London: John Murray, 1863).

White, Walter, *A Man Called White* (New York: Viking Press, 1948).

Willis, James F., *Prologue to Nuremberg: The Politics and Diplomacy of Punishing War Criminals of the First World War* (Westport: Greenwood, 1982).

Woolner, David L., *The Last 100 Days: FDR at War and Peace* (New York: Basic Books, 2017).

Zagorin, Peter, *Hobbes and the Law of Nature* (Princeton: Princeton University Press, 2009).

Zuckert, Michael P., *The Natural Rights Republic* (Notre Dame: University of Notre Dame Press, 1996).

— Index —

— ABOUT THE AUTHOR —

Douglas R. Burgess Jr. is a jurist and historian. His numerous published works have examined the legal linkages between piracy and organized terrorism, the use of the trial to establish dominant historical narratives, and the development of a distinctly American criminal jurisprudence in the seventeenth and eighteenth centuries. Dr. Burgess is a professor of history at Yeshiva University and an affiliated instructor at the Benjamin Cardozo School of Law in New York City. He and his husband recently restored a 175-year-old Hudson Valley home, which they share with their excessively friendly Labrador, Makhni.